THE SUPERWIVES

Legend for Jacket Photo Montage

1. Emmy Cosell
2. Babbs Shoemaker
3. Judith Allison
4. Barbara Nicklaus
5. Judy Gilbert
6. Nancy Seaver
7. Winnie Palmer
8. Vickie Bench
9. Kam Seagren
10. Alice Kiick
11. Daniele Killy
12. Barbara Bouton

The Superwives

Jeanne Parr

Coward, McCann & Geoghegan, Inc.
New York

To Joseph A. Kelly
For courage

An excerpt from this book has previously appeared in the March,
1976, issue of *Viva*.

SBN:698-10716-0

Library of Congress Cataloging in Publication Data

Parr, Jeanne, 1926–
    The superwives.

    1. Athletes' wives—Biography.   I. Title.
GV697.A1P33 1976 796'.092'2 75-41348

Contents

Foreword

At the massive arena in Peking the monotone crowd in their dark mufti applauded with polite restraint when Chou En-lai introduced President and Mrs. Nixon and Henry Kissinger. It was February, 1972, so the coolness of the reception was not due to Watergate—it was too early for that.

Considering the novelty at the time of our détente with the People's Republic of China, these famous Americans could not have been unduly disappointed. But what must have surprised them, though they were too diplomatic to say so publicly, was the thunderous applause the same crowd accorded a slight, singularly unimpressive-looking male figure appearing without benefit of illustrious master of ceremonies. Was he chief of state? Distinguished wartime general? Beloved philosopher? No. He was a member of the people's champion Ping-Pong team. The wisdom and dignity of the East dissolved before this paddle wielder into a pandemonium as complete as the one possessing a Shea Stadium crowd in the bleachers during a Cincinnati Reds World Series clincher.

Also in the sea of dark blue that night sat a smiling woman who wore a peach blossom in her hair. The other women in the audience watched her, fascinated. She was the Ping-Pong champion's wife and undoubtedly envied because she was sharing her life with one adored by millions.

It is interesting to discover that it's no different in China from Miami, Florida, where they worship the Dolphins. We all adore our superstars. I leave the subconscious reasons to psychologists and simply accept as fact that we regard these paragons of maleness as the most talented, sportsmanlike, modest, courageous, glamorous, incorruptible heroes with the fastest legs, the strongest arms, the hardest muscles—and, of course, as peerless sexual performers in bed.

It's easy to see what we've done. We've transformed jocks into national gods and worship our own creations. Is it any wonder we would envy the woman who lives with a superhuman being? What a privilege to associate intimately with greatness. To know this deity better than anyone, to sleep with him, bear his children, dwell in the light of his fame, and build an identity around his. Are these women, each one chosen by a superman, superwomen? Could their lives be *less* than perfect?

During my yearlong investigation I learned a lot about these women, and there were plenty of surprises. It all began innocently enough in September, 1968. I was a real curiosity then, one of the handful of women TV news correspondents. The CBS Sports Department was planning a new five-minute, show called *NFL Questions* with Don Perkins. The format was simple: Women would be encouraged to send in questions about football, and Perkins would answer them during halftime of the National Football League games. They wanted a woman to read the questions—after all, a man wouldn't be so empty-headed as to *need* the answers. It was a gimmick to get more women to watch football.

When I was invited to audition for the show, I explained that I knew nothing about football, had never heard of Perkins (who turned out to be a former Dallas Cowboys star) and cared less. CBS Sports, in its infinite wisdom, replied, "Terrific! That's *just* what we want. You'll be asking the women's questions, and your ignorance of the game will lend charm and credibility to the show."

It was easy work, and the money was good, and besides, I have a policy: When someone asks me to audition, I audition. In the tryout, I remember asking Perkins questions which he answered using English words—but words grouped together in sequences that made them entirely incomprehensible to me. So I plugged away until I understood, and the sponsor was delighted with the outcome. I got the job.

The show went on the air, and during one of the first five-minute episodes I read a question sent in by a woman who wanted to know if the players' wives sat in a special section of the stands. Perkins, to use his own distinctive vernacular, grabbed it and ran with it.

"Y' oughta *see* those wives! They go *crazy* up there in the stands. They're very *into* it . . . devoted fans. What a strong reaction!"

After the show I reminded him that he hadn't actually answered the question. Don shrugged his shoulders and started going over his script. The director came out of the control room and said, "Good show!"

"But we never answered the question," I persisted.

The director shrugged *his* shoulders. "Yup," he said, ignoring me. "Those wives are something else. That's a whole other sports story. And someday it'll be told!"

"Why would they be interesting?" I asked.

"Are you kidding?" The director looked at me as if he were seeing me for the first time. "What stories *they* must have, living with those guys!"

We never did answer the question, but I didn't forget his remark. I made up my mind on the spot that I'd be the one to tell that story. It would take time because sports was not my specialty—news was, and it preoccupied me, particularly since in those days I was the only female in an all-male, chauvinist newsroom. However, now that the seed was sown, events kept popping up to reinforce my interest in superstars' wives.

In the summer of 1968 sportscaster Frank Gifford scheduled an interview with Billie Jean King and promptly fell ill. Someone in the newsroom had to take his place, and since the subject was a woman, it made sense to the assignment editor to send me as substitute. My plea of ignorance was misconstrued as evidence of laziness, and the grouchy editor pushed me out the door along with a film crew.

One of the hit songs of the day was Bobbie Gentry's "Ode to Billie Joe," and I spent the next full hour calling Billie Jean Billie Joe. She didn't understand it, didn't like it, and *never* forgot it. When I took the story back to CBS, the film editor couldn't find thirty seconds without a "Billie Joe" in it, so the piece never made the air. I apologized to Frank, who said, "It's OK," and then added, "I wonder what *he's* like?" (Meaning, of course, Larry King.) Six years later we met and were introduced all over again. Much to my surprise, the queen of tennis grinned and said, "Yeah, it's old Billie Joe."

The year 1968 proved fateful for me. CBS was giving a banquet for Frank Gifford, and I was among the company personalities invited. I was seated next to a bullnecked giant who seemed entirely comfortable in that glittering circle. To break the ice, I asked him what he did for a living. It broke up the ice—and the whole party. The giant's name was Joe Namath. I remember wondering if *he* was married.

Then in the spring of 1974, the makers of Life Savers threw their annual promotion luncheon to name the outstanding sports figure of the year. The award was going to O. J. Simpson. Although I'd resigned my career in favor of marriage, I still had friends at CBS Sports, and I wangled an invitation to Mamma Leone's. It wasn't the free lunch that attracted me. My interest in athletes' wives was developing rapidly, and I decided to launch my investigation with the wife of the year's most outstanding sports figure, Mrs. O. J. Simpson. If there was such a person it seemed fairly logical that O. J. would know, and then I could ask for clearance. It's significant that I assumed he would have to grant me permission before his wife could talk to me.

It wasn't easy. The crush of freeloading press, radio, and TV was more than I could penetrate, so I stood patiently on the sidelines until sports reporters and photographers had exhausted their curiosity. While I waited, I noticed two strikingly beautiful girls who were standing near me, watching O.J. with undisguised admiration.

"Man, isn't he beautiful?" rhapsodized the first.

"For-*get* it!" admonished the second. "He's married."

"So what?" snapped the first. "Since when does a man's wife get in the way of true love?" When she stopped giggling, she took a long, sweeping look at O.J. and said, "I wonder what it would be like married to such a gorgeous man?"

I realized then that that was what I *really* wanted to know—and the only ones who could supply the answer had not been given the chance. Finally I made my way into O.J.'s presence, and when I asked him whether I could interview his wife, my education began. He was obviously puzzled.

"Are you sure you don't want to interview *me*?"

I insisted it was his *wife*. He looked at me with a smile that said, "You poor mixed-up rookie reporter," and shrugged. "Sure, why not?" He gave me her phone number. It was that easy, and later I was to discover that all athletes except a few hockey players and Muhammad Ali were receptive. Mrs. Gordie Howe said no, she was writing her own book; Mrs. Ken Dryden was afraid; Mrs. Bobby Orr wouldn't grant an interview because Bobby wouldn't let her talk; Mrs. Phil Esposito was in the middle of a divorce; and the six people I had to go through to get to Belinda Ali kept saying, "Call back Monday." After twenty-eight Mondays I gave up, but I was trying to interview Belinda in the days ('75) when Muhammad Ali was making headlines with Veronica Porche and no one was about to let her talk. With these few exceptions, the husbands and wives raised no objections and in some cases told me far more than I would ever have guessed.

Before going to the wives themselves, I researched my subject to get some idea of what to expect and firmly to connect in my mind the husband with his sport. I talked to experts and read everything I could, including daily application to the sports section of the New York newspapers, which I had formerly employed only to counteract the awkward effect of leaky garbage cans.

Fortunately, one of my friends and Connecticut neighbors was Emmy Cosell, wife of the best-known, if not best-loved, sportscaster in the country whom she had followed around for twenty years, getting an inside view of the jock scene. I decided she was the perfect one to talk to before I set out on my odyssey. Emmy would know the ropes. Unfortunately, when I called their New York apartment, I learned she was in Hollywood with Howard, who had a part in a movie.

Emmy didn't stay out West long, as she was soon to explain. . . .

Where's Emmy?

I feel sorry for the wife. . . .

The jock's wife never learns how to live independently of her husband. . . . She's a follower. All she does is follow . . . follow . . . follow.

She and Howard were streaking along the Santa Monica Freeway in a big black limousine to the luxurious Beverly Hills Hotel, where they would stay while Howard filmed a scene for the movie *Everything You've Always Wanted to Know About Sex.* For Howard, this Woody Allen picture was a sequel to *Bananas,* in which he also made a cameo appearance. The limousine and script were waiting for the Cosells when they arrived at the airport. There was a note inside. If Howard liked the script, the scene would be shot the next day.

Emmy said that Howard handed her the script and asked her to read it while he watched the passing scenery, which meant he was going to take a nap. Ten minutes later Emmy shook her husband awake and, with the greatest urgency, announced, "Howard, you *can't* make this movie!" Howard turned his sleep-drenched, frowning face to her and said, "You brought me all the way out here to tell me I can't make the movie? Why not? Give it to me straight." (Howard talks that way in real life, too.)

"Because," said the horrified Emmy, "because they've cast you as a child molester!"

Howard was wide awake now and leaning as far forward as the deep back seat of the car would allow. "Can you say that with total unequivocation? Is there no room for doubt in your mind on that score?"

"I'm sure."

Howard's famous voice delivered the command to the chauffeur: "Turn this car around. Waste not a moment. Return me to the airport . . . but now stop at the first telephone booth you see. Do all of the foregoing with as much haste as the law will allow. Ask for no explanation."

When the driver had found the booth, Howard leaped out, made his call and, within the space of two minutes, the limousine was once again speeding along the freeway back to the airport.

"I left the message," he said, patting Emmy's hand. "I left the message."

Woody Allen didn't get Howard's message until the Cosells were on a jet halfway back to New York. Howard was still muttering indignantly to himself, "Difficult, arrogant, aggravating, and vexatious I am. A child molester I am not!"

Then, turning to Emmy, he said, "My dear, you have just saved the reputation of the world's greatest sports announcer!"

Emmy knew it. She smiled to herself, asked the stewardess to bring the lord and master a cup of hot tea, and then she leaned back and closed her eyes.

Modesty resides as precariously in Howard Cosell's psyche as it does in Muhammad Ali's or Henry Kissinger's. Whether Howard learned it from the superstars or vice versa is open to debate, but Howard fits as neatly into the sports superstar category as Uncle Walter Cronkite and Kissinger do the "public servant" firmament.

The difference between Howard and the jocks is that he outlives them in the fame-gathering profession. They are up there only as long as they can hit, shoot, kick, or carry a ball—in short, until their physical equipment wears out. Howard's vocal cords will be vibrating long after his heart stops. So Emmy is a superstar wife. In all the years I've known her I never really recognized that. I don't think she does either. The interview brought it home to me forcibly. I also discovered that just as Howard's niche is infinitely more secure than the jocks', so Emmy's is stronger than their wives. They could learn a lot from Emmy Cosell.

Emmy Abrams met Howard Cosell during World War II. She joined the WAC in 1942 and was assigned to Fort Hamilton, Brooklyn, as a major's secretary. The major's lieutenant in charge of manpower was Howard. He was constantly in and out of Emmy's office, but with Howard an officer and Emmy an enlisted person, their romance was restricted to long looks and veiled smiles. One day, walking with two other WACS, Emmy passed Lieutenant Cosell. Her two friends snapped to attention and smartly saluted. Emmy just grinned at him.

Lieutenant Cosell stopped in his tracks and yelled, "Corporal, don't you salute an officer?"

Emmy kept giggling as Howard repeated the question, trying to put as much authority into it as possible. Then he glared at her, spun on his heel, and stalked away. Thirteen months later they were married, and he's been saluting her ever since.

His friends may find Howard's devotion to his wife neurotic. It certainly borders on obsession. His emotional dependency on Emmy is total. He seems unable to get along without her—not even on out-of-town assignments. To outsiders, though, it appears the opposite. Emmy waits on Howard's every need. She does the packing, the driving (he never learned how), soothes him when he's ruffled, does *everything* but lead him to the microphone. He needs no help in that department.

"I drive Howard everywhere!" she confides matter-of-factly. "They're always opening and closing doors for him. . . . We'll pull up in front of the

studio, and five people will help him out of the car. *I'm* left to find a parking place and get out by myself.''

But should Emmy be delayed at the parking lot, Howard may hold up a camera crew while he asks, "Where's Emmy? Where's Emmy?" It's become a joke with the ABC crowd. Recently at a sports banquet in San Diego Howard was seated at the dais and Emmy was in the audience as usual. An irrepressible urge demanded immediate attention from Emmy, and she passed the word to Howard that she was going to the ladies' room.

"My God," a friend asked, "why does he have to know *that?*"

"Because," an ABC executive answered, "if he looks down and finds her seat empty, he might get up to the microphone and ask, 'Where's Emmy?' ''

If Howard's reliance on Emmy has psychological overtones, it also serves to keep him physically fit. Emmy testifies that he is a hypochondriac. "If he has a headache, he knows it's a migraine or a deadly tumor. If his eyes hurt, he's got glaucoma. If his throat is sore, it's a strep and he's one step away from dying. I realize I'm his security blanket. . . . When I'm around, he doesn't contract any of those fatal diseases."

The Cosells have two daughters, twenty-two year-old Hilary and twenty-nine-year-old Jill (Mrs. Peter Cohane), and three grandchildren. They are a tight little family unit—almost to the exclusion of the world outside. Emmy loves to entertain the grandchildren at their big, rambling country house in Pound Ridge, New York, or have the entire family for dinner at their spacious, sunny East Side Manhattan apartment. When a grandchild is sick or one of her daughters needs her, she stays home while Howard goes on sports assignments by himself. Invariably, though, he calls long distance to complain that he has caught a dread exotic disease and can't work. Then Emmy drops everything to fly to his side. The ABC people greet her at the airport with a "Thank God you're here! *Now* we can get on with our work."

Last year, alone on assignment, Howard really did fall seriously ill, and nobody believed him. Finally, they called Emmy, who had stayed home in New York for a grandchild's birthday, and told her he had the Asian flu. By the time she and Hilary arrived in California Howard had been rushed to the hospital with an overdose of penicillin. While he was being sped through the hospital corridor with the two Cosell women clinging to his wheelchair, a strange woman rushed up and screamed, "My God, it's really you! It's Howard Cosell!"

Howard was not too ill to ignore the obeisance of his subjects. He nodded weakly but regally. His wife and daughter watched in disbelief as the woman leaned over and said, "How do you think the Rams are going to do Monday night?"

That was too much even for Howard. "Ma'am," he rasped, "I am in need of an antidote. I am expiring. Can't we talk about the Rams at another time?''

Emmy Cosell is a slim, nervous woman whose ash-blond hair is generously sprinkled with gray. She is attractive, even elegant in evening clothes, and her sharp features are exceeded by an even sharper wit. A Gentile, she admits she fusses over Howard like a Jewish mother, but somehow she does it without losing her dignity. In return she gets unfailing, worshipful devotion from the scowling bully of the sports world. She figures she has the best of the bargain.

She loves to tell how she has to protect Howard from female fans. ''Don't laugh,'' she said. ''Howard may be a fifty-five-year-old grandfather, but the girls chase him all the time! Once we were in a hotel coffee shop, and two young women sitting across from us kept staring at Howard. One of them got up and had him paged. When he answered, she gave him her room number and told him she was available. The nerve! Imagine! And me, his wife, sitting right there. When he walked back to our table, the other girl gave him a knowing wink. We got out of there in a hurry.''

She explained what I was to hear repeatedly from sports wives: that these ''jock lovers'' frequently file rape or paternity suits against rich superstars. Emmy said that sort of publicity would kill her husband.

''If only they knew what a prude he is,'' she said.

''Women don't find him sexy then?'' I asked.

''That's for them to say,'' she replied, but she told of a recent gin rummy game with Howard losing badly and getting grumpier by the minute. She brought in cheese and crackers, and one of the men teased, *''How* do you tolerate this guy? The crankiest loser and worst gin player in the world. . . . He must be good in bed!''

''Are you kidding?'' Emmy put the tray down. ''Have you ever gone to bed with someone who smells of Malomar cookies and milk?''

During my visit with Emmy in her Manhattan apartment she was nervous about an appointment at her bank. She was $5,000 overdrawn. She explained she had always managed the family finances.

''Howard has never questioned how much I spend,'' she said, adding, ''Of course, he knows after thirty-one years of marriage I'm not going out and buy Tiffany's.'' She put her head in her hands and wailed, ''A five-thousand-dollar discrepancy! The computer at the bank *has* to be wrong!''

Despite their affluence, Emmy has a reputation for being frugal and she admits to having been a penny pincher for the first ten years of their marriage. ''It was good for us,'' she explains. ''We developed values. Instant gratification is dangerous. . . . That's what ruins a lot of young jocks today.''

Before leaving for the bank, Emmy gave me her frank appraisal of the jock scene, drawn from twenty years of observation from the sidelines: ''The whole thing turns me off! In most cases the guys never outgrow their locker-room mentality. They acquire a false love of their image and bodies. I feel sorry for the wife. . . . She stays home and takes care of the children. She borrows his identity, tries to get his love, but he can't give it. . . . He can give only material things—everything *but* what's important. All that money early in marriage spoils a jock. He ends up shallow, sometimes broke, and almost always spiritually bankrupt. The saddest part is, he never learns how to leave the game . . . and the wife never learns how to live independently of her husband. She's a follower. All she does is follow . . . follow . . . follow."

The last time I heard from the Cosells, Howard was on assignment in Europe. His migraine had become intolerable, and Emmy was packing.

Well, Emmy Cosell didn't paint a very cheerful picture, but I decided I was finally ready to see these wives myself—to check out their super-iority—in their own homes, wherever those might be, and with their children and husbands, if I was lucky enough to find them at home. With the help of several sportscasters and journalists, I drew up a list of fifty outstanding athletes. We eliminated all the unmarried, divorced, and unavailable and came up with a list of thirty from every major sport and spread out on the map all the way from Geneva, Switzerland, to Hueytown, Alabama. My God, no wonder no one had attempted to write this book before. I suddenly realized I was going to end up giving all my royalties to the airlines! With a big gulp and a feeling of "Here goes!" I called the number O.J. had given me and then bought an airline ticket to Buffalo, New York.

The Butterfly

As O.J. moved into the arena of superstardom, I realized almost at once that success wasn't without some bitter side effects. We have practically lost our private life.

I have been shoved out of the way, pushed, and stepped on by more than one beautiful woman. I admit I'm jealous. . . . It's the major problem of O.J.'s success that I've had to learn to cope with.

On the plane doubts cropped up. Why would a superstar's wife tell on her husband? Would Jackie tell on JFK? No, but Jackie was as big a star as her husband. Marguerite Simpson* isn't. Wives in her position, living in the long shadows of inflated symbols of superiority, must have complaints. I had been married long enough to know that. Women married to these supermen must have secrets that would be tremendously revealing. Would they tell what it's *really* like? Would they want to tell the worshipers in order to humanize their husbands before they lose them forever. No man is a hero to his secretary or wife, it is said, and honest people want to set distorted records straight, but these women would be living with their superstars long after they gave me an interview. They weren't likely to let anything leak that their husbands wouldn't like. I had a hunch they might not confide in me, might not give me any more information then what I could get from the PR office.

At the airport I saw her silver Mercedes Benz before I saw her. When I admired her car, she said, "O.J. gave it to me for Valentine's Day!" I figured that at that rate he'd have to give her Rockefeller Plaza for their twenty-fifth anniversary. As we drove through the countryside to Williamsville, a new, affluent suburb of Buffalo where Marguerite and O.J. live, she shuddered and talked about the cold, gray November weather.

"I'll be glad when it's time to go back to Los Angeles. About this time I start yearning for warm sunshine."

*O. J. Simpson, running back for the Buffalo Bills of the National Football League. Since 1968, when he was voted the most outstanding player in college football and awarded the Heisman Trophy, Simpson has gone on to become the best known and the best running back in the history of the game. In 1972 he led the NFL in yards gained (1,251) and repeated as league leader in 1973, when he gained 2,003 yards to eclipse the ten-year-old mark set by Jim Brown. The twenty-three touchdowns he amassed for the Bills in the '75 season broke a ten-year record. A track star in college (he is a member of the 440-yard relay team that still holds the world record), Simpson's overall athletic ability led him to victory in the 1975 SuperStar Competition.

Well, we're off to a good start, I thought grimly. *We're talking about the weather!* Then I remembered that the Simpsons are native Californians and consider it their home. Buffalo, with its cold blasts off Lake Erie, is a long way from Los Angeles. But when you have O.J.'s income, you buy places on both coasts and, who knows, someday a jet plane to close the gap. Buffalo is where they hibernate during the football season because it's where O.J.'s team, the Buffalo Bills, is based. Hibernate may be the wrong word for life in a brand-new two-story Tudor brick house. It's also the wrong word for O.J.'s life at any time and place. As almost everyone, including Marquerite, knows, it swings in wide arcs.

As she drove, she chatted about their West Coast home, in the elite movie star colony of Bel Air, in Los Angeles, about their children, Jason and Arnelle, and how, once they were ready for school, she'd probably have to stay in one place. I watched her intently as she talked. She looks like a schoolgirl too young to have two children. She's petite. A size seven figure, dressed that day in faded jeans and a sequined T-shirt. Her coffee-colored baby-fine skin is drawn so tightly across her chiseled features it seemed a smile would tear it. On the contrary, the smile softens and brightens her face, calling on her large, almond-shaped brown eyes to help deliver its brimming warmth. They are wonderfully expressive eyes, communicating the intensity and vulnerability behind them. "Don't hurt me," they seem to ask. "Be my friend." I had the distinct feeling she expected people to take advantage of her. Those who know the Simpsons well say she's sweet, shy and introspective, while he's charming, also shy and introspective. They are an extraordinarily attractive couple.

Both O.J. and Marquerite came from humble beginnings in San Francisco. It was later, after fame and fortune captured them, that they moved south to be near the right football field and to Bel Air apparently to be near the right people. Today Marquerite presides over the Williamsville house for the five months of the football season and their eight-room Spanish-style villa in Bel Air for the other seven months of the year. Life in Williamsville is by far the more subdued. The house is brand-new and practically vacant. The den where we talked had a sofa, a blazing fire in the fireplace against the howling wind outside, and little else. The sparseness of the furnishings had nothing to do with a money shortage. Marquerite simply hadn't had time to finish decorating yet—they had only moved in three months before. She brought in some hot tea, then started at the beginning: her childhood.

"I had a good childhood, but not a complete family life. My father left home when I was small, and my mother raised the three of us all by herself. She was some woman!"

Mrs. Whitley, Marquerite's mother, was an awesome matriarch who sur-

vived a harsh life through sheer determination and deep religious faith. Because of her great strength, she managed to give her three children much more than they might have expected. She worked as a nurse's aide all day, then had to take in laundry, iron, and sew to make ends meet. "She brought us up with discipline and patience. She gave us religion, moral values, and a thirst for education. Today, after getting all of us out of the nest, going through the tragedy of my brother's death, she is taking care of seven-to-nine-year-old retarded children." Marquerite paused for composure and finished with pride glistening in her eyes: "She has been a great influence on my life."

Marquerite met O.J. when she was only fifteen. She was attending George Washington High School in San Francisco, and boys hadn't made much of an impression on her. She'd never had a real date before. And along came O.J. He was attending a rival high school, Galileo, "where Joe DiMaggio got his start." He'd come to George Washington High to scout the football team and had brought his racy reputation with him. Big for his age, handsome, triple threat, good in all sports, lady-killer, the whole works. He electrified the entire female population of the school. Everyone but Marquerite. She found him rowdy, loud, always breaking up parties and getting into trouble.

"One night O.J. and a group of his friends *borrowed* a truck. . . ." Her inflection on "borrowed" saved further explanation. "They were using it to transport beer and booze to a picnic ground where they were going to have a big bash. Well, the police stopped the truck and ordered the fellows to get out with their hands up and stand against a wall. One of the policemen went down the line of five guys, asking for names. When it was O.J.'s turn, he answered, 'My name is Orenthal James Simpson.' "

"Come on," the policeman said gruffly, "give me a better name."

"It's Orenthal James Simpson!" O.J. repeated firmly.

"So you're anxious to get locked up . . . OK, one last chance, what's your real name?"

"It's Burt Lancaster!" O.J. said disgustedly.

That's how Burt Lancaster ended up in the San Francisco Juvenile Court records and according to Marquerite is still there today.

"O.J. was definitely not my type," Marquerite said emphatically. "I was his opposite . . . shy, unsophisticated, straitlaced due to my mother's training—the kind of girl who went to church on Saturday night while the other kids went to the movies." She felt she couldn't, in a million years, bring a boy like O.J. home to her mother, but if she were going to date him, she would have to. That's the kind of woman her mother was, and that's the kind of home she kept. Apparently Mrs. Whitley never allowed another man to enter her life, and it's remarkable that she permitted O.J. to come into her beloved daughter's. But remarkable is the word to describe O.J.'s will to win and his skill as a strategist. Of all the girls who were chasing him, he wanted the one who wasn't interested. He kept calling Marquerite until she finally weakened and went out with him. There weren't many boys who could pass inspection at the Whitley home. "Mom liked O.J. right away," Marquerite recalled, bubbling with laughter, "because' he acted like a choirboy. What a change came over him!" And once he started dating Marquerite, a transformation did take place.

They both went to San Francisco Junior College, where he became a football star immediately and wound up with scholarship offers from colleges all over the country. He accepted the one made by the University of Southern California and was on his way. He could have left Marquerite behind at this point in his burgeoning career, but he didn't. He'd set out to win her, and well, we know how it turned out. In his second semester at Southern Cal he went up to San Francisco to confront the formidable Mrs. Whitley.

"I want to marry your daughter," he said.

"And how do you think you're going to support her?" she demanded.

"Don't worry, I'll take good care of her," he said.

"Uh-huh," said Mrs. Whitley skeptically. "How?"

"Playing football," he said.

"Football! I've never heard of anyone supporting a wife by playing football."

"I will. I'm going to be famous. You're going to read about me someday."

On March 18, 1967 they were married. Of course O.J.'s prophecy came true but to this day Mrs. Whitley thinks it's a peculiar way to support a wife.

So O.J. had won again and was to keep on winning. That year he was on the track team that broke the 440-relay record, and in the fall, when football season opened his initials were plastered over sports pages across the country.

As she told me the story, I had the feeling the more O.J. won, the more Marquerite lost. The first thing she made clear to me on that winter day in Buffalo was how deeply she resented the loss of privacy. "As O.J. moved into the arena of superstardom, I realized almost at once that success wasn't without some bitter side effects."

And then, as the doorbell rang, almost as if on cue, she turned to me with brown eyes widened and shrugged. "You see?" It was a neighbor wanting to discuss last Sunday's game with O.J. Marquerite told him that her husband wasn't home, that he was at practice. "I'll be back later," I could hear the indomitable intruder say. *I'll bet she can't wait,* I thought, and noticed she was shaking her head as she came back into the room and sank down on the couch.

"They come around all the time—people we don't even know. They just walk up to the door and say they want a word with O.J. like they've known him all their life. It drives me crazy! There's practically no time to be together . . . I mean just us. We can't even go out for dinner without everyone bustin' for his autograph.'' Marquerite did an imitation in a fawning falsetto, '' 'Ooooojay, I sure do admire you! Could you sign six of these menus for my kids?' '' It became so bad I finally put my foot down. No more autographs while we were eating. O.J. thought my ruling on this was a little severe . . . after all, he said, what can I do when they ask? Just say no, I told him.''

It took awhile to get it out, but the *big* thing on Marquerite's mind with respect to O.J. is sex. And why not? This swashbuckler is a peacock-gamecock, a Phoenix-Adonis-Apollo—the kind women fantasize about, the kind who attracted Marquerite in the first place—and it gives her a big pain in the heart. The pain is not over her love for O.J. but all those other waiting women. They want her husband and don't see her as a particularly impressive obstacle. When he's at home, Marquerite has him, but he's not home much, and when he's on the road, she rarely goes along.

It's the story of the life of a star's wife whether he be show biz bankable, major politician, big businessman, or athlete. In the world of sports wives called these predators ''jock lovers.'' Marquerite said they stalk her husband day and night. As she spoke of this problem, an unaccustomed frown hardened her face. Her opinion of these women I discovered later is pretty much the same as other athletes' wives who find it hard to hide their disgust and fear. There's no question, jock lovers are determined women who birddog athletes, study team schedules, memorize names and faces, descend in packs on airports, where they rush the stars, screaming, ''Let me touch you,'' call or confront them at their hotels, send them photographs, measurements, and bold invitations through the mail—even go so far as to break into their hotel rooms and push their way into their beds. Sometimes they don't have to do very much pushing. That undoubtedly bothers Marquerite a lot.

It bothers lawyers, too, because healthy sex drives are not necessarily the force motivating jock lovers. They sometimes play a game that is as deadly serious and businesslike as any the superstars play. These women track their prey with remarkable persistence and cunning, then move in for the kill. If the star succumbs, he finds himself in a sticky affair that can destroy a marriage, a scandal, or a sensational ''rape'' case. I had already seen these women flocking around O.J. at that Athlete of the Year award luncheon in 1974. I watched as they closed in and rubbed their slim, supple bodies against him like purring Siamese cats, right in front of all the people and statues at Mamma Leone's. Marquerite has witnessed this scene many times, so she knows why she has reason to be afraid.

''I love my husband, so I'm jealous,'' she told me. ''I have been shoved out of the way, pushed, and stepped on by more than one beautiful woman.

When I see how young and good-looking they are, it hurts more.'' Marquerite realizes she has a problem and is trying to cope with it. It's typical that she sees this as "her" problem, not "their" problem, and that "she" has to cope with it, not "they" have to find an answer together. How is she coping? She lives on a health food diet, plays tennis, studies art and dance, and attends Bible class every Thursday night. "I'm a very religious person," she says. "My religion helps me maintain my values."

Well, almost.

She told me of a time when she accompanied her husband on a flight to the West Coast. This was rare because she usually stays home looking after the kids while O.J. travels. Her reliance on religion must get a workout every time O.J. boards a plane (something he does a lot). On this particular flight a stewardess discovered that O.J. was among her charges. She stopped passing out magazines and almost passed out herself when she saw him. When she spied Marquerite in the seat next to her hero, suspicion and disappointment were clear on her face. "Is that your wife?" she complained dejectedly. "Naw," assured O.J., "she's my sister."

O.J.'s a great practical joker, as Marquerite knows, and the joke was on the stewardess, poor dear. All the time the stewardess sat on the armrest of O.J.'s chair, which was the rest of the flight, the Simpsons were enjoying a private laugh at her expense. The unsuspecting girl whispered into O.J.'s ear, giggled and cooed a lot, and every now and then, whenever the lurching of the plane logically called for it, she fell into a cuddly heap in his lap and there was an interesting struggle getting her righted again. Marquerite enjoys a good joke as well as the next person, but she would have enjoyed this one a good deal more if she could have overcome the urge to kill O.J., the stewardess or both. No question about it, it must have put a severe strain on her religion.

As she told me the story, she shook her head and looked into the fire as if she were seeing a picture of the stewardess attempting to seduce O.J. "It's disgusting, but it would appear," she said with a touch of resignation, "that I have the most desirable husband in the world." I'm sure Mrs. Muhammad Ali would disagree.

Imagine the position of the superstar. He's rich, famous, and probably a physical marvel. Every day his head has to get bigger and bigger. Hordes of beautiful women are offering their bodies as holy offerings to him as to a god. How long can these jocks resist temptation? In time aren't they bound to come to the conclusion that the Lord meant it to be that way?

Realizing that a sense of self-worth will give her the security to deal with this problem, Marquerite assiduously works on "what's going on inside" and then adds, "I'm trying to quit worrying about what I can't control and work on what I can—me!" She's done a good job. She's quite a woman, but the trouble is she still hangs onto O.J.'s coattails and sails through air that is rarefied for him but smoggy for her.

When the football season ends, the Simpsons move west with a sigh of relief, to the glamorous life that O.J. earned for them in the cold, mud, danger, and brutality of the gridiron. The Simpsons now have leisure time, and their world is aglitter with celebrities from the film community, television, and sports world. O.J. moves easily in that milieu. One has the feeling, though, that Marquerite doesn't count them as her best friends. Their circle may best be described as the Celebrity Tennis circuit. O.J. is on the board of directors of the Toluca Lake Tennis Club, along with Johnny Carson, James Franciscus, and Efrem Zimbalist, Jr. Bill Cosby, Dinah Shore, and Burt Bacharach. All consider O.J. one of the club's best players. Charlton Heston, the unofficial chairman of the board, describes O.J. as a cool customer on the tennis court. Others testify he's also cool at the poker table when he and his superstar friends sit down after a game of tennis for a not-so-friendly game of cards. "They usually play until dawn at our house," Marquerite said matter-of-factly. "One night an earthquake was the only thing that stopped them."

In the next hour on that November day in Buffalo we returned to the subject of sex, and it became apparent that it was either feast or famine for most of these wives. Periods of abstinence before a game, during out-of-town games and training camp were par for the course . . . and then to make up for the nights of celibacy, there are periods of indulgence. Later in my travels I was to find out how much many of the wives resented sexual abstinence before a game and particularly forced separation during training camp. That day, I have to admit, when I first heard about it from Marquerite, my jaw fell. "You mean you've never heard of the Tuesday Rule?" She looked at me in utter amazement. "Where have ya been?"

The Tuesday Rule, it seems, is the one the women gripe about the most. It dictates that during the football season players must abstain from sex from Tuesday until Sunday. *That leaves a big Monday*, I thought, doing some quick calculations. I had visions of a thousand hairy bruisers struggling with bedclothes and soft female flesh while springs and mattresses protested squeakily. "Quick," I could hear the urgent voices saying, "before it's Tuesday again!"

"What's the point of the Tuesday Rule?" I wanted to know.

"So the guy doesn't sap his strength . . . ridiculous, isn't it? Some teams actually separate the players and their wives before a game and if they're caught sneaking around, they have to pay a twenty-five-hundred-dollar fine."

"Does it work?"

"During our second year in Buffalo the coach took the players away before every game. We had a losing season anyway. Now we have a different coach, and he doesn't believe in it," she said.

"Sex or abstinence?" I couldn't help asking.

"You know who you should ask? The Dolphins' wives . . . they're *really* burned up about this."

"Who are they?"

Marquerite threw back her head and laughed (over the wrong remark I thought). "Where *have* you been, kiddo? The Dolphins are a football team in Miami, and their coach really believes in forced separation." I made a note of it. By now I knew most of the superstars by name, but the team names still eluded me.

Marquerite's views on the subject were those of most of the wives, as I was soon to discover: Athletes should be able to sleep with their wives whenever they want. They should be able to do their own thinking on the subject. I assume she believed that the wives should have a vote in helping reach a democratic policy decision on the matter. She didn't think the coach should be an arbitrator, making binding decisions.

"What about O.J.?"

"He likes to relax the night before a game. He wants soul food, and we stay home and listen to soft music."

She didn't say what she wanted.

There was another question I wanted to ask, but there are limits to how personal an interview can get, especially with a woman like Marquerite. I finally came up with a weak attempt. "The way women flock after jocks, they must be good in bed," I said, trying to be casual. Marquerite came through. I think.

"The American public is responsible for building these super images in everything, including bed. Jocks have as many problems as anyone else. As far as sex goes, some are super and some are not."

That definitely called for a follow-up question. I squirmed a little . . . couldn't figure how to phrase it and let it pass.

O.J. has always been the star in the Simpson household, and Marquerite has accepted it with quiet reservation. "I realize O.J. is a celebrity. God gave him a gift, to run with the ball, but still, he's just a man. Just my husband. I don't have to act like a fan. I believe I have to stay close to the ground if only to keep *him* there. You don't have to be a beautiful and talented person to be a star. You have to be morally and spiritually a good person. . . . I believe I'm a star."

There have been a few occasions when she's had a chance to shine. One was when she gave birth to their first child. She came downstairs with the announcement that it was hospital time. O.J., always cool under pressure, jumped up and took charge. He'd back the car out of the garage. All *she* had to do, he told her, was to grab her overnight bag and meet him out front. Mar-

querite stepped out the front door just in time to see O.J. gunning the car
down the street toward the hospital. She sat on the front stoop, labor pains and
all, and waited until he'd noticed he was talking to himself and came back for
her.

But there was one occasion when her "star" twinkled merrily all night.
Most of their friends know that of the two of them, O.J. is the practical joker—the one with the "kinky" sense of humor—but after years of taking it on
the chin, Marquerite told me how she finally paid him back, with interest. She
planned a big surprise birthday party for him at one of the leading restaurants
in Los Angeles and invited four of their favorite friends to join them. She
went to a great deal of trouble to get just the right food and wine . . . and
even had a private meeting with the cook, who agreed to bake a four-tiered
birthday cake complete with O.J.'s initials in the middle of a football.

"When they brought the cake in with sparklers sizzling like the Fourth of
July, everyone at the table started singing "Happy Birthday." Then the waiters joined in, and soon all the people in the room turned, recognized O.J., and
started singing 'Happy Birthday, dear O.J. Happy birthday to you. . . .'
O.J. just hates that sort of thing." She giggled. "He bowed his head, and I
knew he was dying of embarrassment." The recollection made her laugh all
the harder. "Everybody started throwing kisses and slapping him on the back
while they were singing, and O.J. winced every time someone did. . . ."
Marquerite put her head in her hands and shook from laughter. "He was
soooo undone!"

"What's so funny about that? " I asked.

"It wasn't his birthday."

Sometimes people remind us of animals. Some of the fussy old ladies who
walk their dogs along Sutton Place look exactly like their poodles. The vulnerable Marquerite, so soft and fragile, reminds me of a butterfly, and butterflies are very big with Marquerite. I discovered this when her daughter, Arnelle, came in to show us a drawing of a butterfly. Marquerite held up the
rough sketch to me as if it were a Picasso and sighed in sheer delight. It's not
hard to understand when you realize that in addition to maternal pride, Marquerite has an absolutely unquenchable passion for butterflies. Their eight-
room house in Bel Air is filled with thousands of the creatures—mounted,
framed, on tables, shelves, window sills, towels, linen, china, dipped in gold,
silver, and bronze and swarming all over the wallpaper. O.J.'s contribution to
this collection was the satiric *pièce de résistance*—a butterfly toilet seat. Marquerite doesn't mind. "I love butterflies," she said, putting her daughter's
drawing down. "They are so exquisite . . . so soft and elusive. I don't want
an epitaph or name on my tombstone when I die. Just a butterfly."

"Where do you go next?" Marquerite asked as we headed back to the Buffalo airport in her pearl-gray Mercedes.

"Well, I'm curious about that forced separation business, so I guess I'll fly down to Florida and see those, uh, Marlin wives."

"Dolphins," she corrected me, hanging on hard to the steering wheel so she wouldn't go off the road. When she got through laughing, she said she would pray for me. I thanked her. I knew I would need it. I almost said I would pray for her. With the pressures she lived under I figured she'd need some prayers and as it turned out, she needed them more than I guessed. During the 1975 football season Marquerite and the two children remained in California in a trial separation while O.J., rushing for new football records and eyeing a movie career, was based in Buffalo.

Mrs. Zonk

He's extremely jealous of me! . . . When we're out for an evening, he watches me like a hawk. . . . God, he won't even let me go into a store with tennis shorts on.

Our friends like us for thumbing our nose at superstardom, and it helps us remember that this fame business is bullshit!

I arrived in Miami on November 24, 1974, the day the Dolphins played the Jets in New York. President Ford and Henry Kissinger were in Vladivostok discussing further limitations of strategic offensive arms. Nobody gave a damn in Miami, they were all listening to the football game. The poolside bar at the Palm Bay Club was ten deep in sunbathers watching the game on TV.

"Kill Namath!" a sunburned woman yelled from her barstool. A bald man sitting next to her put his hand over his ear to soften what must have been piercing vibrations through his eardrum.

"Kill him! Kill Namath!" she shrieked again, slamming her fist on the bar.

As I started to collect my towel and suntan lotion to move to a quieter end of the pool, the man on the deck chair next to mine removed the cotton pads from his eyes, raised himself up on his elbows and turning his head toward the bar roared, "Kill Csonka! Kill him!"

Everybody at the bar turned and glared at us. I looked down between the deck chairs and saw a copy of his New York *Times* next to my New York *Times*—and suddenly had the feeling we were the only two people in Miami who *weren't* Dolphin fans.

Later that day the city lay under a pall of gloom. Namath had killed Csonka, and the Dolphins had lost. I picked up the phone and called Pam Csonka to verify our appointment for the following day. I was thinking of offering my condolences on the Dolphins' loss, but she seemed much too cheerful. After giving me directions she asked, "Whattaya wanna talk about?"

"Well, among other things, the Tuesday Rule!"

"The Tuesday Rule?" she said grouchily. "That's a lot of BS."

I was out bright and early the next morning. The temperature was already 99 degrees, and I was mentally praising the man who invented air conditioning (was it a woman?) while I was driving out of Miami. As I approached Plantation, Florida, I noticed miles and miles of tract housing. The sight of these look-alike ranch homes, spaced a foot apart, annoyed me. The work of a builder with a mania for making life on earth as drab and restrictive as possible. *They ought to put those guys in jail*, I thought as I pulled up to one of the little ranch houses and checked the mailbox to be sure I had the right address. It was. The black letters boldly spelled out CSONKA. What was one of the richest and certainly one of the greatest running backs in football history doing here? Particularly since he had signed a million-dollar contract with the World Football League which promised to pay him his money whether it started, faded, or folded. (It did all three.) It was hard to figure. The house just didn't look as if it belonged to a millionaire.

The door opened, and his daughter stood looking up at me. "Hi, we're expecting you . . . come in." She was a small girl, about five feet three, with a thin reedlike body, brown shoulder-length hair, and dark, brooding eyes. The eyes caught my attention. They were jet-black naphthylamine, as if they had been etched in charcoal. On closer examination I realized they were actually a light blue—it was the thick dark brows and black fringe of lashes that made them appear dark. She was dressed in blue jeans and a halter, and I wondered why she wasn't in school. Suddenly I realized why. This wasn't Larry Csonka's daughter. It was his wife, Pam.*

"Come in out of the sun." She squinted, shielding her eyes from the light. I passed from the bright, hot sunshine into a gloomy, dark room where the temperature must have been under 60 degrees. Slam went the door. My eyes, which were still sending blue sky-scorching sun images to my brain, blinked rapidly, trying to adjust to the change. Then I drew in my breath as I surveyed the room I was standing in. It had a morguelike quality, not only because it was cold, but because it was done completely in blue. Everything, absolutely everything in that room was blue. The rug, the walls, couch, chairs, drapes— there were blue candles, blue ashtrays, blue glass dolphins on the blue coffee table, and blue gauzy inner curtains drawn across the blue shuttered windows. The effect was pure mausoleum.

"I just love blue," Pam explained unnecessarily. "My bedroom is done in blue, too."

"Could we work in the kitchen?" I suggested, praying for a different color scheme. The kitchen was orange. It didn't take long to discover that the house which was "A" typical on the outside is not remotely typical of anything in the history of interior decorating on the inside. It misses being bizarre because

---

*Larry Csonka, professional football player, fullback with the Memphis Southmen, formerly with the Super Bowl Champion Miami Dolphins. Larry Csonka, at six two and 237 pounds, is one of the largest fullbacks in professional football. His size helped him gain more than 1,000 yards in three consecutive seasons (1971–73). He was named the most valuable player of the 1973 Super Bowl Game. In '74 Csonka signed a reputed million-dollar contract to play for the Memphis Southmen of the World Football League (WFL) which folded in October before the '75 season was finished. As this book goes to print, the Memphis Southmen team is applying for admission to the NFL.

most bizarre decor is well thought out. It comes close to the style of the bridal suite at a Holiday Inn, but it's safer to say, it's Csonka-like, and let's face it, the Csonkas are unique. Here's the cast: Larry and Pam and their two sons, eight-year-old Douglas and six-year-old Paul, a Yorkshire terrier named Pepper, a white cat they call HeShe because they didn't know which sex it was when they named it, an iguana slithering freely around the house, and a white rabbit, a free spirit, which comes and goes according to its hunger pains.

Pamela Conley Csonka was born in Akron, Ohio, thirty years ago. She met Larry twelve years later, when she was in seventh grade. They dated steadily through high school and college until they were married during his senior year at Syracuse University. As she was telling me this, I wrote down in my notebook, "Boring."

"Didn't you go out with anyone else?"

"Naw, not really. . . ."

Well, no one can accuse them of not knowing each other well enough before they got married. It also became evident before the day was out, that having known Larry for such a long time, Pam isn't awed by his sudden rise to superstardom. To a lot of their friends back home in Akron, Larry is still "the big Hungarian," and to Pam, who's known him since his mother was washing his ears and his father was working for *her* father at the local Goodyear plant, he's just "her husband."

"I can't be impressed," she said, referring to his success. "Most of this fame business is bullshit."

There are many peculiarities about Pam, but no façades, no affectations. She doesn't like anything phony and is quick to call anything that is bullshit. It's an expression she uses frequently. As if to reinforce this, there is a picture hanging on the wall of the family room that dramatizes the Csonkas' attitude to the three *F*s, fame, fakery, and flattery. In the picture, which appeared on the cover of *Sports Illustrated*'s August edition in 1972, Larry Csonka and Jim Kiick are in their uniforms in an old-fashioned pose as the Butch Cassidy and Sundance Kid of football. Larry is down on one knee with Jim standing rigidly beside him. Nothing seems out of order until you notice Larry's right hand and the middle *finger* which gives the universal gesture that has only one meaning.

"Isn't that a howl?" Pam said, grinning widely. "Can you imagine that picture making the cover of a national magazine?"

I walked over and examined it closely. The faces of Csonka and Kiick are deadpan but there's no mistake about the finger. It seems they were just clowning around at the end of the shooting session, and the photographer somehow caught this pose and submitted it with the rest of the pictures. No one knows to this day if the magazine printed it by mistake or not. If it did, it was the biggest oversight in the magazine business. One has the feeling they knew just what they were doing.

The public's reaction was immediate and negative. Letters poured in from all over the country—most of them written by incensed football fans criticizing Larry Csonka. How dare he corrupt the youth of America? Hundreds of letters came in from coaches of high schools and colleges, expressing their shock and disapproval. Don Shula, the coach of the Dolphins, was the only one who wasn't surprised. He was reported to have made only one reference to the cover and the furor it caused: "Nothing Zonk does surprises me!"

"For weeks the phones never stopped ringing," Pam said with a bubble of malicious laughter. "Everyone was calling to let us know they thought it was vulgar—a dirty thing to do to the clean, all-American football image!" She poured some steaming black coffee in my cup and sat down with her head in her hands, looking directly at me. "Whattaya wanna talk about?" She clearly wanted to get the interview over with.

I asked some background questions that were answered with "Yup, nope, dunno, can't remember," and I knew this wasn't going to be easy. Finally I admitted my ignorance about football. What was this business about forced separation? The Tuesday Rule? Was it true the wives couldn't sleep with their own husbands before a game? How come the Marlin wives put up with this—

"Dolphin!" She corrected me and put her head down on the table. I didn't know if she was laughing or crying. When she came up for air, she worked patiently with me as a teacher might do with her first-grade pupil. Twenty minutes later I looked down at my notes and smiled. . . . I still had to make a few phone calls and check out some facts, but the puzzle was unraveling.

Not all, but most, of the teams in the NFL separate the players from their wives the night before a game. Even for a home game the men are taken to a local hotel to spend the night. This is the coach's way of keeping his eyes on his boys, seeing to it there are no emotional upsets or physical strains and that the men get to bed on time. The Tuesday Rule with its Tuesday till Sunday prohibition is forced separation in the extreme. Most of the wives regard this unenforceable and unbelievable rule as a bad joke. Nevertheless, the football wives say it goes on. But where? I called NFL headquarters in New York and asked which teams practiced the Tuesday Rule? First, Pete Roselle's office said they'd never heard of it. Then they admitted it had been used in the sixties by some teams, but they didn't know *which ones*, and they also didn't know if any of the twenty-six NFL clubs practiced it today. I was told Beverly Warfield knew about the infamous injunction, so I stopped over at the Fort Lauderdale Tennis Club and had a visit with her. She told me that before her husband, Paul, was traded to the Dolphins, they'd had to abide by the Tuesday Rule in Cleveland, where Paul was playing for the Browns. The head coach at that time was Blanton Collier, and he evidently believed there should be no distractions before a game. "We hid from Coach Collier for six years!" Bev said gleefully. "It was dangerous because if we were caught sleeping together, Paul would have had to pay a twenty-five-hundred-dollar fine! When we were traded to the Dolphins, Shula's rule of separation only on the night before a game and during summer training camp seemed like a piece of cake!"

Pam Csonka didn't seem too perturbed by the notion of forced separation either. "The idea is wrong—and most of us Dolphin wives agree on that. It's wrong because that's treating grown men like children, but frankly, I'm glad to have Larry sleep away from me the night before a game. He's extremely nervous and doesn't know how to relax. . . . He just isn't nice to be with. So what's one night? Let Shula have him!"

Under the tough exterior, however, there's the hint of a lonely young woman, a woman attempting to adjust to the solitariness of being married to a superstar.

"Training camp is a drag, but actually I see less of him during the off-season. At least during the season he plays half his games at home. Last March he was so busy with promotions, commercials, and business that I saw him for only three days the whole month. . . . I guess he's gotta do all that stuff now. . . while he's got the big name. It isn't what I prefer, but it's something I can handle."

Knowing that there are just as many jock lovers running after Larry Csonka as there are chasing O. J. Simpson, I assumed I was going to be treated to another tirade against "those women." But it appeared, at least at first, that Pam didn't have Marquerite's problem.

"Jealous of *him* ? He's extremely jealous of *me*! He doesn't like me to dance with anyone, except very close friends. When we're out for an evening, he watches me like a hawk. . . . God, he won't even let me go into a store with tennis shorts on." She looked down at her slim legs covered in faded blue jeans and mumbled more to herself than to me, "I had a chance to do some modeling here in Florida, but Larry put his foot down. He's very possessive of me and wants me home."

That's a switch, I thought. "Do you give him reason to be jealous?"

She looked directly at me, and sparks flew from her eyes. "*No*! But I have good reason to be jealous of him. I have to put up with jock lovers chasing him all over the country—silly people fawning all over him. Why, once he called me from the Playboy Club in Los Angeles to vividly describe a nude swimming party. . . . Yet *I'm* not to go into a store with tennis shorts on. . . ."

"Well, it doesn't seem quite right," I said weakly, trying not to show my amusement at the thought of a husband giving his wife instant replay of a nude swimming party by cross-country phone.

"Larry couldn't handle anything like that when it comes to me," she snapped. "He's admitted it!" And then a little louder. "He's admitted he can't handle it! Once I was really angry because I'd fixed a big dinner and he never showed up—never even called to say he wouldn't be home. Well, I really gave it to him, and after I was all through readin' him out, I said, 'I wish we could trade places just for one week!' and he answered, 'I don't know how you do it. . . . I couldn't. . . . I couldn't handle it if the situation were reversed!' " Pam nodded as if in satisfaction that Larry would own up to his dual standard, but her frown showed some worry.

It's the same old story. What's good for the goose is not necessarily good for the gander (the goose never has as much fun). This sort of double standard (I can play around, you can't) is certainly one which, however irrational, many of the wives adhere to, but it's beginning to look a bit inequitable to Pam, and I got the distinct feeling she and Marquerite shared the same problem. It didn't take long for the subject to come up.

"I could do without jock lovers, not because I'm jealous [she is], but because they annoy me . . . I mean these 'women' "—she said the word with great disdain— "have been happening to Larry since college. I suppose they bothered me at first, but now they're a joke. When I was eight months pregnant, a girl came right up to our house, knocked on the front door and, when Larry answered, handed him a piece of paper with her name and phone number and then winked! 'When your wife goes to the hospital . . . call me!' That's a small sample of what goes on," she said, noting my expression. "I could give ya some shock waves. . . ."

"Well, go ahead. . . ."

"Naw, it's a bore. *They're* a bore. You've gotta be secure with your man, or these women could destroy your relationship. I'm forced to accept it as 'that's the way it is' or get out of the relationship. I accept it."

There are those who believe she "accepts it" because she's a graduate of Marabel Morgan's "Total Woman" course in Miami. This schooling in subservience and submission (if the king makes the wrong decision, the queen still follows him) has attracted various Dolphin wives who have been using the Total Woman strategy. But in spite of Pam's name being widely publicized for taking the course, she denies it, grumbling something about "Aw, I don't even believe in the principle." Nevertheless, when it comes to "put up or shut up," she puts up . . . however loudly.

Her head went back in her hands, and she looked at me as if to say "Let's get on with it."

Pam clearly has the same problem as Marquerite, I thought. When I finished my interviews, I was to find that twenty out of thirty wives had the jock lover jitters.

Ask any of the neighbors on the street what the Csonkas are like, and you'd probably get the same answer I got from one elderly lady ; "A little strange." Then she went on to tell me why. "Why one night I saw that pretty little thing with her two children all bundled up come out and get into their car. She was carrying what must have been TV dinners, . . . and they sat out there in the dark and cold, I suppose eatin' their supper. The car never left the driveway"—the lady sniffed—"must have been out there for almost two hours, and then they all filed back into the house. Peculiar, I'd say. . . . " What the lady *didn't* know was that the power went off right in the middle of a Dolphins game, and Pam simply gathered the kids and their supper and went out to follow the last half on the car radio.

Pam is a loyal "Zonk" fan and was attending all the home games around the time I saw her, but it wasn't long before she didn't have a team to root for. It all started when Csonka and two other Dolphins, Paul Warfield and Jim Kiick, signed up to play with the WFL for the '75 season. The shock waves reverberated throughout the football world and especially in Miami, where loyal Dolphin fans simply couldn't believe their boys would sell out for money.

It's difficult to unravel, but it goes something like this. The World Football League (WFL) was young (formed in 1974), brash (it attempted to sign Joe Namath among others), and very ambitious (it wanted to rival the NFL). The NFL being older (formed in the 1920's) and more famous (it has O.J.) wasn't happy with the new league's attempts to take its big stars away. But the WFL went heedlessly ahead and lured Zonk, Warfield, and Kiick with a $3,300,000 contract to play on its new team, the Memphis Southmen, *guaranteeing* Csonka an estimated $1,500,000. In October, 1975, the WFL, which couldn't live up to its obligations, folded, and Csonka and his teammates suddenly didn't have a team to play for, yet were still under contract (as this book goes to print) to team owner John Basset, who in turn is desperately trying to place the Memphis Southmen in the NFL.

Larry's lion's share of that $3,300,000 contract obviously hasn't affected the Csonkas' life-style. You don't have to know Pam long before realizing she doesn't spend money on clothes, makeup, or jewelry and it certainly doesn't show in her house. Where, then, does it go? Land. In this respect they have much in common (I was to find out much later) with the Catfish Hunters. They're all buyin' up a li'l land. Larry and his agent have handled most of the investments. There's property in Florida, a rustic A frame sitting on some pretty land in the mountains of North Carolina, and a 400-acre farm near Lisbon, Ohio, where his brother is running things until Larry can come home and take care of it himself. Pam claims she and her husband have an entirely different conception of money.

"He's always talkin' in the hundreds of thousands of dollars, it's enough to scare you, and I'm always talkin' about grocery money. I need a raise. Everyone knows there's an inflation out there. I can't complain to Larry; he doesn't talk about piddlin' amounts. Would you believe I have to write to his agent for a raise?"

She started peanut butter sandwiches and said we'd have to gobble them down in a hurry because she had traffic patrol duty after school. While she spread the thick peanut butter on the bread she explained why Larry hated to be touched by fans. "He instinctively wants to act aggressively when somebody pushes him in a crowd. I can understand it," she said, pausing a second to look up to see if I was following her. "When he plays football, he's shoved, pushed, grabbed, and tackled. When he's in a crowd and the fans are doin' the same thing, it's natural to want to come back at them. One time at the airport, in the middle of a huge welcoming crowd for the Dolphins, a gorgeous chick came up and grabbed his thigh and squealed, 'Ohhhh, how *big* your legs are!' Well, Larry almost clobbered her . . . and I guess the feeling frightened him a little. Of course, it doesn't bother him when *I* do it. . . . "
She grinned.

Pam then went on to confirm what I later heard from other Dolphin wives. It seems the Csonkas have frequent wrestling matches in their backyard. "Pam pins him down," I was told, and none too gently, or affectionately. She wrestles to win! She also plays tennis to win and has been known to call Larry a few choice names over the net. Dinah Shore let the cat out of the bag on a talk show. She explained that she and Burt Reynolds sometimes play doubles with Pam and Larry. The men get very chauvinistic. They want to show the women up, so they practically kill themselves getting the ball over the net. But Pam plays a competitive game, and the better she plays, the more Larry runs after the ball, as if he were going through the line in a football game.

"So you're pretty good at tennis, huh?" I inquired.
Shrug.
"What about Dinah's remark?"
Shrug.
Pam is clearly into the "real people" routine, and name-dropping or gossiping about famous friends is taboo. (She must have some good secrets with Dinah Shore, though, because when her name came up, Pam never said a word, but the Cheshire grin was revealing.)

The Csonkas not only like to wrestle in the backyard and show each other up on the tennis court, but often compete for the most original Christmas present. One Christmas morning Pam asked a friend to come over and help her wrap a gift. When the friend got there, she asked where the present was. "The gift's *me*," Pam said, grinning wickedly. Then the two of them used yards and yards of tissue paper taped together to cover Pam from head to toe. They tied a big red satin bow and sprig of holly around her waist, and the friend helped Pam hobble into the bedroom, where Zonk was still sleeping. Pam jumped up on the bed, shouting at the top of her lungs, "Merry Christmas! Merry Christmas! I'm your Christmas present!"

We were about to bite into our peanut butter sandwiches when the phone rang. She got up and shook her head. "It's probably some girl for Larry." When she answered the phone, I knew it wasn't. Pam conversed gaily for a few minutes, then came back in the kitchen. "That was Dick Butkus [former All-Pro linebacker with the Chicago Bears]. He's something else. Once we received a phone call at dawn in our hotel room in New York. I answered, and this sexy female voice purrs, 'Helloooo, this is Barbara. Can I speak to my lover, Larreee?' 'Here, lover!' I handed the phone over to Larry, who was sleeping beside me. Well, it turned out it was a Butkus trick. He was out hitting the bars and decided to get Larry in trouble. So he paid a girl—you know a hooker in a bar—fifty dollars to make that call, knowing I was there. Larry's still waiting to get back at him."

That wasn't the only time Pam was awakened in the middle of the night in New York City. She and Larry once stayed at the Americana while attending a big football banquet. Returning to the hotel at about 3 A.M., they both had trouble falling asleep after the excitement of the evening. Pam started reading the bestselling novel *The Tower* and became engrossed in a chapter describing the panicky flight of those escaping the burning high-rise. Larry fell asleep, but Pam was absorbed. *My God,* she thought while reading, *if people would just keep their heads and not run around yelling fire, everybody would have a chance.* Soon she found herself vividly experiencing the smell of smoke as she read about it. Looking up from her book, she sniffed the air. Impossible! She went back to reading, then smelled smoke again. Startled, she looked up to see thick yellow smoke curling up from under the door and pouring into the room.

"Fire!" she yelled, jumping out of bed and running around the room. "Fire!" Larry woke up and stared at his wife as though she were out of her mind. Then he saw the smoke.

"My God," he gasped as he ran out of the room stark naked, "I've got to warn everybody." He ran into the hallway and pounded on one door after another, yelling, "Everybody get down to the lobby . . . don't panic!" Mission accomplished, he came back to the room, grabbed his wife and a pair of slacks, and proceeded to walk down thirty-five flights of stairs to the main floor. After reading *The Tower,* Pam didn't think the elevators were safe. Exhausted, they reached the lobby in time to find the fire out and the manager feeding the guests coffee and doughnuts. One old lady eyed Larry suspiciously.

"Are you the young man who ran around the thirty-fifth floor waking everyone up?" She asked tartly.

"Yes, ma'am, I'm the one," he said proudly.

"Well, next time yell *'Fire!'* I thought you were a crazy, naked drunk."

We had finished our peanut butter sandwiches, Pam had done her patrolling at the corner, and the children were home from school. Things seemed cooler outside, and I was glad because our interview was drawing to a close. I could almost feel that Pam wanted to wind things up with a definitive statement about herself.

"I don't want to be listed as Mrs. Larry Csonka," she wailed. "I'm Pam Csonka. I want my own accomplishments recognized, whether large or small. I'm learning to fly a Cessna 150! I don't want people to say Larry Csonka's wife is learning to fly. . . . I want them to say Pam Csonka is learning to fly that Cessna.

"I wouldn't say I have an identity problem—but to be honest, there's a certain kind of resentment—not of him or his accomplishments but the *idea* that he's a star."

Suddenly aware that I was leaving and still might not have the picture clear, she put her head in her hands and measured her words. "I guess you might say of me—uh, of us, the two of us—that we won't put up with any bullshit in our lives anymore. I think that's the main thing we've both come to realize. No more bull. . . . No more pretending we're something we're not. We always end up in trouble when we do anyway." She grinned. "I'll give you an example. Last year we put on the dog goin' to a fancy party, and it turned out to be a disaster! You see, Larry bought a 1953 Bentley and spent a great deal of money fixin' it up. We were invited to a very swanky affair in Boca Raton and decided to get all decked out and go in our Bentley—you know, impress the people! We were so proud of that bloody car that we arrived early and drove right up and parked it near the entrance where everyone would notice. But dumb-dumb Larry forgot to turn off the parking lights, which drained the battery. So at the end of the evening the car wouldn't start. There we were, Larry in his black tie and me in a long Venetian lace dress, out there in front of all those ritzy people we were tryin' to impress . . . pushin' our car home! We knew we didn't fit in anyway—a couple of hicks from Ohio—but as we were pushin' that Bentley I knew it was time to stop bullshitting ourselves."

I walked out into the late-afternoon sun—shockingly bright after the dark house. We shook hands, and I thought to myself what a good thing it was their

Bentley had broke down. "One more thing," I said before getting into my car. "Does it bother you that most of Miami seems to be boiling about Larry leaving the Dolphins for all that money?"

"Naw," she said matter-of-factly. "It was a straight business deal. Larry would have been crazy not to take it. He's going to finish his contractual obligations to the Dolphins! We can't live in fear of what the fans think—they can't hurt us!"

Several months later an article appeared in the New York *Times* announcing that the Csonkas had moved several hundred miles north of Miami because of acts of vandalism on their home by angry Miami Dolphins fans.

The fans must have got to them in northern Florida because before the year was over, they left the state and moved to their 450-acre farm in Lisbon, Ohio. I wonder if she'll paint the farm blue.

The Young Fox

The system of football is the antithesis of American ideals.

I'd heard, via the Dolphin wives' grapevine, that Julie Swift* was attractive, bright, outspoken, and pleasantly eccentric, that she was studying law and used a lot of long, impressive words, had great contempt for football, and was the only wife who really understood what the NFL strike was all about. They said Julie was grinding her teeth these days over Doug's contract and I probably would get a lecture instead of an interview. Before I left my hotel for Julie's house, I put in a call to New York, to my friend Dave Anderson, author and spotswriter for the New York *Times*.

"What was the NFL strike all about?"

"Where've you been? That happened back in the summer of '74."

Why do people keep asking me that? "What was it all about?"

"It was a labor dispute. The NFL Players Association went out on strike against management. The football players didn't report to training camp, but after a while they started drifting back, and the strike collapsed for lack of support and was called off."

"Did any of the wives picket?"

"Well, I remember Julie Swift was out there with her sandwich board right up to the end!"

"What did the players want?"

"Among other things they wanted to negotiate on the option clause."

"What's an option clause?"

"Listen, I'm trying to write a book myself. *You're* down in Florida. Why don't you ask Julie Swift?"

Well, they said she was eccentric, I thought as I pushed my way through lush tropical vegetation leading up to the front door, *but they forgot to mention she lives in the middle of a jungle.* I could hear music vibrating through the heavy oak door. A few seconds after I rang the bell someone screamed above the clatter, "C'mon in!"

I was ready for anything after Pam Csonka's house, but Julie Swift has to

---

*Doug Swift, linebacker for the Miami Dolphins of the NFL. Swift has been a starter for the two-time world champion Miami Dolphins ever since he reported to the team in 1970 as a free agent. A graduate of Amherst College in Massachusetts, Swift has the rare combination of size, speed, and intelligence that makes him one of the smartest and hardest-hitting linebackers in the NFL.

have the strangest collection of "things" ever assembled in one room. An enormous wooden *Casablanca* fan rotates above the dining-room table. An Oriental rug, old, beautiful, and threadbare, covers a section of the floor. Above it, on a slanted ceiling, is a tapa cloth, just hanging there covering a large area. (It's from Tonga, I found out later, made of pounded coconut husks and berry dye.) In one corner I noticed that the bamboo wallpaper was torn to shreds; it looked as though someone had jammed a fist through it. Someone had. A wallpaper hanger made a mistake and papered over the entrance to the hot-water heater, and Doug Swift simply put his fist through the mistake. An interior decorator would have had a nervous breakdown looking over that room. Tiffany lamps, lacquered Chinese chests, early American tables, South Sea Island accessories all mixed together in modern Floridian tropicana. Wow! I collapsed on the nearest chair and noticed something I hadn't seen before in the homes of other famous athletes—*books*. Hundreds of books lined the shelves on the four walls. I wouldn't see books again until I visited Barbara Bouton.

The music was blasting—some kind of jazz. A big black woman named Viola, wearing a white starched uniform, was dancing abandonedly along with an eighteen-month-old blond toddler named Alex Swift. He could barely stand up. Viola was really doing her number, a lot of boppin', skat singing, and lurching. The little boy was trying to imitate her. "Come on . . . get down on it, Alex!" Viola laughed and snapped her fingers to the music. Alex gyrated wildly, and his diapers fell off.

Alex is an unusual child, but then *everyone* is unusual in this house. Daddy is a superstar football player who's planning on going to medical school to become a surgeon. Mother is a law student at the University of Miami and has become a student expert in the field of labor law. Viola isn't just a maid either, she's seeing to it that Alex gets the right start in life.

Julie came forward to greet me, a little breathless and apologetic for not being organized. (Being organized is important to Julie.) She led me to the backyard, which was entirely overgrown with greenery except for a postage-stamp area of concrete by the swimming pool. There we sat down on deck chairs and squinted at each other in the late-afternoon sun.

My first impression was: She's a darling! Small-boned and fragile-looking (she turned out to be the smallest of the wives), she has a tiny size six figure and an enchanting smile. Her sun-streaked blond hair fascinated me. Sassoon cut, it was all silk and bouncy, swirling and quivering with her every move as if it had a life of its own. Her eyes are ice-blue and alert. Friends call them "Swift-minded," and they complement a face Helen of Troy *should* have had—a face with the upturned, charming features of a porcelain figurine. But Julie doesn't want to come off as "darling" or "made of porcelain." She'd rather impress you as "foxy" and made of "steel."

She kept looking nervously at my tape recorder as she measured her words and considered her answers very carefully. The conversation was immediately interrupted by a friend, Penny Clark, a second-year law student who came by to study with Julie for their final exam. Penny dropped a lawbook, which must have weighed a ton, down on a metal outdoor table with a thud, adjusted her glasses, and looked me over.

"You gonna write about Julie?"

"I hope to . . . if I get enough information."

"Well, I can tell you she's going to make a great lawyer!"

"Tell me why you think so," I said as Julie disappeared into the house to make iced tea.

"She's got all the ingredients. She's high-strung, sensitive, and very competitive." Penny slammed the words out as if she were serving in a tennis match. "Julie's quick to drive her point home in an argument or discussion. I mean, you should see her debate in class. God! She's always so sweet and polite at first that it's very disarming. It isn't until she's nailed you to the wall that you find out how completely devastating she is when it comes to making her point in any debate. She *never* backs down."

I found myself nodding at Penny, and then I studied Julie, who had just arrived with a tray of iced tea. She was smiling sweetly. She looked so feminine, so vulnerable. It didn't seem possible that Penny Clark was describing the same person. Penny went on talking about Julie as if she weren't there. I heard the words "killer in an argument" and once again appraised the demure little porcelain figure sitting across from me. Impossible.

"Julie's mother," Penny went on, "is nicknamed the Old Fox. She's also sweet-looking. Grandmotherly, but sweet. She always gets what she wants! What a woman! Julie is her mother's daughter—the Young Fox!"

"Mother was a schoolteacher, now she's a guidance counselor," Julie said quietly as if that explained everything.

"I wouldn't get in a heated debate with Julie," Penny went on, looking at her friend with an admiring smile. "Halfway through a good argument she'll come out with something that will destroy it completely. It's kinda like guerrilla warfare. It's not deceitful and never undercover, but the blow is totally unexpected."

"I'll try to watch it," I said, anxious to get on with the interview.

"Guerrilla warfare can be totally deceitful and definitely undercover," Julie countered suddenly. "The only similarity between your opinion of my debating and guerrilla warfare would be in the surprise element."

Just then I noticed that the baby, Alex, was lying flat on his stomach on the concrete apron with his head over the edge of the pool immersed in the water. Alex not only dances, but knows how to breathe underwater. I decided not to scream on the assumption he *had* to come up for air any second. He didn't. I heard his mother say something about "a small defensive force of irregular soldiers making surprise raids. . . ." *My God, wasn't anybody going to stop that kid before he drowned himself?*

"Julie," Penny blurted out, suddenly changing the subject, "is never on time! If she's outside the classroom talking to friends twenty minutes before class starts, she *still* can't make it inside on time. I've often wondered"—she peered myopically at Julie—"why she's *always* late. She's such an orderly person—so organized in every other way."

Alex came up for air! I was overcome with relief. Water streamed down his face and clothes. He gulped, blinked, and promptly rolled over the edge and into the pool—shoes and all. No one paid any attention.

"I *am* an orderly person," Julie agreed. "I'm late because I have so many things to do and think about—things that are more important than being *on* time. I'm late because I have no respect for time!" She smiled broadly, pleased with the way she had structured the sentence. "I get bored quickly . . . distracted . . . I like to get on to something else."

"I wish you'd get on to saving Alex," I said nervously, looking at the pool, where some bubbles on the surface were the only sign he was there.

In a flash Julie reached in and pulled out a wet and laughing child.

"That's some baby!" I said, astonished.

"Oh, Alex is really a person! He has a marvelous personality already." She rubbed the baby vigorously with a towel, and he laughed all the harder. "We have one guy on the Dolphins who doesn't even like kids—he's a bachelor—and he comes over here all the time just to sit and watch Alex do his thing."

Watching everyone do their "thing" at the Swifts' could be interesting, I thought.

"He's an *amazing* child," Julie went on, "just like his father. . . . By the way, did you see Doug's thing—his great masterpiece—as you came in?" Before I had time to answer, she was leading me toward the front door. We stepped out on the grass, and she stretched her arms wide. "There it is. . . . He made it all himself!" I wondered how I'd missed it. It was a massive goldfish pond, measuring fifteen by thirty feet. I could see the fish swimming down below the water lilies. At one end of the pond there was a statue of a faun and at the other a homemade waterfall.

"Doug built it and landscaped it!" Julie said proudly. "He's really the Renaissance type—he could be successful in any one of twenty fields." Doug Swift has been called an iconoclast, a radical, a kook, an egghead by sportswriters and a hippie by his own coach. I'm sure he likes his wife's description of him best.

Julie is more difficult to describe. She plays at all these parts, but I'm not too sure that underneath the role of the "fox" there isn't a sweet, darling, vulnerable woman made of porcelain. (She'll vomit when she reads this, but I have to say it.)

Julie Donaldson was born twenty-seven years ago in Chester, Pennsylvania. Her father was a successful businessman, and her mother was a teacher. Julie was a serious child who went to public schools where she was a straight A student. At Mount Holyoke College she majored in English with a minor in Russian.

Doug Swift went to Amherst, where he excelled in both his studies and football. They met through mutual friends and soon discovered that they had mutual backgrounds. Just about everyone is in a profession! (Doug's father and grandfather are surgeons, and his mother is a pediatrician.) Both were bright and ambitious and had the will to excel. Their relationship, according to Julie, survived the trivia and game playing of a one-year courtship. (A school chum of Doug's said she followed him around like a puppy.) Evidently finding others dull by comparison, they had nowhere to go but marriage.

Julie was late for her own wedding—one hour and forty minutes late. She walked into the church in street clothes, while Doug stood ready at the altar and her mother and bridesmaids waited upstairs to help her into her wedding gown. Why was she late? Maybe she was at the library looking up "guerrilla warfare." At any rate, in spite of her lateness she dawdled at the church entrance, greeting friends and chatting about everything from the weather to football before she went upstairs to change into her bridal finery. It's apparent that even then she didn't have much respect for time (or other people?).

The wedding took place during Doug's senior year at Amherst. He was a football star by then and a very popular one. In those days he and his friends were referred to as the king and his court. "It was easy to understand why they adored him so," Julie explained. "It's because of his uninhibited wit . . . he's really a very funny man. In those days his friends were so attached to him they couldn't understand why they couldn't come along on our honeymoon. Can you imagine? I think Doug would have let them, but I put my foot down." Instead of Doug's court, they each took along twenty books and, according to Julie, spent hours in the Caribbean reading Milton and Joyce. I'll bet!

I think it's fair to say that the Swifts have a full life, between football, negotiating contracts, premed school, law school, and Alex. (For anyone else Alex would be a full-time job.) In the summertime they're able to spend more time with each other, but in the fall when football and school starts . . . whew!

"We'll manage!" Julie said, cracking a piece of ice with her teeth. "We'll just have to get more organized!"

Maybe Viola will have to stop dancing and do some housework.

With an eye on Alex, who was on the loose, I steered Julie onto the subject of football. One hour and fifty minutes later she was still going strong. She hadn't even come to a period. I could synthesize the monologue by saying she doesn't like the game, but her reasons are more interesting than her conclusion. "The irony of football is that so many people equate it with virility, Mom, apple pie, and Americanism, yet the system itself is the antithesis of American ideals!" She walked over and fished Alex out of the water, kissed him on top of his wet head, came back, and sat down. "I hate the system! It's very restrictive. You have a group of businessmen running football, and they set up contracts that deprive players of what I consider their constitutional rights. For instance, my husband's basic contract has been terminated, but he has to work for the Dophins for one more year, and during that time he can't negotiate with another team."

Julie was referring to the option clause stipulating that after the standard contract has terminated, the player must still play for his employer team for one year. If the employer team doesn't renew the player's contract, he has to wait until the end of the option year before he becomes a free agent and able to negotiate with another team. If another team attempts to negotiate at any time before the expiration of the option year, the negotiation is called tampering, and the team is heavily penalized. Tampering is a no-no in football. Once a player completes his option year, however, he's free to negotiate and play for any other team in the league. But there's still another hook. If the player *does* sign with a second team, the Roselle Rule states that the second team must reimburse the first with a player or draft choice to compensate the first team for the lost player. Of course, sometimes a team *wants* to lose a player, then the Roselle Rule doesn't apply. I found out that learning about the "system" is far more difficult than learning about the game.

Anyway, Julie was madder than a hornet the day I saw her because it didn't look as if the Dolphins were going to renew Doug's contract. She was worried that at the end of the option year Doug would have no place to go!

"The only way to beat the system is to quit football!" She sighed dejectedly. "Can you imagine a system where they call job hunting tampering? The owners have it all tied up. If they don't want you, then they see to it no one else can have you. It's a form of indentured servitude!"

"It's a form of what?" I cried over my shoulder as I rushed to save Alex from drowning. It was the third outfit he had soaked since I'd been there.

"Indentured servitude! Some people might think that's strong language, but I don't!"

"It does seem there are a lot of hidden barriers," I admitted, trying to dry a squirming Alex with a wet towel.

"I'll tell the world." And she started counting them off on her fingers.

"There's the draft, the option clause, the Roselle Rule, the Tuesday Rule, and forced separation."

When Julie got to "forced separation," her pretty face looked as though she'd bitten into an unripe persimmon. "My God, *that's* another indignity we have to put up with. Can you believe that these great big, strong men have to have someone over their shoulder saying, 'Come on, little boy . . . you don't know how to take care of yourself, so we'll do it for you. *We'll* tell you when to go to bed . . . and *we'll* tell you when you shouldn't have sex!' "

She had raised her voice, but her diction was perfect. *What a great trial lawyer she'll make,* I thought as she looked at me and shook her finger.

"Do you know any other profession in the world that fines grown men for sleeping with their wives?"

Before I could say no, I noticed Alex was in the pool again. I glanced over at Penny Clark, but she was deep in her lawbook. I was about to go to the rescue when Julie got up and swooped him out of the water without missing a beat. "You know, there's a fining system in football, don't you? Oh, yes!" she said sardonically. "Some teams fine their players as high as twenty-five hundred dollars for sleeping with their wives. . . ." I remembered that Beverly Warfield had told me that before Paul was traded to the Dolphins they used to hide from Coach Collier of the Cleveland Browns and sleep together at the risk of that steep fine. I mentioned this to Julie—that and Bev's suggestion that "Sex was more exciting when it was forbidden." Julie didn't see the humor in it. She stuck right to the point.

"The fines are even unfair *within* the system. The worst teams fine their players the most money. In that respect, the Dolphin wives get a break. The Dolphins are on top, so the fines aren't too high. If Doug decides to spend the night with me, the fine is only around a hundred dollars. It's higher if he's caught with me the night before a Super Bowl. But that isn't the point. Forced separation, particularly the two-month training camp period in the summer, not only is an inconvenience, but creates a lot of tension. By the time you get together with your husband after training camp you have all these, uh, little insignificant problems to solve, and before you know it, you're arguing about something irrelevant like 'Why didn't you get the pool cleaned?' " At the word "pool" we both looked over in that direction at the same time. Alex wasn't in the water. Julie smiled and kept on going. "Most of the Dolphin wives feel forced separation is rough on your sex life, but somehow more of them get pregnant during training camp than at any other time!" Julie started to giggle at her own remark. "It's really a riot! There are a lot of babies born nine months after training camp!"

Penny Clark put down her lawbook and smiled, too.

"Well, I guess Beverly Warfield is right," I started to say.

"She's right!" Julie proclaimed. "What's forbidden is always desired," and then quickly she went back to her point. "I hope training camp will soon be an outmoded concept. Football is ripe for change. I don't think anyone can really believe that sex the night before a game is detrimental to a player's on-field performance. It's been shown to be just the opposite in a recent study. Sex is a *life*-force. It should be good for you before a game, but most certainly it shouldn't be regulated by a football coach!"

"Well said!" Penny cheered.

Julie smiled a smile of complete satisfaction, and I just knew it soon would become her "litigation smile." The audience was over, and we walked inside. The music, which had been going full blast ever since I arrived, had been switched from jazz to a Brahms symphony. The hollow, almost sepulchral tones reverberated through the house. Alex started to cry, and I sat down under the *Casablanca* fan and wondered if I could take it. Julie walked over to the recorder and started fiddling with some dials.

"It's not that I mind my husband's jazz music"—Doug Swift has one of the most fantastic collections around—"but I like *order* to my music, and classical music has order!" Alex, who was still crying, toddled over to the recorder and started pounding on it.

"The trouble is"—Julie looked down at Alex adoringly—"Alex *doesn't* like classical music." She pressed a button. "So we'll have to go back to jazz."

A dreadful noise emerged from the speakers, and Alex stopped crying and started to dance. Julie watched him with a proud little smile on her face. She didn't look like a lawyer anymore, and suddenly I knew the Young Fox—the girl of intellect and steel—was really a soft, loving person and perhaps a frightened wife. She was intellectually concerned about the legalities and human rights aspects of the option clause, but she was emotionally worried sick that her *husband's* contract wasn't going to be renewed.

"Don't let that contract business get you down," I said with forced gaiety as I went out the door. "After all, Doug's a Renaissance man, and he can be successful in at least twenty fields!"

"Yeah," she wailed. "But he's also great at playing football!"

"But you hate the system, remember?"

"Never mind what I hate . . . Doug wants to play football for the Dolphins!"

Six months later I called Julie long distance to find out what had happened. I asked how everything was, and she told me Alex was going to have a sister or brother by Christmastime.

"That's just great! How's Alex?"

"Well, he wasn't talking when you were here, but he is now. Do you know what his first word was?"

"Water, swim, jazz?" I guessed.

"No," she bubbled merrily over the phone. "His first word was 'baseball'! Sooooo we wrapped him up and took him to a doubleheader. He loved it. I think he's going to be a baseball freak!"

I finally got around to the big question.

"Why, didn't you hear?" she said jubilantly. "Everything is super! Doug signed a new four-year contract with the Dolphins in February."

I sure don't want to be around Julie Swift four years from now.

The Survivor

*Football and fame are hard on a marriage. I bet the percentages of un-
happy marriages are higher in football than in any other sport! I have to
admit that it almost destroyed my marriage. . . .*

*Why worship these football players? Why? They're only human . . .
and most of them are stupid jocks—big studs who haven't a brain for
anything but girls and the roar of the crowd!*

After meeting Madames Simpson, Csonka, and Swift, I began thinking that
life as a football star's wife wasn't all that great. When I met Alice Kiick,* I
knew it.

Alice is a fragile, natural-looking beauty who is as tough-minded at the age
of twenty-nine as any woman I've ever met. She has faced a crisis point in her
own marriage, scrutinized it no matter how painful, demanded change, and
got it. At this point, the marriage survives, but then anything can happen between writing this chapter and publication. Alice's background has a great
deal to do with her ability to act and innovate, to dig and weed out whatever
severely complicates a marriage relationship. Most of all, her background has
given her the potentials for personal growth.

Her mother, Mrs. Arthur Chaussart, probably taught Alice more about survival than any other human being. The Chaussarts lived in Superior, Wyoming, a small coal-mining town, where Mr. Chaussart was foreman in one of
the mines and also county commissioner, a job that provided extra funds for
the growing family. He died shortly after Alice, their fourth child, was
brought home from the hospital. Mrs. Chaussart was able to take over her
husband's job as county commissioner, and then, to save money, she decided
to build her own house. She and her daughters sawed, hammered, plastered
during their free time and on weekends. Brick by brick they built their house.
Delighted that they would no longer be encumbered by rent, the family moved
in just in time for the next crisis. Alice's mother lost the election that year and
with it her term as county commissioner, her only source of income. Alice,
who was seven at the time, remembers the gloom that fell on their little
household. "We sat huddled around Mother like a scene from *Little Women,*

---

*Jim Kiick, running back for the Memphis Southmen, formerly with the Miami
Dolphins. Kiick, the "Sundance Kid" of football, gained more than 500 yards in every season he played for the Dolphins. A clutch all-around player, he was signed by
the Memphis Southmen for the 1975 season in a multimillion-dollar contract that included Larry Csonka and Paul Warfield, for the WFL, which folded in October, 1975.

asking, 'What will we do? What will we do?' Mother just held onto us and promised we'd be all right. I can remember her saying, 'We'll survive!' "

At forty-seven, a time when most people think about retiring, Mrs. Chaussart resolved to seek a new career. She gave up the house that had taken so much time and energy to build and moved her family to the big city, Laramie, Wyoming, where she went back to school at the state university and got her teaching degree. That accomplished, she taught school in a rural community seventy miles from town, driving back and forth every day on treacherous roads come rain, shine, or blizzards. "What a woman she was! She was just like the pony express when it came to getting through all that weather. Sometimes her car would be completely covered with snow except for one little peephole on the windshield, but she always made it home to cook our dinner." Alice also remembers how frugally they lived. It wasn't just pennies they pinched. Not one scrap of food was ever wasted, the laundry had to be done all in one day—plugging in the iron more than once a week would add extra pennies to the electric bill—and clothes were never thrown away. Patches were sewn on the patches. "She had ways to save money that most people have never thought of before," Alice laughingly remembers.

The Chaussart girls grew up and got married, and Alice, the baby of the family, went to Laramie High School, where she became a cheerleader—something she has in common with 80 percent of the wives I interviewed. Most cheerleaders meet, go steady with, and marry their high school football hero. They usually never get out of the cheering section unless they're lucky enough to have a background like Alice Kiick's.

Jim Kiick, who was originally from Lincoln Park, New Jersey, was attending the University of Wyoming on a scholarship and met Alice at a basketball game, where she was going through the usual gyrations. He eyed her up and down and, as he tells the story, fell instantly in love. The cheerleader wasn't too sure. After all, she was still in high school, chewing bubble gum and majoring in flirtation.

At first Mrs. Chaussart didn't approve either. "There's only one reason a college man goes out with a high school girl . . . and besides," she said, "he's from New Jersey." Mother evidently thought that everybody who lived in that state was a gangster. Jim's choice also disturbed his friends. "Why waste your time with old bubble gummer?" they teased. "She doesn't seem to like you anyway!"

But Alice gave up bubble gum and her other boyfriends and in her sophomore year at the University of Wyoming married Jim Kiick, the school's football star, who was already making headlines around the country.

Today the Dolphins' famous running back who signed with the Memphis Southmen (of the now defunct WFL) and his wife live in South Miami in a nondescript little ranch house with an adorable 5-year-old son named Brandon and a marriage they hope is sufficiently patched to withstand the emotional and social pressures of the future. When I arrived on her doorstep, I hoped my visit with Alice Kiick would be a pleasant change from what I'd discovered other football wives were going through—namely, their only recently acknowledged disgust at what the game was doing to their lives. But Alice set me straight right away. "Football and fame are hard on a marriage. I bet the percentages of unhappy marriages are higher in football than in any other sport!" And then she went on to tell me how the game had almost destroyed her marriage.

It happened slowly and insidiously, according to Alice. Jim went through the frustration of being the favorite the first three years with the Dolphins' coach, Don Shula, who called him Mr. Reliable in public and then promptly consigned him to football Siberia. Some claim Jim just didn't play too well and had a fallout with Shula. Alice insists it was a personality clash between the coach and Jim. Whatever the reason, Jim Kiick found himself taking a backseat to Mercury Morris, from West Texas State. Nobody had ever heard of Morris, apparently, until Jim sat out a game owing to injuries. The minute Morris got into the game he showed tremendous ability and some outside speed Kiick just didn't possess. Kiick recovered and started playing again, and Morris complained publicly that he wasn't playing enough. By now the sportswriters knew who he was. To appease Morris, Shula started putting him in the game more often and, in doing so, found he had a great football player where before he'd thought he had a good one. It wasn't long before Morris became a regular and Kiick, the superstar, the Sundance to Larry Csonka's Butch Cassidy, became a spot player. It tore him apart. The more he sat on the bench, the more morose and difficult he became at home. It was at this time that the Kiicks' lines of communication with each other ruptured. Jim sulked and stewed in resentment, and Alice wrote angry letters to the coach—letters she never mailed. Their private life became hell.

According to Alice, the star was "replaced," and since it was his whole life, it almost killed Jim. Evidently being replaced is a fear that nags just about every superstar. When the fear becomes reality, it can destroy a career, a marriage, and sometimes a man. Every superstar keeps in the back of his mind the story of Wally Pipp, first baseman with the Yankees from 1915 to 1925. He was tired, and with a batting average of .218, you can afford to sit a game out *once* during the season. His backup man was a fellow named Lou Gehrig, a second-string first baseman who'd been with the Yankees since the season opened but hadn't played a game. That day young Gehrig substituted for Wally Pipp, and everyone knows how *that* turned out. What they may not know is the great Pipp never got in the game again as a regular. It seems replacement is worth worrying about.

Alice remembers how deeply humiliated and frustrated Jim was during the period when he sat on the bench watching Mercury Morris become a star. "That stupid game was eating him alive. I got to the point where I hated football! Hated the game and everything about it, including Shula."

Shula wouldn't exactly win a popularity contest with the other Dolphin wives, but with Alice Kiick, the coach is at the top of her hate list. "Not personally, but because he's part of the whole phony system. I've wanted to call him and ask if he realizes how many players are having trouble at home because he reinforces that winning is the only thing that counts."

Alice shook her head, and I noticed some strands of gray. Most women would have covered them up at her age. She sighed deeply, then went on. "It was a bad period in our lives. There was Jim developing an ulcer over being replaced, all lines of communication were dead, and forced separation took care of our evenings. Football . . . football . . . football. The number one priority in our lives. It had been going on long before Mercury Morris. Every year the Dolphins won more and more, and we lost more personally. Winning all those Super Bowls, winning everything in sight, it had an effect on all the players' wives. "*Win! Win!*" Shula would say, and we all lost track of what was important. Shula's favorite saying is: 'God first, family second and football last,' but you have to believe what he really means is football first. . . . and God and family can come in any order you want."

Even in the days when Jim was a favorite, Alice believed their relationship was more important than football. Her husband evidently did not. It must be said that this is not unusual. Most great athletes have intense self-concentration and dedication to the game, and the demands of total dedication are especially great in football, where tension builds all week long before a game, each game becoming more important than the last, with the Super Bowl looming as the final glory. It's making it to the Super Bowl—the Nobel, Pulitzer and Academy Award of the football world—that's important. The men want to pull it off for Shula, God, and country. The family can wait.

Most football wives wait. Alice decided not to. She got tired of the long periods of strained conversation and tension before a game, tired of summer training camp, tired of forced separation, and mostly tired of her husband's preoccupation with football to the exclusion of everything and everyone else. Just about then the humiliation of being "replaced" and the inability to talk about it constructed the final wall of separation.

Jim Kiick, the falling, fading superstar was so immersed in his own anguish, that he hardly noticed when Alice packed up and left him in March, 1974, for her sister's in Denver, Colorado. For Alice it was instant relief! It was a time of growing and exploring a life without Jim and a time for fun. She went skiing, joined a lecture group, and met new friends. "For once the dinner-table conversation wasn't about football," Alice recalled. "While going up the chair lift at Aspen, my skiing partner asked me, 'Who are the Dolphins?' I almost kissed the guy!''

While Alice was enjoying her newfound freedom, Jim, living alone in their house in Florida, wasn't enjoying much of anything. He was even bored with feeling sorry for himself, and besides, something had happened, or was about to happen, that would alleviate all his problems.

His agent, Michael Keating, had called and informed him there was a good chance he would sign with the now-defunct WFL as part of the $3,300,000 package deal including Csonka and Warfield. It came just in time. One phone call, and his life turned about. What did he care about Shula, Mercury Morris, or the Dolphins? It looked as if the pressure was off. He wasn't going to fade out of sight. He was going to be a superstar again. A rich superstar. But would it be any fun without Alice? After several weeks of apparently thinking about life without Alice, roaming around in a house that constantly reminded him of his wife's glaring absence and missing his son, Brandon, he suddenly must have known the answer. Life, even with the new contract, wouldn't be worth much without his family. He called her up and shouted into the phone, ''I've changed! I want you back! I've put football where it belongs—after you and Brandon. Please, come home.''

One wonders if he would have made that call if Michael Keating hadn't called first. Alice didn't even believe him, but Jim kept the telephone wires from Miami to Denver hot for two weeks before she finally agreed to meet him in Toronto. That week in Canada two negotiations were going on at the same time, and both worked out successfully. Jim signed a new football contract and they both decided to renew their marriage contract—with a whole new set of priorities.

Toronto was the beginning of their new relationship. Alice insists that they literally started life over as different people. ''We aired our differences, put our problems in perspective, and started communicating—really communicating—for the first time in our lives!'' After Jim signed, they headed for Sun Valley and a skiing vacation. ''That was another first.'' Alice smiled in remembering. ''He would never ski before. Skiing is dangerous for football. You know, after that ski trip I started liking Jim as a person, and now I can accept whatever comes in football.''

Oh, yeah! I said to myself as I turned off my tape recorder. *I wonder if you'll still be saying that next season when he's playing his heart out for the WFL.* It turned out even better for Alice, since after October of 1975, when the WFL folded, he just stopped playing.

Alice served lunch in the air-conditioned kitchen, and I gulped down my seventh peanut butter sandwich since my arrival in Florida. ''Now here is something that would have bothered me before,'' she said, handing me a letter, "but now it's difficult to be angry over anything connected with football."

The letter read: "Dear Jim, I'd like to screw you. Please contact me." The address and phone number were clearly printed, and the letter was signed "The Boston Bunny."

"That's going pretty far, isn't it?" I said, putting the letter down.

"That's going far? You don't know *how* far these women can go!"

"Well, it's a good thing you don't take them seriously anymore!" I said, relieved that we could avoid the subject of jock lovers.

"Why should I take them seriously?" Alice said crossly. "Besides, Jim couldn't get sex any better than he gets it at home, so why should he stray?"

I wondered why she put it in the form of a question and decided she may have a new detachment about football, but it doesn't include jock lovers.

Since Jim has turned around and put football in second place, his wife leaves him out of the category she assigns most football players: "Most of the guys are stupid jocks—big studs who haven't a brain for anything but football, girls, and the roar of the crowd. Have you ever noticed how they pick out small women with sensational bodies? They couldn't care less if she has a soul or brain—she *must* have a good body." Alice smiled wickedly. "That makes a jock feel more powerful . . . more masculine. But God, they're really babies inside."

I thought back to Marquerite Simpson, Pam Csonka, and Julie Swift. Yup, they were all small and had great bodies. I looked over at Alice. Small and a knockout! Maybe there's something to it. So far I hadn't heard of a football player married to an Amazon, a lady wrestler, or even a roller derby queen.

Alice Kiick may be small with a gorgeous figure, but she has a lot more. Call it intellectual expansion, awareness, spirit, soul, or any other label you can think of. The important thing is she is growing. "I think we're living in changing and turbulent times. People are slowly getting back to what's real. I deeply believe in the spiritual world—a world we've all ignored for so long. I'm taking a transcendental meditation course. TM's a combination of yoga and psychic meditation, and it gives me complete awareness. I'm also interested in astrology. It all leads to the same thing—oneness. Everything is God. Remember, more than most people I've been living in a physical world, and I've come to believe the spiritual world is the one that's important!"

Today, with the crisis behind them, it appears the marriage will survive. Alice has changed, and so, she says, has Jim. Where once makeup, teased hairstyles, designer clothes, and dreams of becoming a top model were all part of her image, she is now the quintessential nature girl, and the modeling ambitions have been replaced by full immersion in the spiritual world. Her gray-streaked dark hair, cut as though she did it herself and in a hurry, is symbolic of her new approach to life. Alice's appearance, as well as her manner, is without deception. It's as if everything false and plastic had been thrown out of her life along with the old "football days."

There is one story she likes to tell about the past, though. Perhaps more than anything else it reflects her true feelings about "those Dolphin years." It seems that Jim's hometown of Lincoln Park, New Jersey, honored him with a Jim Kiick Week in the summer of '72. Billboards were put up all over town announcing in bold red letters that Lincoln Park was the home of Dolphin *halfback* Jim Kiick. There were speeches, luncheons and, on the last day, a big parade with Jim and Alice smothered in roses on top of an open car. That evening the town gave a big banquet for their superstar. Larry Csonka was invited up for the occasion. The mayor had provided a big black limousine for Jim, Larry, and Alice to ride in, complete with police escort.

That night on the way to the banquet, Zonk stretched his legs in the spacious back seat and said, "The town's sure puttin' it on for you, Sundance!"

"It was sooo impressive!" Alice grins when she tells the story. "After dinner, after all the acclaim, glorification, congratulations, compliments, and general beating of the drums for Jim, everybody left, and we didn't have a way to get home. The limo and police escort were hired only to get us there. No one even *considered* how we'd get home! That story epitomizes my outlook on football and fame. They love you when you're on top, and when it's over, that's how they leave you. Stranded!"

I called my agent, Jacques de Spoelberch, in New York.

"Jacques, I've got to get out of Dolphin country . . . these women have so many complaints a *shrink* would be depressed."

"Well, while you're there, you should talk to Bob Griese's wife," he said in an annoyingly unsympathetic voice.

"I'd just get more of the same. I've *got* enough football wives, I tell you, and I wouldn't change places with any of them—not even if Joe Namath asked me!"

"OK, it's your book. We've got Helen Stewart's permission and telephone number in Geneva. That ought to be a change of pace."

"Switzerland!" I squealed delightedly into the phone. "Goosedown comforters, gorgeous food and wine, skiing in the Alps. . . . Whoopie, maybe I can get a free skiing lesson."

"Jeanne. . . . Jeanne. . . . Jea. . . ."

I hung up the phone and wondered if I should go home first to collect my brand-new Rossignol M3s or head directly for Switzerland and rent skis there. Suddenly I picked up the phone and dialed Jacques back.

"What does Helen Stewart's husband do?"

"He's the world's most famous race car driver."

The Princess

Ten years ago we had a large number of friends from the racing world.
Today they all are dead.

In preparation for my trip to Switzerland I crammed on race car driving. Good thing, too, because most of my impressions were colored by things I'd picked up from bad movies: "Good old boys" weaned on hot rods loaded with bootleg booze, roaring along country roads outrunning revenuers and such; stock car races with banged-up jalopies playing to shirt-sleeve and sundress crowds in the hot sun; sleek, snarling monsters built close to the ground, held up by square-edged fat tires set wide apart, with drivers nestled in cubbyholes scooped out for them. I had a picture of sooty drivers triumphantly lofting huge loving cups, while beauty queens in short shorts kissed grinning faces.

My research taught me that there's a big difference between race car drivers in this country and abroad. In Europe racing has the same prestige as bullfighting has in Spain. It is the sport of kings. I also found out that in recent years Grand Prix racing has killed more drivers than any other category of motor racing. This helped me understand Helen Stewart* when I finally met her, lodged regally in her villa on the mountaintop, looking down at the ordinary folk.

My plane set down in Geneva in the early-morning hours of a Saturday in April. There was nothing to do but go straight to my hotel. I was in a muddle because of jet lag and tried to rest during the morning, but it was one of those splendid, warm, sunny days I will not forget, and the beauty and clean air of Switzerland and the excitement of being there were just too much for a New York girl.

I waited until the decent hour of ten to call, and Helen Stewart asked me to come over at one. She lives in the tiny village of Begnins between Geneva and Lausanne, about twenty minutes outside Geneva, in the foothills of the Jura Mountains. I knew I would be treated to breathtaking views, but I could not have prepared myself for what I found.

*Jackie Stewart, ABC-TV racing analyst, former Grand Prix racing driver. Before he retired at the end of the 1973 racing season, Jackie Stewart established a Grand Prix record for number of racing victories (27). He won three World Driving Championships (1969, 1971, and 1973). He earned an estimated $850,000 a season while he raced and had become independently wealthy by the time of his retirement. *Sports Illustrated* acknowledged Stewart's accomplishments by naming him Sportsman of the Year in 1973.

While the car labored uphill on the narrow, twisting road, I gaped. Each turn opened up a new, sweeping vista of natural beauty. The mustard plant was in full bloom, splashing bright yellow swatches all over the landscape. Flowers and fruit trees added more color than the eye could absorb. I was so busy swiveling my head from one side to the other, I developed a neckache and rarely bothered to look at the road ahead of me. Fortunately, there was no traffic and, as far as I could see, no inhabitants. I felt all alone in this fairy-land.

Finally, on top of the numerous hills, I came suddenly around a curve . . . and Clayton House, the Stewarts' retreat. The fact is, I didn't see Clayton House because it wasn't visible from the road. What I confronted was a large wrought-iron gate left open (for me?), which bore a sign identifying the property, if it can be called that. I found out later that Clayton is a contraction for "Clay," Jackie's British Clay Pigeon Trapshooting championship, and "ton," racing vernacular for 100 miles per hour. Tall hedges hid the estate from those traveling along the road.

Once past the gate, my attention was drawn to the vast, impeccably groomed lawns, gardens, and formal hedges clipped into designs that would be more in character at Disneyland.

I saw the house and garage at the same time, although they're detached, but it was the house on the right that hypnotized. *Here is grandeur,* I said to myself. It was a two-story French Normandy villa, creamy beige in color, with cocoa shutters setting off tall windows. Geraniums, giant pansies, tulips, and jonquils overflowed window boxes and huge cement pots.

On the left, I took in the three-car garage, the same color as the house, and wondered what kind of cars an ex-racer and his wife drive. I had visions of Helen Stewart trying to decide which one of three to take for a run into the village. Was I disappointed or not when I discovered they were *Fords,* snuggled neatly together side by side? I don't know what I expected—probably expensive, powerful sports cars. After all, Clayton House was reputed to be worth more than $1,000,000, and I had no reason to doubt it now I'd seen it with my own eyes. The Ford Motor Company samples somehow didn't fit into all this luxury. Oh well.

Let me just say that during my odyssey I saw many of sport's nouveau riches, but none who live more opulently than the Stewarts. Even Aly Khan, in his halcyon racing days, couldn't have lived any better. Here's one woman about whom you could accurately say, "You've come a long way, baby!"

I knew something of the Stewarts before I knocked on the door—information given me by Americans living in the rich jet set Swiss colony. I knew, for instance, that the Stewarts are considered a valuable private property, a direct link to the fairyland that Switzerland is to the rest of the world. They adore

Jackie and speculate about Helen. There is no consensus about her. To Jackie's friends, he is exactly what he seems to be—open, straightforward, pleasant. His heavy Scots burr is real, not affected for its charm. Elocution lessons have all but wiped out any traces of a Scots accent in his wife's case. Helen *is* enigmatic and not easy to capture in words. Fitzgerald could perhaps do her justice, for he knew how to write about rich, beautiful, indolent women. To some in Geneva, she's a simple, unpretentious Scottish girl, while to others she's a snob interested only in the rich, titled, and famous. On the one hand, she's described as a tragic woman who has watched all her close friends die, and on the other, as a woman cold as ice. She is weak and she is strong, depending on the observer's point of view.

I hoped, as I knocked on the great carved wooden door, I would find out for myself. The girl who answered looked like the baby-sitter. Young, glowing, without a touch of makeup and light-brown* hair which hung straight down the middle of her back. She was barefoot and in blue jeans. But the blue jeans turned out to be St. Laurent and the girl . . . Helen.

She has a "Deneuve" look, a hybrid of courage and fragility and without exaggeration, beauty. There was the coolness everyone remarked, the manner of a supremely confident woman. There were also signs of a woman who has been pampered all her life, first by a doting father, then by an enamored husband, who could gild his affection with the help of a half-million-dollar-a-year income.

The phone rang, and she politely declined an invitation to a dinner party. She spoke in a soft, cultured voice with no trace of an accent. Sorry, but she and Jackie were flying to the South of France for a holiday. He had been working too hard, poor darling. Later, as she showed me around the house, trying not to appear pretentious, I had the feeling she was trying to create an impression of modesty amid opulence. We stood out on the terrace in back, looking down on a sparkling aquamarine pool. The pool house which opened to it was larger than most people's homes. White wicker furniture; pads and pillows done in apricot and lemon spilled out of the sliding glass doors and onto the tile pool deck. There was a bar and an open hearth for outdoor cooking. It didn't look as if anyone had ever used it, and I had the uncomfortable feeling very little use was made of *all* this.

Inside the house I was shown only the ground floor, which contained a living rooom, formal dining room, den, guest room, and cheery kitchen done in brown and orange tile. All the rooms were oversized with marvelous antiques, richly woven fabrics, fine rugs, accessory touches from world travels, just enough prints to achieve that English lived-in look—yet somehow it seemed

*I thought her hair ash blond. Jackie was adamant. Light brown!

unused to human traffic. Helen admitted that although they're frequently invited out, they seldom entertain in their own home.* "I like things peaceful for Jackie when he comes home from his travels."

I knew instinctively that the decor was all Helen's, and although I did not meet her husband, I had the feeling he did not fit as comfortably in this house as she did. Some people make a god of taste. It seemed evident from the understated but expensive interior, best described as "well bred," that Helen does too. Her taste is simple. The best of everything. The den was the one room that was clearly Jackie's. It held all his trophies and scrapbooks. The furniture was tweedy, the colors were brown, beige and black, and it looked like something Helen had created especially for her husband.

The Stewarts have two sons: Paul, who is ten, and Mark, eight. The rest of the household is composed of a Scots nanny, who takes care of the boys, a woman who cleans, a cook, Ruth Kinnear, the secretary who handles all correspondence, and a gardener.

Helen led me outdoors, where we sat on white-cushioned deck chairs, looking over rolling countryside. The view was so staggering it beggared description—a broad green-and-yellow patchwork quilt with cows serenely munching in the distance. The tiny village of Begnins was almost lost in it all. Lake Geneva glistened deep blue in the sparkling sunshine, drifting white sails dotting it. In the distance loomed the quiet majesty of Mont Blanc, perennially capped with snow, at 16,000 feet the highest peak in the Alps, situated where Switzerland, France, and Italy come together. The combined wealth of all mankind could not buy this spectacular prospect, and the Stewarts have it, whenever they wish, merely by turning their heads. Someone like Jackie Stewart, who lives on the edge of fiery death almost daily in his work and is paid handsomely for the risks, would not settle for less. Neither would his wife.

"I love it here," she said almost to herself. "It's beautiful and safe. It's peaceful and soothing after so many years of living off highs and pain."

Those trying years came crowding into her mind so easily still. Yet they were the juiciest years for Jackie, the ones that made everything else possible.

A maid appeared with a tray of hot coffee and disappeared as silently as she came.

Helen talked of her years with Jackie thoughtfully, reliving emotions, while her eyes unseeingly gazed out on the miracle of natural beauty before us.

It isn't the classic "love-at-first-sight-with-complications" story, but it's close enough. Helen was born thirty-four years ago in Helensburgh, Scotland, a small town about twenty-five miles northwest of Glasgow. She was Helen

*Jackie claims they never go out and frequently entertain in their own home.

McGregor then. Her parents owned the local bakery that provided the family with good, solid middle-class living. She lacked for nothing, she says, but she did not have everything she wanted either. That, or much of it, was to come later.

Helen was always shy because she was reared according to the maxim "Children should be seen but not heard." She says she's gotten over her self-consciousness but still doesn't feel at ease with those she doesn't know well. She was not entirely at ease with me.

She studied ballet, tap, and Highland dancing and took elocution lessons not "to lose my Scottish brogue" (which she did), but to learn to project her small voice. She quit school at fifteen, worked in a bank for two years, and entered the family business because banking was boring. She really would have preferred going off to Glasgow or London, but "girls didn't do that sort of thing in those days." It worked out for the best because she met Jackie. She was sweet sixteen and ready to fall in love.

She had gone to a favorite hangout for young people with a girlfriend who was to meet a blind date. Jackie, of course, was the date. He didn't particularly like the girl, and she was not impressed with him, but Helen took one look and decided instantly that one of the things she wanted from life was Jackie (and she believed she had every right to expect what she wanted). Of course, Jackie wasn't what her parents had in mind, and they said so and did their best to break them up.

Mr. and Mrs. McGregor were crushed when she took up with this young playboy whose family owned a garage in a neighboring town and who was always getting his hands greasy tinkering with motors and racing cars. Mrs. McGregor sniffed that he would probably end his days cracking up on some distant racetrack. What kind of career was racing to support a wife as beautiful and promising as their daughter Helen?

As Helen remembers it, "I knew the minute I met Jackie that he was different somehow from all the others [like herself?]. I could sense this immense energy pouring out of him . . . he was strong!"

He also had a dashing red Austin-Healey sports car, plenty of money to spend, and a working knowledge of all the places of interest in the Glasgow area. The couple courted for two years, broke it off once, and eight or nine months later ran into each other accidentally and rediscovered their love. The engagement was announced on Helen's twenty-first birthday. Eight months later they were married, without the blessing of Mr. and Mrs. McGregor. Helen's father gave in grudgingly when he realized there was nothing else for him to do, but her mother withheld her forgiveness, even after seeing her two grandsons. She finally came around only after Jackie officially announced his retirement from racing on October 14, 1973.

Hardly had the newlyweds settled down to the routine of married life than

Jackie started racing in local competition. His talent was quickly recognized, and soon he was being paid for what he had always wanted to do as a hobby. In a year's time he was spotted by Ken Tyrrell, owner of a British team of racing cars, who invited him to come to England to test a new car—an invitation that led to a happy working relationship that endured until Jackie retired at thirty-four. It also made them both rich.

Listening to Helen talk, I felt she had made herself an extension of Jackie. She described herself and her life obliquely—by describing Jackie and *his* life. It wasn't clear whether or not she did this by design, but she did it. I think she enjoys being a puzzle and possibly fears others getting close. Not hard to understand. Many of those who'd succeeded in penetrating her reserve and winning her affection have died violently because of the nature of Formula One race car driving.

When death strikes hard and close repeatedly, it can't help affecting the survivor's nature. Helen McGregor met and built her life around a race car driver, and death soon became a frequent caller to her circle. She was young and unprepared.

World championship racing is the riskiest of sports—a life only for daredevils resolved to tempt the Reaper. They expect it everywhere and are more or less willing to accept the consequences as fair payment for thrills received. Their wives don't and aren't. Helen came to this sporting life through the Scot with the corduroy tam and the charmed life. He survived the odds long enough to complete ninety-nine races before he retired and grow extravagantly rich in the process. Helen should be able to relax now, and perhaps she will one day, but the clutching fear she lived with for so long won't fade so quickly. The recollection of all those deaths so close to home in such a short time won't let it.

When her parents wounded her by rejecting her marriage, she compensated by nestling ever closer to Jackie. "From the beginning," she told me, "I was involved with the team. My place was in the pits, keeping time of every car on the track. In practice runs, Jackie would often stop to get a timing on another driver, and I'd get out my little black book. But it was more than that. I knew he wanted me there. I was his security, his touch of reality in that circus atmosphere."

Helen was part of a coveted inner circle—not just an adoring wife cheering and boasting, "That's my husband," from the sidelines. This close relationship fascinated some and exasperated others, all of whom admit the two grow closer with the years.

At first she was too new and naïve to be afraid. The rude awakening came at the Monaco Grand Prix, where Helen saw her first accident. "First I heard the sound of tires screeching, then an awful thud as he hit a cement barrier. There was an explosion right in front of me, and then the smell of smoke and burning rubber. I saw them trying to pull the driver out of his car, but the wind was whipping up the flames, and they had to stand back. I thought, *My God, aren't they going to do something?* And then, the worst horror of all, a man turning away and drawing his fingers across his throat.''

The victim, who so abruptly introduced Helen to the real meaning of car racing, was an Italian named Lorenzo Bandini. ''I never dwelt on death before Lorenzo,'' she said ''and it never left my thoughts afterward. It haunted me all the time.'' Helen admitted she never spoke of her fears to Jackie, but she said, ''It hung ominously over us—our thoughts and words. It was there when he kissed me before a race. He knew I was frightened, and I knew that he knew.

''I asked Jackie, after he quit racing, how he felt when he drove away from the house during those years, and he said he felt *terrible* and often wondered if he'd come back. If I'd known *that*—how he felt—I'm sure it would have affected me. Through the years I learned to accept the risk. I never asked him to stop, but I was nervous and upset, and I can tell you I didn't enjoy it. If a woman enjoys it, she doesn't truly love the man she marries.''

As he roared over the course, Helen sat in pits, feeling alone, choked with tension. ''There were times when it was so oppressive I couldn't eat for forty-eight hours before a race,'' she recalled. ''People used to comment that I never showed any emotion! I was frightened, but I was also concentrating so hard people took it for aloofness.'' Once when she was sitting in the pits taking a lap chart of the race, Roman Polanski, the internationally famous filmmaker, came over to kiss her cheek and wish her well. She froze, not even acknowledging his presence. Looking like a man slapped in the face, Polanski turned and walked away. ''I know he didn't understand it,'' she told me, ''and later I had to explain to him that I simply didn't want to break up my concentration. You see, during a race, I was with Jackie on every lap and corner, visually and mentally while he was going around that track.'' Helen leaned back in her deck chair and slipped on her dark glasses, and I took a deep breath as if to ingest the gorgeous scenery during the pause. *How lucky they are*, I thought, *to look out their window every morning and see all this beauty.*

''Ten years ago,'' she went on, ''we had a large number of friends from the racing world. Today they are *all* dead.''

She started reciting names, counting on her fingers at the same time. ''Jim Clark, Bruce McLaren, Piers Courage, Jochen Rindt, Jo Bonnier, Joe Siffert, Lorenzo Bandini, Jerry Birrel, Mike Spence, Ludovico Scarfiotti, Joe Schlesser, Pedro Rodriquez, Peter Revson, Graham Hill* and . . . '' her voice

---

*Dead in a plane crash November 29, 1975.

trailed off and I knew she was fighting emotions as she whispered the name of "François Cevert."

"Oh, would you like to see his picture?" She leaped from her chair and dashed inside, saying, "Wait until you see him, so handsome, smashing. . . ." She returned to our spot on the terrace with a fat scrapbook and opened it to a photo of an extraordinarily fair young man who seemed to look out adoringly at someone.

"I took that picture!" Helen explained, looking at it adoringly. "He was the most charming man in the world! We just loved him. The birds were crazy about him, too," she said with a slight grin. "It was always amusing to watch them go after him, but he preferred to be with us." She turned the page showing photographs of the three of them, smiling happily on a beach. "He was so vital—so in love with life!"

François Cevert was more than the "other driver" on Jackie's team. For eight years he had been so close to the Stewarts in work and play that he was considered part of the family. Friends remember the three as inseparable, and Jackie undoubtedly considered François heir to his world championship title when he retired.

It was April, 1973, when Jackie Stewart made his decision to quit racing after the Watkins Glen Grand Prix the following October. At that time his two sons, Paul and Mark, were attending a little school about 4,000 feet straight up from their home. Jochen Rindt's daughter, Natasha, and Jo Bonnier's kids were attending the same school. After Jo died at Le Mans, the word got out that racing fathers die. It was only a matter of time when the kids told the two Stewart boys that their father would be dead too. Heartbroken, the boys brought this information home to their parents and it had a lot to do with Jackie's decision to quit. He didn't tell Helen or François. In fact, he kept it a secret to all but his team manager, Ken Tyrrell. That fall, before coming to America, the team had raced in the Canadian Grand Prix, where François had suffered an accident and couldn't walk very well. The three left for Bermuda, where the Stewarts helped François get back on his feet and ready for Watkins Glen. For two weeks they swam in the warm salt water, walked the beaches, and spent lazy, therapeutic days in the sun where François' leg healed and all three did some unwinding.

Lying on the beach with cotton pads over her eyes, Helen listened closely to Jackie as he and François discussed the next race. Would he quit racing after Watkins Glen? She must have wished desperately for that announcement. A bundle of nerves, saddened by the loss of so many friends, frightened by the odds, she must have seen the next Grand Prix—Jackie's 100th race— looming as a titanic threat. Could he be lucky one more time—could he make it one hundred?

Helen and François tried unsuccessfully to manipulate Jackie into telling them his plans. "One minute he'd say something that sounded like he was quitting, and François and I would look at each other knowingly; then he'd say something that implied he was going to go on racing. It was a frustrating game."

Neither found out. The canny Scotsman wasn't talking. But his decision was made, and Ken Tyrrell had the word. He was to come over to Helen after the race at Watkins Glen and say, "OK, Helen, he's all yours now!" and then Tyrrell was going to turn to François and say, "Now *you're* number one!" He was never able to deliver either message.

Helen paused for a long time before recalling what happened at Watkins Glen. The drone of a power mower wafted in from the distance. A bee buzzed about her head, unnoticed. Finally, in a barely audible voice, she summoned up the sequence of events on that fateful day of October 6, 1973, the day before the Grand Prix.

"I sat on the pit wall overlooking the racetrack. Both Jackie and François looked so tan and fit as they slid into their identical blue cars to start the practice run. I had my black book and stopwatch out and was waiting, ready to record the lap time. François looked up at me on my perch and winked, then started his engine with a roar that is always deafening, even with earplugs. He flipped down his visor, blew a kiss, and gave a tiny wave—a thing he'd never done before.

"Jackie followed a few moments later and they began circling the track some distance apart. . . .

"I clicked the watch each time they passed. First time around François recorded the fastest time ever at the Glen. Then came Jody Scheckter, a young South African. Jackie's car streaked by at around one hundred and seventy miles an hour, and I entered the time in the column on my pad. More cars passed, and I clocked their main rivals.

"Seconds ticked by, and I realized that François was late, but there was no sign of Scheckter either. My throat went dry, and stomach muscles tightened as I looked from my stopwatch to the empty track. I became aware of an eerie silence. All the cars on the track seemed to have stopped. Without uttering a sound, I screamed Jackie's name in my head. The quiet filled me with panic. It was the same kind of silence that had spread over Monza the afternoon Jochen Rindt was killed. *Please God, don't let it be Jackie or François.*

"A blue car appeared. It was Jackie. Relief flooded my entire being, then turned to terror as I saw the truth on Jackie's face. My mind couldn't accept it. The beautiful François with all his charm and vitality—so in love with life. But it was true. Jackie looked me straight in the eyes and said, 'It's François.'"

That was the end for Jackie, as he told the officials, "We've withdrawn from the race, and I have retired from racing." His family finally heard the announcement they'd so longed for. There was no joy.

I thumbed through the scrapbook in the late afternoon sun while Helen went to tend to something in the house. Picture after picture of the French race car driver, all taken by Helen. The last one in the book had a simple inscription across the bottom of the page: *"Au revoir, François."*

Helen came back without her dark glasses, settled in her chair and said, "Isn't it beautiful here? I don't ever want to leave. . . . Of course, someday when we're old, we may go back to Scotland. . . ."

What a luxury it must be for her to think about growing old and planning for the future with Jackie with such certainty.

"Lunch!" a maid announced. We moved a few feet away to an umbrella-shaded table. It was a delectable sight. The centerpiece was a large bowl of the pansies that grow in such profusion there. The cloth was blue linen. We were served fish, fresh asparagus, a green salad, and French wine, a big improvement over the peanut butter sandwiches and paper napkins I'd grown accustomed to. Helen picked at her food.

"I try to watch my weight—Jackie likes me thin," she said. She had nothing to complain about, I noted enviously as I dived into my food. It was almost too much. The food, the wine, the flowers, and the gorgeous 'scape before us with the mountains looming majestically in the background. One could hardly challenge their decision to remain in beautiful tax-free Switzerland, but since some of Jackie's money was made in America, I thought I'd ask if she ever considered moving to the States.

"America?" she said in disbelief. "Heavens, no. Why would we want to live there? It's so plastic. Everyone eats canned food, and all the men wear baggy pants."

Helen admitted that she and Jackie have few close friends left because the people they loved most were drivers who have been killed. But the myth that they see *no one*, live *alone* on a mountain which was once populated with friends from the racing world, is untrue. They hobnob regularly with the jet set world—with Stavros Niarchos, the Greek shipping magnate, with Fiat's Gianni Agnelli, Ford's young Edsel (Jackie was an usher at the wedding)—and they were very close to the Aga Khan and still see the Begum. They also pal around with such superstars as Truman Capote and Andy Warhol, and cameras have given us glimpses of Helen escorting her friend Elizabeth Taylor around Monaco during the Grand Prix, and it is well known that Princess Grace and Prince Rainier are good friends. Grace loves to drive around her postage-stamp sized country with Jackie at the wheel and undoubtedly has much in common with the fashionable Helen, who may not have the title, but who has the manner and cool beauty of a princess. It is not well known, but nevertheless true, the Stewarts see a great deal of Princess Anne and Mark Phillips. Jackie and Mark Phillips are extremely close, and because of that personal relationship and Princess Anne's penchant for privacy, they try to keep their friendship with the royal couple a secret. Helen slips every now and then with remarks like, "Anne's a good driver!"; "Her wedding was in quiet, good taste"; "Anne's mother, Queen Elizabeth, is the woman I admire most . . . she's family-minded."

Fortunately, after a quick mental review of her experiences with the English royal family, one adventure was cleared for public consumption: "A funny thing did happen when we were in England at the royal wedding. We were there for all the parties, including the great ball the night before. I'd spent the entire day at the hairdresser, having my long, straight hair piled into curls—you know, one of those elaborate styles. Well, by the time I got out it was bloody late. I rushed back to our hotel room, ran into the bathroom and turned on the bathwater, and what do you think? *Someone* had forgotten to turn off the shower handle! I was drenched. *Drenched.* On the way to Buckingham Palace that night, Jackie looked me over and said, 'For someone who spent six hours at the hairdresser, I can't see what difference it's made!' It's the first time in my life I told him to *shut up!*"

One can easily understand Helen's love of royal weddings, beautiful people, and fashionable parties. It was a party she *didn't* have when she was four years old that still sticks in her mind today. Her brother, Evan, who was eleven months older, had a birthday party with all his little friends coming over to tea. Helen thought it a wondrous event, and it touched off a spark in her childish imagination. She wanted a birthday party, too, when it came her turn, but her mother refused, saying she was too young. It seemed enormously unfair to Helen since her brother wasn't *that* much older. She begged for a party, but her mother was adamant. The night of her birthday she lay in bed and promised herself it would *never* happen again—and that she would somehow make sure she would always be in a position to get the things she wanted out of life. "As I went to sleep I got the feeling that it would be so. I didn't know how it would happen. I simply knew with complete certainty that my life was going to be very special."

She wrote her script when she was four years old, and it's come true in every way. Her life is special.

Helen is nonchalant about fame and publicity. She acknowledges with a shrug that racing people claim she was responsible for much of the front-page publicity Jackie received during races. "I don't know why the photographers were around me all the time. Maybe it was because Jackie is a three-times world champion driver." Of course, it had nothing to do with the fact that she's a photographer's dream and wore one outfit more smashing that the previous one to the track. "All I know," she said in her clipped, crisp accent, "is that I didn't pay any attention to them."

If that's true, some meticulous collector rescued hundreds of pictures and news clippings of Helen that now appear in her bulging scrapbooks while she was not paying any attention to the photographers.

At dinner that evening in a charming restaurant in the Hôtel Du Lac at Coppet, a waiter almost swooned at the sight of Helen. Another rushed up with the back of a menu for her to autograph. There seemed endless fuss over the selection of the proper table for their favorite celebrity, one with just the right view of the lake. Helen handled it with just the right touch of pride and humility. "It's all because of Jackie," she said, nodding toward the waiters. "It hasn't anything to do with me." *Not any more,* I thought, staring at this incredibly elegant woman, *than Jackie's car has to do with his winning a race.* She spoke of how his fans admired him. Adulation, not based on simple sports loving hysteria, but on a keen appreciation of the risks involved in Grand Prix racing.

"Jackie's popularity hasn't diminished at all," she said, "even though he no longer races. Just last winter he roared down the icy roads of our little village and slammed into a parked car. The owner ran out of the garage shaking his fist and swearing until he noticed that it was Jackie. He froze. The more Jackie apologized, the more the man beamed and said it was an *honor.* The poor man never had his car repaired—he would rather brag about who put the dent in his fender."

Now that Jackie has retired, his fame can be expected to moderate, and in time there won't be as much fuss for the Stewarts to put up with.

Nevertheless, the high income continues to pour in unabated. But now, to Helen's relief, the gnawing fear of danger is gone. Jackie travels even more than before, all over the world, promoting Ford cars and Goodyear tires, doing commercials and broadcasting for ABC's Wide World of Sports. Helen doesn't go with him as much now, but she proudly points out that when he's away he calls every day.

"He just called me from Vienna," she said. "I forget what he's doing there."

During their separations, she says, she occupies herself with photography and skiing, but the moment Jackie comes home, she is *all his!* Because he's away so much, she sees to it "that he has no irritations when he is home. I organize my time so I can be completely free to sleep late, to take off with him, or do whatever he wishes. If that seems slavish, I can only say that's the way I am."

As she talked, she twirled the stem of her wineglass around and around. I noticed her nails, natural without color, but like everything else about her, polished and perfectly groomed. I brought up the subject of fashion and she said, "I'm not interested in it." I looked over her St. Laurent pants, cashmere jacket, and Gucci scarf knotted with studied abandon around her throat and gulped. "Everything really good that I have Jackie bought for me," she hastened to say. "He loves to buy me things. He presented me with a fantastic necklace when he first quit racing. It has three strands of pearls for the three world championships, ninety-nine diamonds for the ninety-nine Grand Prix, twenty-seven rubies for the twenty-seven wins, and a crash helmet of onyx in the middle. . . . Of course"—she sniffed—"I hardly ever wear it. I don't care much for jewelry either."

I let it go, put my notebook down, and enjoyed my dinner. Helen noticed the reporter was off duty and had a little smile on her face for the rest of the evening. I didn't know if it was a smile of victory or relief, but I know I left Switzerland knowing very little more about Helen than the rest of the rich Swiss colony whose favorite occupation is speculating about this beautiful woman. Was she trying hard to make an impression, trying hard not to make an impression, or just not trying?

I said good-bye to the Stewarts' secluded haven, so far removed from the frenzied, crowded, and often ugly world and took off for the States and my next stop—Hueytown, Alabama.

The Southern Libber

I used to take pills . . . and I finally had to admit that I was a drug addict. My husband became a very busy man about the time this all started. I couldn't take the responsibility that went with his career. I felt completely inferior, inadequate.

When I left Switzerland and the gracious elegance, refinement, and felicity of Clayton House and made my way to Hueytown, Alabama, where the Allisons live, I couldn't have found a more startling contrast. I knew that Jackie Stewart and Bobby Allison were in a related sport, but I didn't expect to find such unrelated life-styles. Allison's Knoll is the official name given to it, but the neighbors in Hueytown call it Gasoline Alley. I stopped my car before I turned in the driveway. There it was—thirteen acres of gentle rolling land as pretty as you'll find in that part of the country, clustered with maple, dogwood, sweet gum, and magnolia trees. And right in the middle of this setting and to the right side of the house was an astonishingly bright blue garage seventy-seven by thirty-three feet littered inside and out with transmissions, camshafts, wheels, axles, engines, fenders, car doors, and everything else usually associated with junkyards.

Allison's knoll, I wrote on my note pad, *is situated on an acre of car parts.* This was going to take a bit of getting used to.

Judith* and Bobby Allison live in a four-bedroom ranch house that has a small living room and family room but an *enormous* trophy room running the full length of the lower level. It traces and celebrates a long, active, successful career of coaxing top speed out of race cars, ranging all the way from the most dilapidated souped-up stock car to the most sophisticated Indy special. It was a career that made him a million and almost cost Judith her life. She's just barely coming out òf the woods now.

A redwood deck, the size of a modest parking lot, juts out from the back of the house over a creek cutting through the backyard. The deck supports a swimming pool forty-four feet by twenty-five feet, a Ping-Pong table, a picnic table, and enough assorted outdoor furniture to accommodate Judith, Bobby, their four children, and the army of admiring friends in and around Hueytown.

---

*Bobby Allison is only the second man to earn more than $1,000,000 in stock car (NASCAR) racing. He has won more than 40 races in his career and in 1972 was voted the Martini-Rossi Driver of the Year, an award which is emblematic of the best overall performance by a United States driver.

When I arrived, the Allisons were getting ready to go to Florida on a holiday in their private plane, a brand-new red, white, and gold Aero-Star that seats six. My heart sank. How was I going to gain insight into this woman in the midst of such turmoil? Judith had the answer. "Let's go to town for lunch," she said.

Judith doesn't follow the latest fashions like her Northern sisters. She wore an inexpensive cotton pantsuit and sandals. Her blond hair was short, permanented and framed a slightly puffy but still very pretty face.

As we drove down Hueytown's main street, people tipped their hats to the Allison car. It was probably the only Mark III in the area and not likely to be mistaken for another's. Besides the Lincoln, the Allisons have a Chevy station wagon and a Matador, the model Bobby drives in stock car races.

Suddenly I was thrown forward with a jerk as Judith slammed on the brakes unexpectedly for a red light. "Sorry," she said. "I was going a little too fast."

I didn't think so, but she pointed out, "You should never go too fast in the South. It's against nature. There's a slower pace to life down here than what you're used to. People are so slow here we don't even have amber lights on our traffic signals. That's why everyone crawls along."

I thought of how her husband did not get where he was by driving slowly or worrying about amber lights *or* nature. and steeled myself for any more traffic signals that might shift from green to red without notice. There was no need because Judith took her own advice, and we crawled along at about eight miles an hour and parked finally in front of the best, and possibly only, restaurant in town.

"Hi, Judith," drawled an elderly man as we got out of the car. "Sure proud of Bobby winning that race in California." (The week before Bobby had won the Los Angeles *Times* 500 Charity race in Ontario, California. First prize had been $12,000 in cash and a Datsun 260Z.) Judith nodded to the old gentleman and turned to me, again feeling the need to explain. "People are friendlier here than in the North. You can live all your life up there and not know your neighbor. Here everyone is warm and friendly."

There was no denying the warmth and friendliness of the people in the restaurant. Friends, neighbors, waitresses, busboys, and even the cook came out to pay their respects and congratulate Judith on her husband's recent win. Everyone in town seemed to know about it but me.

"Sure is nice, honey, about Bobby," trilled our stocky waitress. "I jes' had a feelin' he was goin' to win and beat that no-good Northerner, Richard Petty!" Petty is from North Carolina.

Pointing a spoon at me, the waitress asked of Judith, "What's she doin', honey?"

"She's interviewing me, Dolly, so you'll have to leave us alone."

Dolly let the admonition slide. She was too busy being warm, friendly, and curious.

"Where you from?" she wanted to know, turning her unwavering eyes on me.

She had caught me with a mouthful of food, so at that precise moment I was in no position to be warm and friendly in return, but she pushed on unabashedly.

"Atlanta?" she suggested hopefully, being more considerate than I deserved.

"No," I finally managed to get out. "New York."

In Hueytown, being kind to New Yorkers is apparently a challenge even to the most congenial practitioners. Though she had cooled perceptibly, Dolly was willing to go more than halfway, perhaps because she felt sorry for me. "Well, you did come from Atlanta."

I started to deny it, but Judith sprang to my aid again.

"There's an old saying that around here you don't go straight to heaven when you die, you have to go to Atlanta first. Everything that comes or leaves here by air has to go by way of Atlanta."

I turned to Dolly, smiled, and said, "You're absolutely right. I came from Atlanta."

That settled and Dolly mollified, she left us to our own devices. Over shrimp salad, Judith told me of life with Bobby, one of the country's top stock car racers. Her story shook me up considerably.

Racing under the banner of "Bobby Allison Racing, of Hueytown, Alabama," stock car driver Bobby Allison reached the $1,000,000 mark in lifetime earnings on the Grand National Circuit in 1973.

Judith Allison, caught up in the whirlpool of her husband's success, is more cautious than most superstar wives in accepting the publicity and recognition that have come with her husband's career. She believes fame can act like a cancer from which few recover without great spiritual, physical, and mental loss.

"We are unconscious of what fame may do to us," she told me. "It takes us away from reality. It blinds us and eats away at us until the humanism is gone. Success is the most dangerous thing that can happen to a human being."

I'd heard these words from other wives, but I was not expecting them from Judith. What could possibly have happened to her to have aroused such a distrust of success? Other wives of superstars had emphasized the more obvious symptoms of their predicament: the loneliness, the threats from jock lovers, injuries, forced separation, and sexual abstinence. They had only hinted at the subtler complication induced by their husbands' fame, the loss of self-esteem that could furtively strangle a marriage because the husband was catapulted into prominence and adulation while the wife marked time. The dichotomy put an almost intolerable strain on the fabric of the marriage. In Judith, as I was to learn, the lack of self-worth manifested itself to a greater degree than in the other wives because she felt the gap between what she was and what her husband had become had widened almost beyond the bridging point. Marquerite Simpson had hung on by turning to religion for refuge; Alice Kiick had got into spiritualism and astrology; Julie Swift studied law. Some, unable to cope, sought divorce, withdrew from life, or turned to drink. Judith Allison turned to pills. Then she added alcohol for good measure.

At the age of thirty-two, with her husband's career at its peak, Judith Alma Bjorkman Allison confessed, after years of inner conflict and torture, that she was addicted to pills. She admitted her well-kept secret in a letter she sent to her priest, her doctor, and her husband. All three were astonished.

The confession was the start of a long, brave climb back to health and sobriety after eleven years of the agonizing torment of addiction to pills. Looking back, she believes that the pill habit was only a symptom of the disease. The disease was lack of self-esteem.

Judith was born in San Jose, California. She had three sisters, an overworked mother, and a father who was a free-lance electrician. Most of her childhood memories are of moving from town to town. Her father would take electrical contracts wherever he could get them, but the periods of employment were usually short, so the family followed him to Ohio, Idaho, Georgia, New Jersey, and finally Florida. They constantly changed towns, homes, and apartments. She remembers the continuous adjustments to new friends and new schools. "It was a nightmare. I fell behind in my studies and I was painfully shy. If I was lucky enough to make a new friend, we'd move, and that was the end of that. Moving so much mixed up my credits, and my high school record was a mess. I must have had twenty different math teachers for the same course and still flunked it. When I finally transferred to a public high school in Hollywood, Florida, I should have been a senior, but they told me I couldn't graduate for four more years. I stuck it out for a while, then quit for good in the first semester of eleventh grade. I just gave up. But it's bugged me ever since that I didn't finish my high school education."

It didn't bother her at first. She was thrilled at being free of the classroom. An education seemed unimportant and unnecessary. She began living with a married sister whose husband was a race car driver, and they often took her to the track. She loved the races and soon knew the names of many of the drivers, including Bobby Allison. She'd seen photographs of him but had never met him until one day at the track she saw a car lose control on a turn, skid into a retaining wall, and erupt into flames. Instinctively she jumped up and began to scream, "Bobby . . . Bobby Allison." She was amazed to learn that it had been his car and that he had managed to escape without injury. That afternoon she was introduced to Bobby, and her life was instantly full of excitement, racing, and love. Who needed an education?

They were married in 1960, shortly after she'd turned eighteen. They settled in Hueytown because it was central to the seven major tracks on which Bobby would be racing. During the early years of their marriage, while Bobby was driving his way to fame and fortune, she was content to remain at home and have babies—four of them: Davy, now thirteen, Clifford, twelve, Bonnie, ten, and Carrie, seven.

In the middle sixties Bobby began to win huge amounts of money and was fast becoming one of the country's top drivers. But fame proved very difficult for Judith to handle. She felt threatened by the personal visibility Bobby's fame brought her. She tried to hide what she considered embarrassing flaws in her personality, background, and education. She anxiously imagined that unfavorable comparisons were being made between herself and other women. So instead of being herself and enjoying her husband's successes, she allowed her insecurities to plunge her into depression and despair.

"I gradually started losing interest in just about everything," she recalled. "Bobby wanted to take me with him to the track, to press parties, to all the functions he was now attending, but I didn't want to go. I didn't want to be compared to all the young, beautiful girls that hang around superstars—all of them, I was sure, smarter, more secure, better dressers, and better conversationalists than I. I was convinced that other people had lost respect for me. I blamed my husband's career. I felt he was more interested in racing than in me. I would ask myself, 'How could a handsome man, a famous man, idolized by millions be interested in a little, plain, uneducated nobody like me?'"

Her negative attitude resulted in physical and mental strain. An allergy developed and grew progressively worse. She was forced to take medication to ease her pain. Then she needed pills to soothe her hypertension, which led to pills to help her sleep, which led to pep pills, headache pills, and muscle relaxants. Within a few months she had become totally dependent on pills to ease her ailments and hide her inadequacies, or what she saw as inadequacies.

An eleven-year diet of pills and alcohol brought her to a partial breakdown. She was emotionally and physically exhausted and was contemplating separation, divorce, and even suicide. One night, in desperation, she drove to a friend's house and confessed. She stayed there for two days, and persuaded by the woman, she wrote everything out in a letter and sent copies to her doctor, priest, and husband. The letter read:

Eleven years ago an allergy started and it has progressively gotten worse. I had to take medication for it and that was the beginning of my problems. I now admit that I am an addict. My husband became a very busy man about the time this all started. I couldn't take the responsibility that went with his career. I felt completely inferior, inadequate. He was always away from home. Maybe what we didn't realize is that I probably drove him away even more with my insecurities.

As I'm writing this down, I'm trying to break the pill habit. It breaks my heart to write this because up to now I have never considered myself an addict. Now I realize I must find the courage to quit. It isn't going to be easy. Every morning I wake up with a sick feeling that covers my whole body. A gnawing in my stomach, a heaviness in my chest. God knows, I need my pills. My face is puffy and it itches, my eyes are almost swollen shut, my head is throbbing. I couldn't sleep last night, so I am exhausted.

One reason is that I was hoping my husband would call me, but long after the time he usually calls, the phone was silent. I couldn't sleep. I looked at the phone and begged it to ring. *Let it be Bobby.* I finally dropped off to sleep; then he called and woke me up. I was glad, but then that awful feeling invaded me like a wave; it washed over me and left me weak and lost. It went like this: I asked Bobby how the filming went. He said they'd really had a good time and had gone to dinner after work with four or five guys and a woman that's in the film with him (was she beautiful? I wondered). He went on to say that they would finish the film tomorrow, but there would be a party tomorrow evening and he wanted to stay over for it. I told him that would be fine, but I didn't mean it. I immediately felt left out and alone. I was jealous. It kept me from going to sleep, and I felt that it was all Bobby's fault. And yet I had been the very one who told him to tell me everything, to be completely honest with me because it would cause less trouble later. I still think it's better to know than not to know, but now I must do my part and not let jealousy take over.

I woke up in the morning feeling terrible. Depression had taken hold. God, how I needed my pills. I drove to my best friend's house. I hope I can finish writing this and then have her type it for me. She and a few other friends have really stuck by me. I don't even think they know how much they've done for me; they have pointed out my good points, helping me find myself, finding self-worth. The one thing I wanted more than anything was to be accepted by people as having some intelligence. My friends reminded me that getting degrees doesn't necessarily make you intelligent. I think I'm getting better on this subject; the doctor I went to the other day was talking about confidence and at the end of our conversation he said, "You've got a college education, haven't you?" It was the first time in my life when I didn't hedge or feel embarrassed. I said no and right there I knew God was with me.

I've got the shakes right now while I'm writing this. I'm fighting myself because I know I can go to my mother's home across the street from my home and get a nerve pill (I left all my pills over there), but I'm not going to do it. I'm thirty-two years old and have a great husband and four wonderful children. I want to love them and enjoy them while I have them. I know I have a serious problem, but with God's help I'll make it.

One year after that letter was written, Judith was doing fine. She never went to her mother's for those pills. At first she fought the craving hour by hour, but with the passage of each day, she became stronger. Now her health has improved, confidence has replaced self-doubt and she is slowly accepting and liking herself for what she is. It's been an ordeal and she still looks forlorn at times. The pills and liquor have taken their toll, but with recuperation it is still possible to see the beautiful woman there. She has a winsome smile that dimples both cheeks, but her pale-blue eyes seem shy and show fright and suffering.

"I'm very involved emotionally with Bobby's racing," she said. "Now that I'm well, I'm really with him in every way before and during a race. Just before a race, whatever is going on in Bobby's mind is going on in my mind. I know his fears, his problems with the car if he has any. I get withdrawn from the rest of the world and completely concentrate on Bobby, on his car. I don't want any interruptions from children or friends."

The resemblance to Helen Stewart's description of watching Jackie racing was startling.

"After the first few laps, my stomach's in a knot," said Judith. "I'm better off if I'm keeping score. It gives me something to do. If I'm not involved in scoring, I usually stand up on top of our camper and eat myself to death."

She said she eats everything she can get her hands on, peanuts, hot dogs, candy, apples, popcorn, anything. Then, after a while, if all is going well, she settles down to what she calls the rhythm of sound and sight. She imagines herself in a car taking laps.

"If there's an accident, it really unnerves you, breaks the rhythm. When you find out it was another car, you're still exhausted, but happy your man has pulled through, even if he doesn't win. The tension for me is never over until the race is over."

She recalled that recently in a race in Ontario, Richard Petty was monopolizing the race until his car got in trouble.

"My heart was in my mouth as I watched Bobby move forward and pull away. The last thirty-five laps he had about a half of a straightaway lead, but instead of relief, which I should have felt, my stomach went back into knots. He was winning, but I always have an apprehension just before the end that something might go wrong.''

During Judith's losing bout with pills she rarely accompanied Bobby when he raced. She stayed home and let jealousy, fear, and hatred eat at her vitals. But now she says she attends three-quarters of the races, leaving her children with her excellent housekeeper or with the Allisons' best friends in Hueytown, the local barber and his wife.

In the early years of marriage, when Judith traveled with her husband, she was so afraid he might be killed in a race that she'd reach for her pills to pull her through the day. "The fear was becoming neurotic, but I think my Catholic beliefs pulled me through," she said, her hand shaking slightly as she raised her coffee cup.

"Three years ago I really came to terms with my fears of death. I got to the racetrack during the last week before the race. The track was slippery. They had three weeks of rain and wrecks. I saw a friend, Swede Savage, get killed. He hit a wall. The car caught fire, and he was thrown clear, but too late. He was on fire, too, and burned to death right before our eyes.

"There were several more serious accidents before the week was over. I got very emotional, uptight, and nervous about everything. If my husband made love to me, I was certain it was for the last time. I cried, and I prayed, and Bobby came through all right. I gained a deep faith during that week. It got me over my neurotic fear of death, and I think I really found God." Judith's religious dedication is strong. It's visible all over her house. She took up needlepoint, as have so many superstar wives, and most of the themes are religious.

She says she still has fears, but not "the neurotic kind." She still fears fire because the first time she saw Bobby his car was on fire and she saw Swede burn to death. "Fire is a bad way to go, and most drivers die in flames.''

When she came to terms with the fear of death, she says, she also came to terms with the reality that her husband is a race car driver and not a golf pro or a salesman. "OK. If he's going to die, it would be better to live a full life as a driver than to live in constant fear or to force him to quit. Better he should die doing what he wanted to do than live doing what he didn't want to do. Death isn't the worst thing that can happen. A divorce, separation when you love a person can be worse than death. Life sometimes can be worse than death.''

She was twisting her hands nervously. Once again my thoughts turned to Helen Stewart. Both Judith and Helen were married to racers, but one was afraid of death, and the other, because of her agonizing personal experiences, feared life more.

I had heard about the euphoria drivers feel after winning and wondered if their wives shared it. Judith did. "I really feel high when he wins. I want to celebrate—make love! But, you see, when Bobby wins a race, he doesn't need sex. Winning is a form of sex for him. It's so fulfilling and gives him so much satisfaction that when it comes to sex, I find him much more needful when he's not winning. Some guys take a week to come out of the euphoric state, but Bobby is high for the evening after a victory, and then it's back to business the next day. It's a mentally exhausting state to be in when you win a race. It takes a lot to slow down for most drivers, but when Bobby loses a race, he's off the minute it's over. Sometimes it's almost better. I mean, we're, uh, closer when he loses—when things don't go right."

During the slow drive from the restaurant back to the house we made every green light. I doodled on the back of my notes while she chatted about life in Hueytown where everybody knew *everything* about everyone. I suddenly was aware I had printed the word "Brave" and drawn a circle around it.

"Do you think you've finally found that elusive bluebird?" I asked as we turned in the driveway.

"The bluebird of happiness? Well . . . let's say I have found myself. I've been through it all." Her pale-blue eyes looked straight ahead, and her voice was firm. "It was bad . . . so bad I thought of suicide more than once, and for a while I hated my husband. I thought he wanted to make me feel inferior, angry, envious . . . jealous. But after I wrote that letter and started getting professional help, I could see that I was doing it all to *myself.*"

She stopped the car, put the key in her purse, turned, and looked directly at me. "Now I know who I am, and I accept myself the way I am. It's taken many years to be able to do that, but today I believe I can stand on my own two feet as a person. I've started to do things without Bobby's help. In the past I was just his reflection. Now I'm proud of the things I can do. Is that peace? Happiness? Yes, I guess it is!"

"Why have you told me all this?" I asked.

"Because by telling you and getting it out to the public, I might be able to help someone else—perhaps another wife who is suffering like I was and for the same reasons. I would like to think that all I've gone through could be of some help . . . some value for someone else."

Later that day, as she was driving me to the airport, we started laughing about my plane having to stop in Atlanta. "I'm going to take flying lessons this summer and learn how to fly our family plane. Next time you come down I'll fly you out without stopping in Atlanta."

I remembered that Pam Csonka also took up flying and wondered whether it was significant. I suggested to Judith that she might end up a women's libber. She threw back her head, and I saw her really laugh for the first time. "Just

last week at the race in California, I started to think about how independent
I've become. I'm decorating our house myself, planning a trip, and soon I'll
be getting my pilot's license. We were out to dinner, and I turned to Bobby
and said, 'You'd better be careful. I'm a real women's libber now! What do I
need you for?''

''What was his reaction to that?''

''He threw up his hands and said, 'Write me another letter!' ''

It was a short hop to Greensboro, North Carolina, where Bobby Allison's
leading competitor, Richard Petty, and his wife, Lynda, live. And yes, we
had to go to Atlanta first.

Just Simple Country Folks

Any woman who marries an athlete has to know she is second to his career. If she doesn't understand this from the beginning, the marriage won't last a week.

No amount o' money can change us 'cause we're just simple country folks. Money buys things—not character, strength, and happiness.

Lynda Gayle Petty* is thirty-three years old and looks every minute of it. She's short and plump. She lets her gray hair show prominently through the short dark strands that had an exclusive franchise before the four babies came into her life and Richard became so all-fired famous.

She has a girl's skin, smooth and eggshell white, enhancing cornflower-blue eyes which have forgotten how to sparkle.

There's not a stock car racing fan in the world who doesn't know of her husband and hardly a soul in the southeast quarter of the United States who hasn't heard of him. He is considered one of the two top stock car racers in the nation (Bobby Allison is the other) and has enriched himself beyond his wildest dreams. But it's done little for Lynda. Outside of her tiny circle of personal friends and relatives, no one knows about her. She is nobody's hero, and the potential benefits of wealth have passed her by. She doesn't know how to spend graciously. She has a maid but does most of the housework herself while the maid sits and rocks and gazes out the window to keep from having to watch disagreeable work being done. If Lynda had ten domestics, she would still do the work and have to add a recreation room to the house where they could all pass the time. She is a nervous, fidgety housekeeper who is never still. Small, quick steps whisk her here and there to do countless small tasks to which she seems to assign undue importance.

Lynda has had little opportunity to grow. She claims she doesn't want to. Her childhood was cut short, and adult responsibility crushed her too soon. She married Richard in her senior year of high school and graduated directly into motherhood and domesticity. It seems to suit her, and Richard shows no sign of dissatisfaction. Lynda knows that and is honest with herself.

---

*Richard Petty, professional racing driver. Richard Petty is the first and only driver to win more than $2,000,000 in car racing. He owns every important stock car (NASCAR) racing record worth having, including the greatest number of victories—164. Petty has won the NASCAR Grand National Championship a record total of five times. He has won the prestigious Daytona 500 five times in his career. Petty's 1974 earnings came to $278,175.

"My husband is married to his profession. He comes around here and clowns, and we know he loves us, but let me tell you, racing comes first. Sometimes I think the nuts and bolts that go into his cars mean more to him than anything. He lives and breathes racing one hundred percent. Any woman who marries an athlete has to know she is second to his career. If she doesn't understand this from the beginning, the marriage won't last a week. I knew what I was getting into when I married him. His career comes first—that's fine with me. I'm busy here at home."

When the subject of jock lovers came up, contempt boiled out of her. "Those women?" She sniffed. "When a man takes off with one of them, somethin's wrong at home. If a man is a Romeo, like Joe Namath, well, Romeos shouldn't get married."

Richard does come around and clown as Lynda says. He's an inveterate tease, and she's the perfect ploy because she takes him seriously. Maybe with reason. It's hard to tell.

When I arrived at the Petty house and was ushered unceremoniously into the kitchen, the only room I had a chance to see, children, mostly babies, were everywhere, all in a bad mood. There were Lynda's four and an equal number of nephews and nieces. Most were crying, and Lynda was flitting from countertop to sink, making lunch or changing diapers, sorting laundry and changing her daughter's muddy clothes or answering the telephone. Richard entered the midst of the bedlam, stamped his foot, and howled like a wolf.

"Ah want some attenshun ma-se'f," he bellowed.

The tiny children were so startled they forgot what they were crying about and gazed up at him with astonished, unblinking eyes; the torrents of tears stopped.

"Now behave yoreselves, y'heah?" he warned as he swooped up his daughter and perched on a chair, the little girl on his lap.

"Betcha the other wives gave you tea and cakes and sat you down proper in the livin' room," he said to me through a wide, white, fun-loving smile that must have charmed thousands. "Well, yo're lucky to git any tenshun at all 'round here. *Ah* nevah do."

He set eighteen-month-old Rebecca down and poured himself a cup of black coffee to give his wisecrack a chance to sink in.

Lynda ignored it and kept working. I asked him about the dangers of car racing, and he said he never thinks about it and has never been injured. "But Ah got m'finger broken playin' football in the front yard," he said as he lifted Rebecca back on his lap. "Y'see, stock car racin' is a sport where either ye gits killed or don't git scratched at all."

"Why, that's not true," interjected Lynda without looking up from a pile of clothes she was sorting. "You had a bad wreck at Darlington [South

Carolina] back in 1970. Have you forgotten? The car bounced off a wall and flipped over twelve times.''

"Wull, Ah may have got scratched up a bit that time."

"Scratched?" contradicted Lynda. "You dislocated your shoulder."

"Okeh," he said, turning to me the better to plead his case, "but she sure was a nervous wreck. Beat me to the field hospital, cryin' and whimperin' like a hurt puppy.''

"I was not a nervous wreck neither. I got there first like he said, but when I saw he was conscious, I knew he was OK and I went home."

"Tell her about the time you drove off in my car, Lynda."

"She don't want to hear about that. Wasn't nothin' to it."

"Tell it, Lynda, or I will.''

"Well, it wasn't nothin'. I don't know why he brought it up. It was a souped-up old thing with fender skirts on it.''

"*That* was my byoo-tee-ful old car. She took her girlfriends ridin', and when she crossed the ole bridge outside of town, she took the guardrail right along with her.''

"Did not! Just bumped into it a bit."

"Haw! She scraped the fender skirt all up and down and then got so frightened whut Ah might say, she went over to her daddy's garage and found some black enamel paint and tried to fix it up herself.''

"It wasn't such a bad paint job."

"She thought Ah wouldn't notice. Can you feature that? She thought Ah wouldn't notice.''

Then on the matter of whether Lynda gets lonely when Richard travels, Richard said, "She sure does. Cries like a hound dog."

"No, I don't. I don't have time to get lonely." She was at the counter now, preparing lunch, and the evidence all pointed ominously to peanut butter sandwiches. "I travel with him just about everywhere he goes, and when we're home, like now, well, he drops in on me too much.''

"Aw," protested Richard.

"Yes, he does. His garage, the body shop where they make racing cars, and his offices are just down the street. It don't take nothin' for him to pop in here for coffee or lunch or somethin'.''

"Somethin'? Whut d'ye mean *somethin'*? Whut's this nice lady s'posed to think when you say a thing like that?''

Lynda blushed.

"Oh, hush. Lonesome?" she said, pointing the peanut-buttery knife at him. "That man is *never* out of my sight. I feel sorry for those baseball and football wives. Now *they* have to endure long separations. Those men go away for months at a time. Sometimes I wish Richard . . .''

"Haw, haw, haw," railed her husband.

"Their days are prob'ly OK, but their nights must be awful."

"Ah'm gettin' outta here before she starts to cryin' or worse," said Richard. He put down Rebecca, picked up one of the sandwiches from the counter, and strode out the back door.

That was the signal for the crying to resume. Lynda patiently fed, cleaned, and bedded the children. Peace settled over the house, and Lynda sat down next to me and talked as we munched our sandwiches and drank hot, strong coffee. It was the only time I saw her sit still all day.

"You mustn't pay Richard any mind," she said. "He's thataway most of the time. It's his nature to tease and carry on. But he's a good man, religious, don't use bad language or drink or fool around with women, and is mighty serious when it comes to racin' and business. That's why he's on top and hasn't gotten hisself killed. He tries not to show it, but I know him. He gets all keyed up before a race. That's when he puts aside all his jokin' and foolin' aroun'. He's so occupied with his car and whut he's gonna do the next day I jes' leave him alone. I feel he needs all the rest and relaxation he can get. He needs his energy."

The Pettys live in a fifteen-room $300,000-house with a swimming pool and tennis court on the edge of a four-hundred acre farm. They moved into it recently, discarding their red-brick ranch house in Randleman, a tiny community fourteen miles south of Greensboro. The place had got so small they had to move; otherwise they would probably still be there. The new house is only a few miles away at a community called Level Cross. You can be sure it wouldn't be more than a few miles away. Lynda and Richard are bound to this land the way darkness is to daylight. They were born on it and have never lived out of sight of their parents' homes. Sisters and brothers have their homes sprinkled over the adjacent countryside. No question, this is Petty country.

They were still living in the smaller house when I went to see Lynda. It was fussily decorated. She had stapled plastic sprays of lilies of the valley on the wastebaskets. She also had more than a hundred dolls ornamenting the mantel, glass cases, bookshelves, and table tops in every room except the kitchen. There were antique dolls, London bobby dolls, Civil War dolls, Vietnamese dolls, Hawaiian dolls, Indian dolls, Chinese dolls, and a few that defy easy definition.

Like Marguerite Simpson and her butterflies Lynda has a strawberry fixation. The kitchen was full of them. Lynda had them on the china, glasses, linens, place mats, soap, wallpaper, curtains, salt and pepper shakers. She had strawberry candles and hot pad holders, a strawberry-shaped floor mat at the sink, plastic strawberries in a bowl, and real ones in the refrigerator.

Money and fame have not touched the Pettys' inner core. "We've stayed the same," said Lynda. "If you put me in with the Kennedys and folks such as that, I wouldn't fit, and I know it. They wouldn't care much for our ways neither, I don't reckon, and that's the way it should be. I don't want what they've got. If you're not careful, you can be pushed into places you don't belong. You ask Judith Allison, she'll tell you the same thing [she had]. When people try to change it can be disastrous. It takes strength to stay the same when you become famous. Like Abe Lincoln and Stonewall Jackson. No amount o' money can change us 'cause we're just simple country folks. Money buys *things*—not character, strength, and happiness."

She was telling me about how Richard learned to drive from his father, Lee, who was a top racer himself in his prime, how Richard is the biggest winner in stock car racing, how Richard and Bobby Allison abide each other, but that's about all, and how her husband not only races but has a franchise to sell auto parts and equipment to others who race.

Richard burst through the door at this point.

"Hey, whut's goin' on in heah?" he boomed. "Whut'd y'all find to talk about all this time?"

"Whad d'you want now, Richard?" asked Lynda good-humoredly.

"Jus' a cup o' coffee is all. Cain't a man come into his own kitchen after he's been a-workin' hard all day?"

He poured out the coffee as the children started crying again, awakened by the sudden outburst. The maid rose from her rocking chair slowly to do some ironing, and Lynda reverted to being a wound-up Judy Doll, rushing from one chore to another.

The damage done, Richard settled down at the kitchen table and cupped his coffee in both hands, sipping it gently and breathing in the aroma. He glanced over the edge of the cup at me and asked, "D'ye git down this way very often?"

"Nope," I answered. "I live in New York City."

"Well now," he said, his face looking serious for the first time that day, "that's a durn shame."

I missed my plane that evening because Lynda drove me over to inspect their new house, which is so large that even her dolls could have separate rooms, and by the time we finished the tour there wasn't anything flying out of Greensboro. Stuck in a hotel room without anything to listen to but Lynda's tape or read but the Gideon Bible, I called Jacques and complained loudly that my odyssey was beginning to be a drag and boredom had set in.

"Well then," his voice came back, "it's the perfect time to go to Cincinnati."

"Who's in Cincinnati?"

"The zaniest wife of them all—a real character. You might have to go on Valium, but you won't be bored."

Big Momma

When I first got married, I worried about the groupies, then I said to myself, "Karolyn,* he's got to find someone much better, and that ain't gonna be easy!"

People say wives of superstars are living in their husbands' shadows. Well, most of the time I get in front of his spotlight. I've got a big mouth!

River Front Stadium in Cincinnati was crawling with security—plainclothesmen, the FBI, secret servicemen and just about every policeman on the local force. It was the 1970 All-Star game, and President Nixon had come to Ohio to see it. The officials at the brand-new stadium were not as concerned with the President's arrival as they were with the prospect of an appearance by a stripper named Morgana.

Morgana had a passion for baseball players and had been showing up on baseball fields all over the country, rushing out in mid-game and hugging and kissing one of the startled players. The voluptuous, dark-haired beauty had made all the talk shows for her daring, and her name was fast becoming the biggest joke in baseball history.

"Wonder who she's gonna hit next?" was a frequent question in the locker room.

With the presidential party safely conducted to their seats, the police breathed a sigh of relief and started looking for Morgana. The very thought of a stripper slipping through security and running out on the field in front of the President of the United States was too embarrassing even to contemplate.

Plainclothesmen stood by every gate, armed with her vital statistics—39–24–36, dark hair, heavy eye makeup, and sexy.

"She'll never get by my men!" The chief of police snarled through clouds of cigar smoke. "She may have made it in other cities, but *not* Cincinnati!"

Two women were making their way into the ball park, strolling along with the crowd toward Gate 15. One was tall, exceedingly thin, with dark, Spanish-looking features. The other was short and looked as though Fellini had de-

---

*Pete Rose, professional baseball player with the Cincinnati Reds. In 1963 Pete Rose was chosen Rookie of the Year in the National League. Since then he has gone on to become the finest switch-hitter in the game. He has batted over .300 for ten years in his career (1965–75) and had the highest batting average of both leagues in '68, '69 and '73. Rose has played in all but two All-Star games since '65. In '73 he was chosen the Most Valuable Player in the National League, and in '75 he was named the Most Valuable Player in the World Series.

signed her. Heavy blue luminescent eye shadow coated her lids; silver dangling earrings were lost in a mop of reddish brown hair, snarled as though it had come out of a clothes drier. Her large breasts were undulating under a tight, décolleté pink knit dress that stopped six inches above the knees, and she sauntered along as if she were body-proud, a confident but mischievous smile on her face. People waved at her, and she waved back with a "Hiya," her fingers forming a V—the wave often accompanied by a big wink.

As they approached the gate, a plainclothesman spotted them. He checked Morgana's description against the one in the pink dress, then moved in closer to eavesdrop on a conversation between her and two men.

"Well, who's it going to be this time?" one of the men asked.

"Don't you know, baby?" The woman laughed.

The plainclothesman tilted his head and caught the words "Come on, Morgana, who're ya gonna kiss this time, Bench or Seaver?"

"It's gonna be Rose, baby, all the way!" She gave a wink and whirled her hips.

The detective wasted no more time. He'd heard enough and called in on his walkie talkie—he'd found Morgana. In thirty seconds the group was surrounded.

"OK, no trouble now, young lady, we're takin' you in!"

"What the hell is going on here?" the gorgeous brunette cried as she tried to throw off the uniformed man already clasping her shoulder.

"Come on, baby, you're not gettin' into *this* ball park! You're goin' downtown."

"What the hell is the matter with you guys. Are you *serious*?"

"Come on, Morgana, come along quietly."

"Morgana?" she gasped and turned to her friend. "Petuka, tell these goddamn fools who I am!"

Petuka Perez looked up with wide innocent eyes and said, "I don't know her."

"Petuuuuuka!" The girl with the blue lids wailed at her friend in disbelief.

"I don't know her," Petuka repeated quietly.

A policeman on the Cincinnati force was watching the scene from the sidelines. Suddenly he knew he had to stop the arrest. "Let her go," he said firmly. "That's not Morgana—that's Mrs. Pete Rose."

"What the hell is wrong with you, Petuka?" Karolyn Rose growled as they hurried to their seats. "You're suppose to be my best friend. Why in hell didn't you hlep me?"

"I didn't know you at the time," Petuka said. They both sat down and roared with laughter.

The first time I saw Karolyn Rose was in the new Pete Rose restaurant, in the Oakhills section of Cincinnati. All the walls in the gymnasiumlike dining room are lined with oil paintings of baseball scenes by Gene Lockcler, and I noted, as I was ushered through the lunchtime crowd to a table in the rear, that the place had the ambience of the old Toots Shor's.

A curvy brunette with heavy green eye paint poured coffee into my cup and said, ''Mrs. Rose will be right with you, she's substituting for a waitress who's sick.'' Then she disappeared through one of the double doors to the kitchen and immediately came back out through the other—sat down and grinned. It was 12:45 P.M. Karolyn didn't stop talking for two days.

There's no question she looks like a stripper, with her mop of auburn hair piled on the back of her head and heavy layers of green eye shadow on her lids, but if you can get by the grotesque eye paint, you look into direct, unflinching hazel eyes that confidently challenge everyone to a duel.

Karolyn and I passed a few minutes in trivial conversation while we were sizing each other up. I knew it was going to be difficult if Karolyn didn't like me, and I had a hunch she was the kind of woman who related to men and, in general, didn't trust other women. It came out early in the interview and without any mincing around.

''I don't really like other women. I've got a theory about us females. . . . I don't think we really *like* each other. Oh, we say we do and we put up with each other for propriety's sake, but deep down we don't trust each other. We compete all the time.''

Watch out, I told myself, *female reporters have to be at the top of her list.* Karolyn took the lead and started talking about her family in between jumping up to greet friends, giving orders to the hired help, and bantering with a tableful of ballplayers across the room.

''I could kill that kid of mine!'' she said, waving at someone.

''What kid?''

''Petie Junior. He's gonna drive me up the f——— wall. He takes batting instructions at the field house, and that damn kid swears a blue streak when he doesn't hit the ball. It sounds bad comin' from a five-year-old. I don't understand it.''

''It must be very embarrassing to you,'' I said with a perfectly straight face.

Karolyn asked the waitress to come over and fill up my coffee cup. ''Give her a roll with it, what the hell, she might give me a better write-up.''

The ice was broken.

I soon found out that she's a nonstop talker with a special talent for mixing up her nouns and verbs, and it's useless to attempt to correct her. If you haven't already got it by now, she uses four-letter words instead of adjectives and often. Her speech would make a longshoreman blush. Only five feet two, she has a temper as fiery as her husband's. Friends quake when Pete snaps out in anger, but they hide when Karolyn gets into the act. When the Roses fight with each other, it's like watching someone throw a match in a gas tank. Wham! Karolyn not only holds her own, but can outtalk, outswear, and outshout the meanest man in baseball.

Depending on her mood, she can charm, ignore, embarrass, intimidate, tease, or melt your heart when she lights up with one of her million-kilowatt smiles. This warm, tough, sensuous woman, who is completely spontaneous, has more zip, zing, and zizz than ten females put together.

New Yorkers would call her delightfully zany. In Cincinnati they call her a character. Karolyn, they say, shaking their heads primly, "is a character!"

She was born thirty-three years ago in Cincinnati, the Roman Catholic daughter of a German-born carpenter and a vaudeville show girl named Pearl. What a combination. That union explains a lot about Karolyn. The Englehardts, with their son, Fred, Jr., and daughter, Karolyn, settled down in a middle-class neighborhood and sent their children to Catholic schools. The neighborhood may have been middle-class, but that didn't rub off on Karolyn. They haven't devised a class to put her in yet. When she was twelve and attending St. John the Baptist Catholic School, she had the leading role of the Virgin Mary in the school's Easter passion play. She upset the cast, shocked the faculty, and had the audience roaring with laughter when kneeling in one of the holiest scenes, she kept winking at the wise men.

After high school ("They got me out in record time") she went to work for the American Book Company in Cincinnati. Before she quit, the boss got an ulcer, records were irrevocably scrambled, and everyone who worked there was weak from laughter.

Maybe "Lucy" might have done it on TV, but it's doubtful anyone in real life would ever get her fingers caught in the typewriter roll. Karolyn did. She rolled them in with the paper, and before she could cry out in pain, her boss came out of his office and asked when the letter she was typing for him would be ready. She couldn't answer. Her face was locked into a grotesque smile, trying to hide the pain. He asked if she was sick.

"No," she answered, smiling through clenched teeth.

"Well, you look it!" and he went back into his office.

With her free hand Karolyn called the typewriter repair service, and the next time her boss walked out he saw his entire office staff standing around convulsed while a repairman took her typewriter apart. The boss was handed a fifty-dollar repair bill, and Karolyn was handed a pink slip, her career in the book company finished.

In 1963 she went to Florida and stayed with friends. One day they took her to the racetrack where, in the clubhouse, she was introduced to dark-haired, mean-looking, tough-talking Pete Rose. Karolyn's friends thought that since they were both from Cincinnati, they should know each other.

Karolyn looked hard at Pete. "Your name sounds familiar."

"Well," said the already-famous baseball star, almost swallowing his gum, "it should be."

"Do you play football for the local tavern back home?"

"Naw," Pete growled, eyeing her suspiciously. "I play baseball for the Reds."

"The who?"

"The Reds! The Cincinnati Reds!"

"The Reds, huh? I've never heard of 'em!"

"Where have you been?" he shouted. "Has your head been in the sand? We're the most famous ball club in—"

"Well, I don't give a shit!" Karolyn yelled back before he could finish, and then, to the astonishment of their mutual friends: "I've never heard of ya. Maybe that's because you've had your f——— head in the sand!"

That was their beginning. Years later Karolyn told that story when she was the guest speaker at a meeting of the Society of Cincinnati Engineers. To the horror of Pete's agent, a circumspect little lady named Ann Smith, who went along because she was scared to death of what Karolyn might say, one of the engineers asked Karolyn how she met Pete. She told the story with relish while Ann squirmed in her seat.

Six months after their first meeting they got married, and they've been yelling at each other ever since. Karolyn's mother, Pearl, sums up the marriage this way: "Neither one could have married anyone else, because no one else could stand either one of them. They've *got* to stick together!" The Roses were married in a Catholic church, and it was probably the only time in their lives that both were quiet. Well, almost. Pete kept looking at Karolyn and whispering, "Are we married yet?" The Catholic ceremony, he found out, goes on and on.

In best Mike Todd style, the Roses had their reception at Cheviot Stadium. Big drums of punch, hundreds of cases of champagne were hauled in, and five hundred wheels of pizza were baked for the occasion. "Pizza doesn't go with champagne," someone complained. "It does today!" Karolyn countered. Thirteen hundred people received invitations and how many more showed up because of last-minute "Why doncha come to our wedding?" nobody can guess. Cheviot Stadium was jammed. The biggest names in the sports world went down the receiving line. "Hiya, Mickey!"; "Hey, Joe, when you gonna get caught?"

Karolyn, who flips over celebrities, had to be restrained from getting autographs as the superstars came down the line. "My God, I just kissed Joe Namath!" she swooned.

"Cool it, honey, cool it."

When they came back from their honeymoon, a friend asked Karolyn where they'd gone.

"We went to Tijuana."

"Tijuana, Mexico?"

"No," Karolyn said, deadpan. "Tijuana Hotel, Fort Knox."

Pete, who was in the Army Reserve, and his bride spent their honeymoon at Fort Knox, Kentucky, while he was on a six-month tour of duty. To think of Karolyn that close to Fort Knox makes one tremble. Fortunately for the country, before she hatched a plot to count the gold, they left for Florida and spring training.

After a few years a house in the suburbs couldn't contain several million megatons of energy, so Karolyn went back to work. This time for Station WNOP in Newport, Kentucky, a thousand-watt AM jazz station headquartered on converted oil drums floating in the Ohio River.

"I'm a Howard Cosell woman! I tell it like it is!"

The people who live in that area also report that she did *all* the talking when she was interviewing and that during a "live" interview with Muhammad Ali he had to interrupt her with a poem in order to get a word in before the show's end. Ali went out of the studio that day, shaking his head. "I always thought *I* talked more than anybody."

Even as he was going out the door, Karolyn was introducing referee Don Dumphy on the air as the "blow-by-blow man." During the commercial Don said, "You can't say that, Karolyn, you can't call me a blow-by-blow man!"

"Of course I can." Karolyn grinned and went on to repeat the introduction. A few weeks later the radio station asked her to announce a list of sports events going on in the area. Last on the list was a hockey game, and she went off the air with, "Puck-off time is seven forty-five."

Karolyn isn't with the station anymore, but when you go to Ohio, you still hear sportscasters imitating her.

Today the Roses have two children: ten-year-old Fawne Rene, who, like Jim Bouton's daughter, loves baseball and wears her father's baseball cap around the house, and five-year-old Pete Edmund Rose, Jr., who's a chip off the old block in the departments of baseball and swearing. The kids are their father's most vocal fans at a game—besides Karolyn, of course. *No one* is louder than Karolyn.

In the past the Rose house in the snazzy section of Oakhills was the meeting place for every sports figure who came to town. The guys would drink beer, gossip, swap stories in the basement, where there's a pool table, pinball machine, baseball machine, hockey machine, bowling machine, bar in the corner, and a life-size model of Pete in the bathroom. Now the gang goes to Pete's new restaurant if they want to see the Roses. Karolyn spends most of her time there. She moves around the place like greased lightning. One day she's a bus girl, the next a waitress, sometimes she works as a cashier ("That's a good way to go out of business," Pete grumbles), but most of the time she plays hostess and does what comes naturally. Talks.

"God gave me a marvelous gift," she says of her loquaciousness. She has something to say to everyone who comes in the restaurant. "Hiya, kid." She pats the head of a twelve-year-old boy. "Are ya gettin' ready to root for the Reds?" "Well, Willie," she greets an ancient white-haired man who can barely walk with a cane, "I'm gonna put you back at Ethel's table, and stop tryin' to make the waitress, will ya?" She chats with women about their children, teases young people about their love life, and with men she's positively great, exuding sex appeal, eyes sparkling with mischief at her quick-witted best as she banters and jokes with them all.

While I drank my coffee, she was up and down like a jack-in-the-box. "Hiya, Ed, you're gettin' a fat ass. . . . Hiya, Mary, why doncha put him on a diet?"

Speaking of a diet reminded me that the roll I'd eaten simply wasn't enough, and it didn't look as if Karolyn were ever going to settle down long enough to have lunch.

"I'm hungry," I announced when she sat down once again.

"Well, Jesus Kee-rist, why doncha order some food? There's no need to starve in the middle of a restaurant?" She stuck a menu in my hand. "Number two and four are lousy. Try the roast beef."

"Karolyn, I have to ask you something that doesn't seem quite appropriate for you"—I almost choked on my roast beef—"but all the wives get the same question. . . ."

"Shoot."

"Well, uh, do you ever get lonely?"

She looked at me as if she didn't understand the question. "Lonely? How do I have time to be lonely?" The problem of jock lovers proved more of a challenge. "When I first got married, I worried about the groupies; then I said to myself, 'Karolyn, he's got to find someone much better, and that ain't gonna be easy!' "

One night Pete called after an out-of-town game, and he was teasing Karolyn about the gorgeous women hanging around the ball park. He was undoubtedly looking for a reaction. He got one. "Listen, sweetheart," she said, "you gotta find someone much better . . . now how are ya gonna do that? *But* if you do, have the guts to pick up the phone and tell me. . . . Then I won't have to bother to go to the airport and pick you up!''

"I've never been bothered with those dames since." With those words Karolyn got up and walked over to a table across the room and exchanged greetings with four men. I wondered where Pete Rose was. He probably had the day off. Everyone in the restaurant seemed to know one another, and they all were having a good time. All, that is, but the man sitting at the table to my right. He was alone and not paying attention to anyone or anything. Slumped in a chair with his head down, he was concentrating on a big box of baseballs, signing each one carefully and putting it back in the box.

But of course! It was the great man himself. Suddenly I realized that he'd been sitting there right next to us all the time and he and Karolyn hadn't exchanged a word.

I introduced myself, telling him that I was there to interview his wife. Just in case he hadn't heard.

"Yeah." He never looked up from his baseballs.

"Gee," I said in another attempt at sociability. "That's a great idea to give signed baseballs away! Really good PR for your restaurant."

"Whatta ya mean, *give* them away?" he growled. "I don't give these babies away—I sell 'em! They cost a lot of money! Are ya crazy?"

When Karolyn returned, she found me sitting red-faced and quiet. "Now let's see, where were we?" she boomed. "Oh, yes, on those little bitches—groupies. Now, I honestly have to tell you that I feel all women are jealous, and every husband is jealous of his wife. It's human nature. I'm jealous! And the wives who say they aren't are lyin'. Jealousy is part of life, the spice of life. If there weren't any of these girls around, groupies, it would be dullsville!"

"The football wives sure aren't crazy about them!" I said, remembering Marguerite Simpson's hurt eyes.

Karolyn shrugged. "I'm glad I'm not a football wife. . . . I'd beat the hell out of Pete if he said, 'Don't touch me' before a game."

Her opinions are not nearly as unorthodox as her actions are outlandish. When Pete received the 1973 Most Valuable Player award, Karolyn was beaming proudly at his side while sportswriters and television reporters questioned him about his performance. Pete acknowledged the accolades as humbly as possible for a guy not known for humility, answered all the questions and ended up by saying that he thought the Most Valuable Player award went to the right fellow. With the cameras still rolling, he turned to go when Karolyn grabbed the microphone and yelled, "Now I get to sleep with the Most Valuable Player!"

It wasn't until lunch was over that she introduced me to her husband. Pete Rose, the irascible, arrogant, hot dog baseball player, famous all over America for his on-field aggressiveness and his short-fuse temper, put down his baseball, barked, "Hiya," then went back to work.

Above our table in the restaurant was an oil painting by Lockcler, of the famous fight between Pete and Bud Harrelson. The title of the painting was "I Play Hard." Karolyn caught my glance and explained that it happened during the Eastern and Western Division play-off at Shea Stadium in New York.

"Bud called Pete a name, and that did it!" A quick glance to my right told me Pete was listening intently.

"I wasn't there," she went on, "because I don't go to out-of-town games, but you can be sure if I had been, I woulda been in the middle of it!"

Pete nodded vehemently and went back to signing baseballs.

Neither Pete nor Karolyn wanted to discuss the fight or what followed, so I had to call New York and get the information from a friend at *Sports Illustrated*. It seems the New York Met fans were so irritated with Rose after the Harrelson fight that when Pete took his place in left field the next day, he was showered with garbage and bottles. Rose, who seems to thrive on adversity, responded by hitting a game-winning home run and dashing around the bases with his right fist triumphantly raised. This made the Met fans madder than hornets. Harrelson later forgave him, but the fans never did. Someone in the crowd shot a paper clip into his neck, bottles came dangerously close, and at one game a piece of ice whizzed by his right eye. In California the Reds had to give Pete special protection. The more the crowd booed, the more belligerent he became, and before the season was out, he was the most unpopular man in baseball and the fans the rowdiest in many a season.

Why does a crowd behave like this? I called my friend Barbara Newman, psychologist on the staff at Marymount Manhattan College, and asked her. She quoted something I couldn't make heads or tails out of from Freud's *Group Psychology and the Analysis of the Ego* and Le Bon's *The Crowd*. Simplified, it comes out like this: Psychologists found that the individual feels powerful in a crowd. One can set aside personal responsibilities and act out aggressions and hostile impulses because of the belief that in a crowd he/she is anonymous. The referee, or a player like Rose, does something the people don't like. Collective action sets in—spreads through the crowd like a contagious disease. Even those who have no grievances join in. They boo, jeer, and throw things. The shrinks say the reason is to appease boredom, anger, frustration, or maybe even a desire for adventure. Pete Rose thumbs his nose at the crowd. This provides a ready-made opportunity for people to vent their feelings. The more overtly aggressive (known to us neophytes as troublemakers) can now manipulate the crowd into action it would not otherwise take, and this is what leads to violence.

Karolyn admits she doesn't understand what gets into the fans. "They can yell and boo all they want. I'm glad to see 'em involved. But damn it, I get mad when they throw things! I don't want anybody to hurt him." Many of the Reds' wives complain that even before the Harrelson fight it was embarrassing to sit near Karolyn at a game because she yells, stomps, swears, and puts her fingers in her mouth and lets go with an ear-piercing whistle. "When she does that whistle bit," one of the wives complained, "and you're sitting next to her, it can do permanent damage to your nervous system!" She has also been known to take a little nip from a flask that looks like a transistor radio when the score gets close.

But since the Harrelson fight she does a lot more than cheer at the game. She keeps an eye on the crowd, and if somebody gets out of line—watch out! One day Karolyn was sitting with the other wives behind home plate. Someone threw a golf ball at number 14. "Some son of a bitch threw a golf ball at Pete!" Karolyn screamed. "I'm goin' into the bleachers and find out why a dumb bastard would throw a golf ball at him!" She stormed out of her seat and made her way into the bleachers, bosom heaving and fists clenched.

"What are ya doin' here, Karolyn?" a man in the crowd yelled.

Karolyn, who usually loves to banter with the bleacher bums, went by with a nod.

"Hey, Momma," another yelled.

"What you want, Daddy?" she responded.

"You want that guy who threw the golf ball?"

"Yeah," she shouted, "I'm gonna kill him!"

"He's right over here in the red shirt—"

Karolyn squeezed through a laughing crowd and made her way to the man in the red shirt, whose chin was sinking lower in his collar every second. "So you're the dumb bastard who threw the golf ball at Pete Rose!" she boomed out for all to hear. "Well, you————head, everyone in the stadium saw your ball go astray and hit the backboard instead of number fourteen! Clumsy ass, that's why Rose is in the big leagues and you're not!"

The Harrelson/Rose fight left its print on the Roses. You know it did by the very fact that they won't talk about it. It's probably the one irritating factor in their otherwise carefree, kookie, flamboyant lives. In spite of their toughness and pretense that it doesn't exist, they can't shake it. During baseball season it must spook them, and I'm sure Karolyn is frightened that one day a fan will hit his mark.

Meanwhile, back at the restaurant, Karolyn was stuffing my papers and tape recorder into my briefcase. "Come on, we're goin'. I've got an appointment in an hour at my house."

"Good-bye," I said to Pete as Karolyn charged ahead.

"You've got a runner, honey," he said with his eyes on my legs.

"If you want a house tour, you'll have to take it by yourself. It bores me to look at it. The only thing important in here is Ralph." Ralph, I found out, was a huge wooden hippopotamus lying by the fireplace. Up above Ralph, on the mantel, there was something even more interesting—a huge picture of a naked baby lying on its tummy with Pete Rose's head superimposed on the neck and and underneath in gold letters MVP.

I asked Karolyn to stand in front of the fireplace so I could take a picture of her with the Most Valuable Player. She posed with a naughty smile on her face, and it was perfect except when I tried to snap the shutter nothing happened. Karolyn dropped her pose. "What's the matter?"

"I'm out of film," I apologized.

She disappeared and came back with a small yellow package and resumed her pose. I tried again. This time the flash didn't go off. She disappeared again and came back with a flash pack. All set, I took my time in lining up the shot on my viewfinder.

"What's the matter?" she said suspiciously out of the side of her mouth without moving an inch. "Do I have ta take the picture for you, too?" Later, when I ran out of ink and asked her for a pencil, she said, "God, don't you have *anything?* I'm gonna worry about you on the road, honey!"

Except for the picture of Pete over the mantel, most of the pictures around the house are of the children. Karolyn is more obvious in her affection for her offspring than she is toward Pete, but insiders know that their fights and name-calling have always been part of their mating game. Pete calls her dummy, and it isn't worth repeating what she calls him. Others recoil while the Roses grin as if they've just told each other, "I love you." They have.

When out-of-town games separate them, Pete has been known to call Karolyn several times a day. Their conversations go something like this. Karolyn answers the phone: "Hello, this is Frankenstein."

"Whatcha doin'?" Pete barks into the phone.

"Puttin' bombs in mailboxes."

"How're the kids?"

"Asleep."

"That's good. I'll call later."

"Can't wait."

Click.

"We don't have much to say. What the hell can you say to a guy over the phone that you've been married to for eleven years?" But Karolyn said much more to me. "He's the greatest! Charlie Hustle! He's the only one I know who'll run to first base on a walk. [Mickey Mantle and Whitey Ford gave him that name and for that reason long ago.] I love him, but I wouldn't exactly say I get up at dawn to run his bath. I'm not his geisha! People say wives of superstars are living in their husbands' shadows. Well, most of the time I get in front of his spotlight. I've got a big mouth!'' The question in their case is whether Pete has suffered a loss of identity, not Karolyn.

Karolyn was telling me how she loves bargains—how she took a fox coat Pete bought her back to the store and exchanged it for two cloth coats "Now what the hell am I gonna do with a fox coat?''—when suddenly we were interrupted by two women, one of them crying. Karolyn jumped up and put her arms around her, and the three went into the living room, where there was more crying and Karolyn's voice crooned, "It's gonna be all right. . . . Big Momma promises.'' This was Karolyn's appointment and the reason she had rushed home. One of the wives was undone by her husband's being traded. She came to Karolyn (whom I learned all the Red wives call Big Momma) for comfort and advice. It didn't seem to go with the image Karolyn was trying to project about not liking other women. When they left, she said, "This trading business is shit!''

"I didn't know you had such a gentle side . . . especially for women, Mrs. Rose,'' I teased.

"Well, even *I* cry a lot when our friends get traded,'' she said gruffly. "We've been lucky. . . . We've always stayed right here in Cincinnati!''

Karolyn doesn't worry about trading or about the day when Pete retires. She claims that about the time her husband turns in number 14 she'll be packing her bags to go on the road with her son, who she hopes will be in the major leagues if he stops swearing long enough to learn how to bat. "Baseball is my love. I wouldn't want any other life. Still. . . .''

"Still what?'' I asked.

"Ya know, most women would like to change places with Queen Elizabeth or Jackie Onassis, but frankly, I always wanted to be a roller derby queen or a go-go dancer! God, what fun!''

Every now and then the go-go dancer in her comes out. During the 1972 World Series in Oakland, Karolyn and her good friend Petuka Perez were on NBC's *Today* show. "Do you ladies have any superstitions?'' Joe Garagiola asked.

Petuka said, "Well, I'm not really superstitious, but I wouldn't think of going to the ball park without my charm bracelet on. . . . I'm convinced it brings my husband good luck!''

"What about you, Karolyn?'' Joe asked. "Do you have a good-luck piece?''

"Yup!'' said Karolyn with a naughty grin on her face as she started pulling off her tight-fitting sweater.

"Now wait a minute, Karolyn. . . . *Karolyn . . . puleeeeeese!*''

"My God!" shouted the director in the control room. "Get ready, camera two, to go back to Garagiola. That woman is peeling off her clothes!"

There was an incredulous pause—a mass intake of breath—as Karolyn's sweater went up and over her head. Joe Garagiola looked on with a sickening smile as the camera wavered indecisively, then zoomed in on her chest.

There, in big red letters on a T-shirt, was BIG RED MACHINE 14.

"That's my guy's number!" She beamed.

"That's some good-luck piece," said the relieved director.

Petuka Perez turned to the audience with large, innocent eyes and said, "I don't know her!"

Everybody held his breath again when Pete was picked the Most Valuable Player of the '75 World Series. Karolyn didn't disappoint them. She wore her Big Red Machine 14 T-shirt on all the talk shows.

But this was the spring of '74, and after two days with Karolyn I needed to go home and rest. It was while I was recovering in the country that Jacques called to remind me that Nancy Seaver was practically my neighbor in Greenwich, and wouldn't it be a good idea et cetera et cetera. . . . I called, and she was at the ball park.

A Hell of a Good Pitcher

What kind of woman do I consider myself to be? A hell of a good pitcher!

I hate being alone. . . . I guess you can call me a baseball widow, and most of all, I hate the question "What's it like being married to Tom Seaver?"

It was a hot, muggy day in June, '74. The first game of a doubleheader between the Mets and the Phillies at Shea Stadium. The starting pitcher was warming up in the bullpen. Thousands of fans were sitting in the hot sun fanning themselves with their hats or programs. The red lights on the TV cameras signaled the start of the game, and the hum of noise died down as a sports announcer's voice drifted across the press level.

"Seaver's going into windup . . . the pitch is low and away . . . seems like forty-one is having control problems and walks the first batter. Now Seaver is setting up to throw to power hitter Boone . . . and fires a blazing inside fastball!"

Thunderous cheering from the crowd. With field glasses one could observe that Seaver's face had that settling-down-to-strike-Boone-out look. The crowd roared its approval. Suddenly Seaver stopped, took out a white lace handkerchief and daintily mopped her face. First baseman Lynn Dyer used the time to run a comb through her hair, and from the sidelines a male voice yelled out to shortstop Harrelson, "Yvonne, honey, keep your ass down and be ready for that ball!"

The occasion was a rematch between the Met and Phillie wives in between a regular scheduled game at Shea Stadium. Nancy Seaver* pitched a three-hitter, and the Mets won 4 to 2. Angie Jones was mad. She didn't get a hit. "I'll never live it down—the old man won't let me!" The ballplayers started teasing their wives from the sidelines: "What were you thinking about when the ball hit you on the head?" "Hey, gals," another yelled, "are you going into the training room for your rub now. . . . Can we watch?"

On television sets across the country people watched beautiful blond Nancy Seaver being interviewed after the game.

*Tom Seaver, pitcher for the New York Mets of the National League. Since winning the Rookie of the Year Award for the National League in 1967, Seaver has become one of Baseball's most consistent 20-game winners. The mark of good pitching is a low earned run average (ERA), and Seaver has twice had the lowest ERA in baseball (1971 and 1973). He won the Cy Young Award, representative of the best pitcher in the league, in 1969, 1973, and 1975. In October of 1975, Seaver became a weekend sportscaster for WCBS-TV in New York.

"On the whole," she said just as her husband had so many times before, "I think our team was stronger this year!"

Three days after the game, in an interview with Nancy, I asked her what kind of woman she considered herself to be—easygoing, social, sophisticated, a dedicated mother, or a professional wife?

Her answer was: "A hell of a good pitcher!"

Nancy Lynn McIntyre Seaver is a smashing-looking thirty-year-old woman. Tall, with a perfectly proportioned size ten figure that is glowingly copper tan. Her honey-blond hair has recently been razor-cut boyishly short to frame a face that can do no wrong when the camera focuses on it, which is often. She was born in St. Joseph, Missouri, and was eleven when her family moved to Fresno, California, where she attended public high school. Tom Seaver was on the baseball and basketball teams, but Nancy claims he was so short and homely she didn't even know he was alive.

After high school and a stint in the Marine Corps Tom caught up with Nancy McIntyre once again at Fresno City College, where they both were in the same English class. It's the same old tired story of shy young man who pants after the most beautiful girl in school and she doesn't give him the time of day. Every time he approached those cool blue-green eyes and that icy manner he was, as the saying goes, all hands and feet. On the last day of school he tried a new tactic.

Finals were over, and Nancy had just finished her last exam that morning. She was waiting for a friend to show up at a designated spot on campus to walk her home. It was one of those typical June days in Fresno with the temperature breaking the country's high for the day at 110 degrees. Nancy, dressed for the weather in shorts and a halter top, was standing in the shade of a tree at the far end of the football field. All of a sudden something hit her and knocked her flat on her back. She couldn't breathe, couldn't see anything, and was so frightened her heart started pounding in her chest.

"I was just lying there," Nancy remembers, "*gasping* for air with terrible thoughts whirling around in my mind. Had I been shot? Had a tree fallen on me? Something dark was hovering over me and finally came into focus. It was Tom Seaver looking down at me with a ridiculous smile on his face."

Now we go to this side. He too had just taken his last final and was celebrating with his buddies—most of the baseball and basketball teams—at the far end of the field, where they were playing touch football and drinking beer in the 110-degree heat—a combination deadly even to the strongest constitution. Through his blurred vision he picked up a tall blonde at the other end of the field. Messages filtered through to his overheated brain, Nancy . . . Nancy. . . . And she's all alone.

Brandy McCarthy, a good friend, followed Tom's gaze and then dared him

to "tackle" Nancy. "You haven't been able to get her any other way!" he teased.

Tom put his beer down, and with teeth clenched, perspiration streaming down his red, determined face, eyes on his target, he started running. He ran straight down the field and with a mighty flying tackle crashed into Nancy.

Minutes later Nancy was able to piece together what had happened. "Even then," she recalls, "this lunatic let me get up by myself. It wasn't until I doubled up in pain that he reacted. He grabbed me by an arm and leg, threw me over his shoulder, and carried me to his car, where he unceremoniously dumped me in the back seat and then drove me home to my parents. To this day I can hardly believe it!"

The caveman approach worked. Two years later they were married, and she says he hasn't knocked her down since. Today the Seavers, their five-year-old daughter, Sarah, a baby girl, Ann Elizabeth born November 15, a black Labrador puppy called Hotstuff, a poodle named Slider, and Ferguson the cat, all live in a ninety-five-year-old gray shingled and fieldstone house in Greenwich, Connecticut. A wide old-fashioned veranda goes all the way around the exterior, overlooking two acres of rolling lawn with a tall sugar maple tree sheltering the house like a big umbrella. It looks like a scene Norman Rockwell might have painted for the cover of the old *Saturday Evening Post*. The veranda, I told myself as I pulled my car in the driveway, would be a perfect place for the interview. Much to my disappointment we went down the street to the Greenwich Country Club pool. It's a nice place if you don't want to talk. Children were screaming and splashing, mothers yelling caution to youngsters, teenagers in bikinis gyrating wildly to rock music blasting from a transistor radio, and on top of it, Nancy Seaver has to be the most popular girl at the club. When I got home and played back the tape, it sounded like sixty thousand Zulu tribesmen doing a war dance. In between the jangling collection of noises was the faint high-pitched voice of Nancy.

"I'm so proud of Tom!" she exclaimed as she applied lotion to her tan body. "He just got his degree. It's taken him ten years, but he made it!" And then not trusting me to figure it out, she explained, "The reason it took him so long was that he had to skip semesters, even years, and in the end his own graduation because of baseball. We're sooo happy—well, almost. Just when you think you have it all, something comes along and spoils the enjoyment." She was referring to a muscle spasm in Tom's left hip that was giving him not only pain, but the first slump he'd had in his pitching career. The problem was the hip wasn't serious enough to keep him from playing but painful enough to keep him from playing well. Nancy spent the day trying to convince me (herself?) that all those boos at Shea Stadium didn't bother her.

"I take the boos in stride. It isn't a mean boo like they have for Pete Rose. It's more like a 'Come on, Seaver, you've had a bad day . . . get outta there!' kind of boo. That's the way I interpret it," she said with a slight frown. "Those fans know they need Tom Seaver. They're not going to. . . ." Her voice trailed off, and she slipped into the swimming pool. After a few long strokes which took her to the other side and back, she popped up where I was sitting, dangling my legs in the water, and said, "I know *everyone* has a slump, even businessmen. But when Tom makes a mistake, it's viewed by thousands of people—and he can't help it if his hip is bothering him!"

If this bothered her, I wondered what she'd do if she had Karolyn Rose's problems. Nevertheless, it must have been strange to be booed by the very fans who cheered Seaver so wildly in the '69 World Series. For Tom and Nancy there will probably never be another year like '69. Even my hard-news-oriented producer for the WCBS evening news assigned me to Shea Stadium during that Series to do color stories on the crowd. I watched the proud New York fans, including Governor Rockefeller, Mayor Lindsay, Jackie, who was explaining the game to her husband, the late Ari Onassis, movie stars, sport stars, and astronauts, go absolutely berserk in the final game when the Mets won. It must have been sheer euphoria for the ballplayers and their wives. I remember Nancy Seaver in particular, as she was pointed out to me as the most beautiful and best known of the wives. Nancy always wore a knit tam to match her outfit, which quickly became a trademark. The fans, as well as the press, could always spot the girl with the jaunty tam on her head and the dazzling smile. She was not only the most photographed wife, but in those days a "Met celebrity" in her own right, her husband being one of the few who could top her popularity. In fact, Nancy and Tom were almost loved to death by their fans.

The day after they won the Series the Mets were given a ticker-tape parade in New York. Nancy and Tom were sitting on top of the back seat in an open car, waving to the crowd, acknowledging thunderous cheering and being drowned in a sea of confetti. Suddenly the crowd moved in. They wanted to touch their hero, touch Nancy. Bodies were crushed against the car. Fans reached up to shake their hands; others tried to tear buttons off their clothes; someone grabbed Nancy's head by the hair and pulled her tam off—the car started to rock. The police moved in just in time, but when the Mets arrived at the Four Seasons that day for the luncheon John and Mary Lindsay hosted, Nancy was still deathly pale. Later, in a television interview with me, she said it was the most terrifying experience in her life.

"I . . . we like being popular," she said in a small voice. "But today was too much. I really thought we were going to be crushed to death. I know they didn't mean us harm. . . . I guess it was sweet hysteria."

The boos which have replaced the sweet hysteria may be less frightening, but more perplexing, and it's also a bit pessimistic when Nancy sighs and wonders if there will ever be another year like '69. She's given up wearing tams and going to every Met game and usually goes to the ball park only when Tom is pitching which, when I saw her in the summer of '74, was every fifth day. On those days she's very calm and ·ladylike, the antithesis of the gum-chewing pitcher of the Mets' wives baseball team. Karolyn Rose would call it *not* being involved, but if Tom is having a bad day or those irascible Met fans are booing him, Nancy starts cracking peanuts loudly. During the '74 season she cracked a lot of peanuts. In '75 she didn't crack one!

Nancy ordered iced tea, and we sat at a poolside table and watched Sarah gurgle into her straw, while she told me some things about herself that she thought were safe to print.

"I love Charlie Seaver [Tom's father, who was an amateur golfer], Billie Jean King, Arnold Palmer—he's my favorite superstar—Henry Aaron, the Mets, my softball team, the way I pitch when I have good stuff, golf, need-lepoint, and the entire year of 1969. In particular, I liked the day a big black cat came out of nowhere and walked across the field and into the Cubs' dug-out. What an omen! And I also loved it when there was an argument over a play on the field that very same day, and Leo, lipping it up and shaking his fist, ran out on the field to interfere. Someone in the stands waved a white handkerchief, then another and another. Pretty soon it looked like it was snowing in the stadium—thousands of white handkerchiefs fluttering back and forth. They were telling Leo to surrender, and he did!

"I'll tell you what I hate. I loathe the trading that goes on in baseball. It's tragic. You commit yourself to a friendship, and the next thing you know the guy is traded and shipped out. Baseball players and their families live in great fear of this cruel practice. Being a baseball widow isn't much fun. I hate being alone, but most of all I hate the question 'What's it like being married to Tom Seaver?' Ugh!"

"How about what's it like being married to pitcher Nancy Seaver?"

"To tell you the truth, sometimes I don't even know who I am. It's because of the goldfish-bowl atmosphere of being married to a man who's public prop-erty. The public is supposed to have the right to know about our private life, so it's exposed. I'm not sure I like that. There's a part of me that doesn't want to stand bare in front of everyone. It's made me hold back, hide things. I don't trust reporters. They distort what you tell them. I don't trust people. What do they want from me? So I hide who I am—sometimes even from myself."

The Nancy Seaver who shows is an attractive, cheerful young woman who looks as if she should drive a station wagon, belong to the Greenwich Country Club and the Junior League. Her life, except for her brief pitching career, is full of the undramatic pleasantries and the humdrumness of suburbia. Behind the wall, contained and suppressed, is the woman we would like to meet and know. One can only hope that Nancy will someday find her.

There was something I did sense, however, with this happy housewife—that was stardust in her eyes. My hunch is that she and Tom would like to be the Lynn Fontanne and Alfred Lunt of the TV commercial world. They do more commercials together than any other couple in America. Turn on TV, and you see the Seavers selling gasoline, aspirin, and deodorants (Nancy got to hit Tom on the head in a Brut commercial); turn on the radio, and you can hear them pitch food and fuel oil; thumb through magazines, and they're selling cottage cheese. One cottage cheese ad brought a great deal of criticism. It showed the Seavers in the kitchen of what was supposed to be their Greenwich home (it wasn't because they don't allow it to be photographed), posing with set smiles and staged nonchalance. ''After the game,'' the ad reads, ''it's Friendship time at the Seavers' .''

Many people think the only friendship time at the Seavers' is when they're putting their friendly money in the friendly bank and that their dalliance in the world of commercials is highly objectionable, not proper for the all-American incorruptible hero of baseball and his sweet wife. Their critics are probably just jealous. There's nothing wrong with a little honest exploiting that the money it puts in the Seavers' pockets won't make up for. Besides, they have great company. Look at all the famous people pitching products. If Sir Laurence Olivier can sell cameras on television, we may, as Russell Baker pointed out, be approaching a time when an invitation to perform a sales pitch will be the most distinguished accolade our society can bestow.

In the meantime, a lot of people think it's pretty awful! ''The Seavers are nice people but phony on TV. . . . Nancy sounds insipid. . . . They should stick to baseball!'' are just a few of the comments. ''The happy couple next door is a massive public relations pitch that the Seavers are beginning to believe themselves,'' a former Met wife told me. One of Nancy's friends in Greenwich, however, insisted that the Seavers are *really* happy, wholesome, and friendly people—exactly like their image.

Somehow I'm not sure. I'm not sure whether Nancy is a damn good pitcher or pitches because it's damn good copy. But she *is* quick to deny the wholesome part. ''There's such a rush to stereotype us! We've come off as a typical all-American-as-apple-pie couple. Yuk! On the other hand, we're not exactly swingers. We're not into alcohol, drugs, or swapping wives, but I hate it when they describe us as Tom Terrific, Nancy Nice, and Sara Sweet. It's . . . it's positively sickening!''

''Sarah Sweet'' came up and announced she wanted to go home. The tiny blond girl skipped alongside us as we cut through a corner of the golf course and asked me if I knew her daddy. I acknowledged that I did, and she shook her head. ''Everyone knows my daddy, but he's always at his office.''

Nancy straightened me out. ''Shea Stadium is his office.''

When we got back on that nice peaceful veranda, Nancy admitted she was a baseball widow and that Sarah was right—Tom spends most of his time at his office. Like most women married to a famous athlete, she feels the lack of companionship in the marriage but is conditioned to put up or shut up with the frequent separations. For baseball wives the loneliness comes when the team goes on the road trips for the eighty-two games played out of town each season. Each road trip lasts from a week to twelve days, and during that time every baseball wife learns how to be mother, father, maid, plumber, repairman, accountant, banker—and most of all how to cope with long, lonely nights without a mate. Nancy doesn't say, but one wonders if sitting home alone after the children are in bed, twisting a huge diamond solitaire around on her finger that once was the center stone on the Hickok Award belt Tom received as Outstanding Player of the Year in '69 is compensation for the absence of her superstar husband.

The consolations are a beautiful house in the country, membership in the prestigious Greenwich Country Club, all the fringe benefits money can buy, and a circle of young, attractive friends. Having more of everything than her contemporaries at age thirty hasn't produced, in her words, "one ounce of guilt," but then, perhaps that's because she's already paying a very high price.

With all those commercials she's doing with Tom there will probably be even more material substitutes for "togetherness" in the future. It's hard to tell what deep down in her impenetrable center she really wants, but my guess is that Nancy Nice is going to become Nancy Rich!

Recently a story leaked out, confirmed by Nancy, that she called Tom after a game and told him she had found her dream home. "It's everything I've ever wanted in a home—big, beautiful, and right on the Sound at the end of Meads Point. It would be a super summer house!" she enthused.

"How much is it?" Tom asked, thinking of a cottage on the water.

"Four twenty-five."

There was a pause. "Four hundred and twenty-five thousand?" He laughed weakly after she confirmed the figure, then teased, "Well, I can't afford it right now—you'll have to wait until the end of the season."

"*Yes*, but by that time," Nancy wailed, "Catfish Hunter may have bought it!"

I made an appointment to see Mrs. Catfish and find out.

A Flower of the South

Jimmy's buyin' a li'l land back home.

You have to be from the backwoods to understand Helen Hunter.* She's rich but lives poor because she had always been poor and she's not the type to change. Not quickly anyway.

She speaks with a slow, high-pitched Carolina drawl because she has lived all her life in Hertford, North Carolina, and that's how people talk there and she sees nothing wrong with it. She's come into contact with fame, but she hates and is confused by it because somehow it means being disturbed by strangers and being taken away from home when she doesn't want to be. It also means that her husband, Jimmy, is not allowed the luxury of failure that most humans have.

"He had a slow start his first season with the Yankees, and the fans booed him, and the press got on his back. Everybody figured he *owed* them, that he was supposed to win every time out because they were paying him so much money. I was still down home, and he'd call me, so sad and depressed. He jes' didn't have nobody to talk to. It wasn't easy on the phone, but I'd tell him to keep his grit up, that he was a lot better 'n what he was showin'.''

By the time she'd joined him he had started to win and give the fans their money's worth.

Jimmy "Catfish" Hunter pitches a baseball better than most, and people are willing to pay to watch him do it, and sportswriters give his name wide circulation, and this has brought this country boy fame and fortune; but he and Helen are still country folks who don't want to change. They sprang from a languorous land. The lazy Perquimans River runs by their house. So the rest of the country will either have to get used to them as they are or go to hell. Or ruin them.

It was well into morning, and the heavy dew that had hung like fog over the water had burned off in the sun. The riverbanks looked dark and cool, protected by cypress, beech, birch, ash, and maple trees. Under the green cover the

---

*Jim "Catfish" Hunter, pitcher with the New York Yankees, formerly with the Oakland A's. Catfish Hunter won 20 games or more for five consecutive seasons (1970–'74). In 1974 he posted the lowest earned run average (ERA) in the American League and won the Cy Young Award as the best pitcher in the league. At the end of the 1974 season Hunter signed a three-year contract with the New York Yankees for a reputed $3,5000,000 and went on to win 23 games for the Yankees in 1975.

rustling of rabbits, opossums, and raccoons could be heard. On the east bank, in the shade of the trees just off a natural rock reef, a small motorboat, the stern weighted down by the motor and a slouched-over man, rocked gently in the rippling tide. A broad-brimmed hat pulled down over his eyes cast his face into shadow. He was still and concentrating on the point where his fishing line entered the nervous water. The best time was over. He'd be coming in soon now.

Helen was in the kitchen, surveying the mess. Dirty dishes were piled in the sink, the countertops were sticky, and glasses with rusty dregs of apple cider were scattered about in disarray. These were the remains of a family party held at the Hunters' the night before. A family party at the Hunters' means a lot of people. Catfish is one of nine children, and Helen one of eleven. All those brothers and sisters have families of their own now living in the area, and they never miss a party.

The last family get-together of this size was among the Hatfields and the McCoys, but it wasn't for a picnic.

It was morning, and Helen had her hair up in pink plastic curlers. She was trying to decide which corner of the kitchen to tackle first. Two-year-old Kimberly Ann was on the floor, smearing grape jelly on everything in the vicinity of her toast. Five-year-old Todd was beating the dog for eating his cereal. The front-door buzzer sounded, and Helen was relieved.

"Come on in, it's open. Yer jes' in time," she yelled. She assumed it was one of her sisters come over to help with the cleaning.

Nobody came in. The buzzer persisted. Helen wondered who it could be at this hour. Wiping the suds off her rubber gloves with a towel draped over her shoulder, she clip-clopped to the door in her bathrobe and red mules. She threw it open, and her mouth fell in shock. There stood a determined band of reporters, photographers, and television cameras stretching down the front lawn all the way to the magnolia tree. She looked at them, and they peered back as she tried to think of something to say. At that moment she heard Jimmy's familiar step as he came in the back door, cut through the kitchen, ambled down the hallway, and stopped directly behind her.

"Why didn't you tell me half of New York was comin' down here today?" she hissed.

Catfish, who had just signed a $3,500,000 contract with the New York Yankees, looked out the door at the clamorous press corps, then at his wife. He studied his shuffling feet and grinned sheepishly, knowing it would be all right.

"Ah plumb forgot, sugah," he said.

The constant presence of the press is one of the worst by-products Helen has found of her husband's spectacular career.

"Reporters weah me out. They're always pressin' and pushin' and tryin' too hard. Used to be, Jimmy could nevah say no to them 'n' they run all over 'im. Now his bein' such a success and all, he's learned how to take care of hisself. But me—Ah cain't handle it."

Another thing she can't handle is Jimmy's long absences.

"Ah'm not wild about baseball, nevah was. If it wasn't fo' Jimmy bein' in it, Ah wouldn't pay it no mind. But Ah listen to all the out-of-town games. It makes me feel closer to my husband. It's like he's in town, out to the stadium playin' and when he's through he'll be comin' home. Of course, he doesn't.

"The kids and Ah are alone more 'n half the time. Even when he isn't playin', in winter, when we're all home in Hertford, he's either off huntin' deer or quail, or fishin'."

Helen puts up with it, but not without an occasional squawk. Her attitude is: Baseball he can't help—hunting and fishing he can. Neighbors in Hertford have heard her complain to Jimmy from time to time. One woman confided, "When she's mad enough, she yells so's you can hear her real clear over those twenty yelpin' hound dogs of their'n."

If she's lost and lonely in Hertford, it borders on despondency in Norwood, New Jersey, the Hunters' home during the season. There she's surrounded by the Yankee enemy. She won't even go into the town itself.

"The shoppin' center is only a block away, and it'll do me fine till Ah get back to Hertford."

I suggested she might find New York City amusing when she got bored with being cooped up in her house.

"New York? No sirree, not me. Ah wouldn't drive in that city for anything. Why, the taxi drivers scare me to death. Ah'd be dead in a minute if Ah evah crossed the George Washington Bridge."

Helen is a young, unspoiled flower of the rural South. She has dark hair kept in a neat permanent, large brown eyes, and smooth, clear skin partly inherited and partly because she has sense enough to stay out of the hot sun. She's five feet three inches tall and has kept the trim figure that won her a spot among the cheerleaders in high school

Her family, the Overtons, always lived in Hertford, and most of her six brothers and four sisters still do. They were always poor. Her father was a butcher, her brothers worked from daylight to dark at a relative's farm, and all the women worked in a nearby shirt factory.

"The only toys we ever had in those days that I can remember were horses made out of the cardboard sticks they used for blocking the shirts in the factory."

Helen and James Augustus Hunter had been aware of each other's existence from before kindergarten because everybody in Hertford knew everybody else. When she reached the seventh grade, Helen began to notice Jimmy "in that way" but kept it under control. When she entered Perquimans High School, Jimmy was two years ahead of her and was playing baseball. She became the school's prettiest cheerleader.

"It was jes' nach'ral for Jimmy and me to get married," she said. "The Sadie Hawkins Dance was comin' up at school, and Ah wanted to ask Jimmy. Ah went up to 'im and got to blushin' and stammerin' and couldn't hardly look 'im in the eye. He jes' stood there and let me carry on. Every time Ah'd try to get the words out they got all twisted and Ah'm sure Ah was mumblin'. Anyway, Ah was about to give it up when Jimmy (he was shy, too) said yes. Ah don't know how he knew what he was sayin' yes to. And we both bolted. In opposite directions. That was one of the worst experiences of my life. But it worked out jes' fine."

For the next two years they saw each other "as much as possible," which translated to every other Saturday or so. Jim worked at a gas station weekdays after school, played baseball Friday nights, and on Sunday there was church, family, and chores. That left Saturday, but Jimmy frequently went hunting or fishing with his brother. When he didn't, he went over to Helen's.

"One of those huntin' trips, he got shot. When Ah heard about it Ah hightailed it over to the hospital, cryin' all the way. Ah thought he'd been killed and nobody wanted to tell me the truth. When Ah got to Jimmy's room, all his relatives was standin' around the bed, so's Ah couldn't see him. Then Ah knew it was all over. Ah liked to had a heart attack. Ah pushed them people out the way, and there was Jimmy grinnin', his right foot all bandaged and propped up like they do in hospitals. That fool'd had his toe shot off, that was all. Ah could've died I was so mortified."

Jimmy also lost the feeling in two surviving toes and had to hobble around on crutches for months afterward.

Inexorably the country courtship led to the inevitable. In 1966 Helen and Jimmy exchanged vows. No one is quite clear on who asked whom the formal question, or if anyone did. The wedding was a family affair, and relatives filled the preacher's house to capacity, and the overflow trampled the front yard.

Following the feast, the newlyweds took off on their honeymoon. They went to Salisbury, North Carolina, where they said hello to Clyde Kluttz, the agent who got Jimmy into major-league baseball, saw the sights, and otherwise did the town.

They returned to the security of home to claim the wedding gift of Jimmy's father, a tiny bungalow which stood guard over the far edge of the Hunter property. Jim and Helen swept out the chickens and, with the help of the family, made the place "right livable."

Helen lost no time going to work in the shirt factory, which would not be unusual if it weren't for the fact that by this time Jimmy was playing for the Kansas City A's, thanks to Clyde Kluttz, and was drawing $75,000 a year— more money than any Hunter or Overton had ever seen before. He'd started with the A's as soon as his toe healed well enough from the hunting accident to permit him to pitch. Charles O. Finley, the team owner, sent him to the Mayo Clinic to have the last remaining pellets removed from the foot, and when Jimmy was released, Finley called a news conference to introduce his new star pitcher to reporters as Catfish Hunter. As expected, a sucker rose to the bait and asked, "Where did you get a name like Catfish?"

That caught Jimmy short. It was the first he'd heard of it. Before he could open his mouth to make the disclaimer, Finley broke in and said, "One day he ran away from home, and his mother and father looked all over for him and finally located him a few miles away, pulling a catfish out of the canal. The name's stuck ever since."

Jimmy didn't think much of the story and considered correcting the part about the existence of a canal near his home, but he never said a word.

Now everybody calls him Catfish except Helen and the folks back home, who, if they couldn't think up a better story than Finley's, would rather not tell one. If Hunter hears someone hollering "Jimmy" at the ball park, he takes another look because he knows it's somebody from Hertford. Sometimes Helen wishes Finley had given the name Catfish to Clyde Kluttz, who she thinks could have made better use of it than Jimmy.

So it wasn't necessity that drove Helen to the shirt factory. She did it because that's what *all* the girls in Hertford do. It was winter, and Catfish wasn't off playing ball, but he was bulldozing some property a neighbor wanted cleared, and he was away all the time anyway, so she figured she might as well fill her spare time at the factory with her friends. And so that's how the newly rich, newly marrieds spent the first weeks of their marriage while waiting for spring training to begin. They saw nothing unusual in it at all.

Baseball gave Catfish the roar of the crowds, broadening travel, and millions of dollars. It gave Helen a headache. She found out that the crowds were fickle and the roar turned to boos when he lost. Travel took her away from Hertford, the only place she felt comfortable. As for the millions of dollars, she had as clear a concept of that much money as a tortoise has of the theory of relativity.

Travel to Helen meant renting a house in Amorea Island, Florida, during spring training at Bradenton, then taking an apartment in Independence when the A's moved to home base in Kansas City, then settling in Walnut Creek, California, when the team moved to Oakland. *If that's traveling*, she thought, *the tourists can keep it.* Then, in 1974, Catfish won a contractual dispute with Finley and became a free agent, the dream of every top baseball player. He was now able to sign with any club that wanted him and most did. He accepted a $3,500,000 contract with the New York Yankees. Helen approved. Not because of the money—that much was meaningless. It was because they could now move back to the East Coast and, she thought, Hertford.

By now the Hunters had two children, and that little bangalow on the edge of the Hunter land, still "home," was no longer big enough. They built a new house six miles outside town. It was a two-story farmhouse with enough surrounding land to take care of the immediate family, relatives and twenty howling bird dogs and deer hounds. The kitchen is fifty feet by twenty-five feet, big enough to handle a family reunion.

Helen admits that her life revolves around Jimmy's and doesn't want it any other way.

"In the South, you have to understand that some women kowtow to their husbands, and some are waited on hand and foot by their men. Anything in between is a women's libber. In my country, that's not a very popular thing to be. Ah'm certainly not one of them and don't aim to be. Ah believe it's my job to work to please my Jimmy. Ah cook the food he likes, corn beef and cabbage and kale greens. Ah wear bright colors because he thinks it makes me look bright and gay. Ah make sure music is blastin' on the radio or stereo when he comes home. Country music. Right now 'Drag Me' is his favorite."

She still does her own cooking and cleaning. She never trusts her children to a baby-sitter unless it's family. She said, "Ah can do without fancy clothes and jewelry," as though she were speaking of the devil, "but Ah could sure use a good Southern Baptist church," something in short supply in New Jersey.

I asked why she lived that way now that she could afford any luxury she wanted, and she said, "We were very poor most of our lives, and Ah guess we just haven't gotten out of the habit."

I thought about the $3,5000,000 Yankee contract, plus many thousands more from selling trucks, automobiles, and dog food on television and had visions of millions moldering in vaults because the owners didn't know how to spend it. I couldn't bear the thought, so I asked what they were doing with it, fully prepared to be told to mind my own business as I deserved. But Helen looked at me with her honest, open face and said, "Why, Jimmy's buyin' up a li'l land back home."

A li'l land back home meant many thousands of acres. Helen said he's been buying up property since his first pay check with the Kansas City A's, and the closest she could come to the specific number of acres was "lots and lots."

The acres that mean most to her, though, are the ones that hold up her new house. The trouble is she can only live there in the off-season. The rest of the time she and her faimily have to live in the New York metropolitan area. It might as well be hell's backyard as far as Helen is concerned.

It was May, 1975, and Catfish came to New York two months ahead of Helen to find a place to live. Millions or no millions, the rents were too high to suit Catfish, so he decided to buy a place in Norwood, New Jersey. It was a split-level three bedroom tract house not usually associated with millionaires. He bought it because the builder was a good friend of a ballplayer who lived right across the street.

I visited Helen one week after she'd arrived to take up residence. The two small children hadn't adjusted to the move yet and were clutching and whining. The room was empty of furniture except for a single sofa occupied by folded towels and diapers. I considered sitting cross-legged on the floor, but Helen noticed my discomfiture and brought a chair from the kitchen for me. It was broken, so I sat down gingerly. It took me a few minutes to get used to the idea that I was in the home of the signer of one of the most lucrative contracts in baseball history.

Because of her shyness and sensitivity to her Carolina drawl, Helen is withdrawn and taciturn in her Yankee home.

"Ah gets razzed all the time about mah accent, so Ah finally said to Jimmy, before we moved to Norwood, Ah said, 'First Yankee makes fun o' the way Ah talk, Ah'm gonna shut up.' "

It happened immediately. Neighbors, probably meaning to be kind, came over to welcome her to the neighborhood and said they just loved to listen to her talk. It had the exact opposite effect to the one intended. She clammed up in embarrassment and later grumbled to herself, "They're the ones who talk different."

Helen revealed that a friend from home was moving up and she wouldn't be as lonely as before. "It's not as bad as Ah'm makin' it sound. Ah get along fine with the other players' wives. Ah was worried at first they might laugh at me, think we was country freaks or something, but they've been right nice. Why, one of the wives, Ah forget her name, told Jimmy he was the biggest star on the team. On the New York Yankees, can you beat that? Well, Ah jes' cain't get it into mah head that people consider him all that big."

The social world that Jimmy's fame and wealth has opened up to the Hunt-ers is of little interest to them. Jet setters they are not. If they were of a mind to drop names, which they aren't, the only one in their collection would be Monk Harrington, state senator from North Carolina. Catfish is involved in a business deal with him. Helen thinks it's probably real estate. "Ah don't know what else it would be."

The Hunters' idea of social climbing is someday to get to know Richard Petty. "We bumped into him once at Greensboro, when we went to the North Carolina Hall of Fame. He's from around there. Trouble is nobody introduced us. Probably thought we already knew each other. So Ah ended up gawkin' at him, wishin' Ah could meet him and shake his hand."

"Speaking of shaking hands"—reaching out my hand as Helen finished the story—"I've got to get back to New York before the rush hour."

"Mah God"—her pretty face scrunched up in a frown—"y'all going to cross that George Washington Bridge?"

" 'Fraid so."

"Well, it's been right brave of y'all to come ovah heah to talk to me."

On my way up to Boston to see Carol Yastrzemski, I was worried about two things: Helen going back to the shirt factory and how in blazes to pro-nounce Carol's last name.

Mrs. Yaz

I'm concerned about Carl's retirement. Everyone thinks we are millionaires without a care in the world, but I'll tell you what happens to an athlete. . . . He makes a tremendous amount of money over a short period of time and is taxed to death. . . . How do you save?

Imagine being forced to retire in your thirties because you're over the hill.

The town of Lynnfield, just outside Boston, is a typical New England suburb. The houses, which are big, expensive, and mostly all alike, are on single acre lots with tall maples and oak trees. I drove up a steep driveway and stopped in front of a white Colonial that was different from the others. It had black shutters. Two yardmen were in front cutting down a tree. They watched with interest as I got out of the car juggling my notebook, tape recorder, and bulging purse.

"Is this the Yastrzemski house?" The grubbier of the two men threw his hands up in the air in the universal gesture of "who knows?" and without saying a word went back to sawing the tree. I rang the bell. "Is this the Yast—"

"It is!" a stunning blonde answered before I could get out the name. "And you're right on time. . . . Come in." I looked back toward my car, which was full of luggage, and then over at the two workmen. "Maybe I'd better lock my car first. . . . We'll be inside for several hours and since you have yardmen around—"

She followed my gaze and burst out laughing. "Oh, that's just Yazi and his father!"

"Who?"

"Yazi, my husband."

"That's Carl Yastrzemski?" I wondered out loud looking over at the dark-haired young man who was once again giving me the helpless who-knows expression. As I turned to go inside, I had the distinct impression that behind my back there was great amusement.

Carol Yastrzemski* yelled out the door, "She thought you were a workman, Yazi!"

---

*Carl Yastrzemski, professional baseball player for the Boston Red Sox of the American League. Yastrzemski has been a consistent .300 batter and All-Star performer for the Red Sox for more than a decade. He led the American League in batting in 1963, 1967, and 1968. His 1967 performance has rarely been matched in the history of

I stepped into an immaculate house, furnished like so many homes today, for show—the furniture new, the prints smart, and the arrangement studied. There was one room that had escaped the decorator look, and it was a large family room at one end of the house where they all lived when they weren't sleeping. It was cozy and warm—a beamed-ceiling, grandfather-clock kind of room with deep, comfortable chairs and an enormous mahogany bar at one end that looked as if it could be the scene of some great parties. Over a row of bottles in the back was a wooden plaque with the inscription "The Yaz's."

Carol saw me gazing at the plaque. "I don't blame our friends for shortening our name. . . . When I first met Carl, I couldn't pronounce his name, much less spell it. When a girl trades a name like Casper for Yastrzemski, she's gotta be *crazy!*"

"Have you always called him Yazi?"

"A-huh."

"Does he have a nickname for you?"

"Not for you to print."

And so the interview began or almost. The phone rang, and Carol swung onto a barstool and started a very animated conversation with someone. I noticed that she had a smashing figure, like all the other superwives, and later she told me she was a size seven, which somehow after four children seems unfaithful to motherhood. She isn't beautiful, but with her small, fantastic figure, short-cropped blond hair, tan skin, light-blue eyes, and white, even teeth, she's strikingly attractive. My observations were interrupted by the grubby workman—I mean . . . Carl . . . Yazi.

"Who is it?" he asked his wife. She kept right on talking, paying no attention to him.

"Who is it?" he repeated, hovering over her. She was looking up at a fixed point on the ceiling, as if he weren't there.

It was driving him crazy. "Who is it? Come on, who is it?" he nagged.

I was feeling a little skittish, sitting three feet away from this little family comedy. Why did he have to know? Why didn't she tell him? Was it a call from her lover? No, she didn't seem the type.

"He *has* to know!" Carol said, looking directly at me. "You can mark that down in your notebook. He has to know who it is every time this phone rings!" She turned to him with a sardonic smile. "It's Susan."

He shrugged and without saying a word went back outdoors.

the sport. Yastrzemski won the Triple Crown that year by leading the league in home runs (44), runs batted in (121) and batting average (.326). He was voted the Most Valuable Player in the league that year and helped carry the Red Sox into the World Series. Yastrzemski batted .301 in 1974 and was voted to the All-Star team, which he made again in '75, when he was one of the outstanding stars of the World Series play-off.

Carol Casper was born, reared and educated in Pittsburgh, Pennsylvania, one of three children whose parents belonged to that group who make up a good bit of the population in America, white, Catholic, and middle class. She was just out of high school when a friend got her a blind date with Carl Yastrzemski, who was home on vacation from Notre Dame. Nothing very spectacular marked their meeting or courtship except that he proposed on their very first date and they were married a year later. Immediately after Carl signed his wedding contract, he signed a professional league contract with the Boston Red Sox, and in all these years neither has been canceled.

The Yazes have been living in Lynnfield for the past thirteen years, along with four other members of their family: fourteen-year-old Mary Ann, thirteen-year-old Michael, eight-year-old Suzanne, and five-year-old Kara. Transporting this flock around is a major problem and one that Carol has in common with Barbara Nicklaus. They both spend more than half their waking hours chauffeuring. Carol drives Mary Ann to piano lessons, Suzanne to tennis lessons, Kara to ballet, and Michael to karate lessons. Back and forth . . . back and forth. That's where the resemblance to Barbara ends, for I had the feeling while visiting Carol that I was looking at an instant replay of Nancy Seaver.

Both Carol and Nancy are deeply entrenched in suburbia, both are blondes with short-cropped hair, gorgeous tan bodies, and similar tastes in clothes. Nancy sticks to pantsuits, and so does Carol, who admits her husband complains he hasn't seen her legs in five years. Both are outwardly cheerful and bright, as organized as the "Stepford Wives" and extremely guarded and self-contained. Their differences are narrow. Nancy practically lives at the Greenwich Country Club; Carol claims that golf bores her and gets her exercise playing tennis. Nancy likes needlepoint, and Carol loves bridge.

The big difference between them is that Nancy resents the time Tom spends away from her, and Carol, it appears, is grateful when Carl travels. "I'm probably the only wife you'll meet who doesn't mind that her husband travels," she told me. "When Carl goes on the road, we don't have to eat dinner at four in the afternoon. I *love* out-of-town games!"

"Four o'clock? Why so early?"

"That's when baseball families eat. Yazi has to drive to Boston and be ready to play ball by seven thirty. It's a drag! God, what a relief to have him gone so we don't have to stay on *his* schedule."

She's also one of the few wives who aren't just ga-ga, or pretend to be, over their husbands' sport. Carol can take or leave baseball, and the thought of playing on the wives' team leaves her cold. "It's OK for Nancy Seaver to get out there and pitch, but not for me. I'm not going to make an ass of myself in front of thousands of people."

She's not particularly interested in watching her husband play either. Although she admits going to all the games when she was first married, today she attends only a few. "I guess I'm what you call a front runner. I only like to go when they're in a winning streak and the game is bound to be super-exciting." Just as she isn't a fanatic over America's favorite sport, she also doesn't have very normal cheering habits when she *does* get around to going. Carol found out that every time she left her seat to go back to the stands and have a beer, the Red Sox would forge ahead. Usually, her husband would make a spectacular play the minute she left. So it got to be customary for her to leave her seat the minute the Sox fell behind and spend her time in the stands. The crowd caught on and started cheering her the minute she got up to go. She'd walk out and have her beer, and sure enough the tide would turn and the Sox would soar ahead. Reporters have asked her if that didn't amount to believing her presence brought the team bad luck and she's shrugged and said, "Call it what you want. The Red Sox get hot after I leave!"

Friends say Carol has a keen mind, stinging tongue, double-edged wit, and some shocking opinions about baseball. Beth Havlicek, one of the more prominent members of the Boston sports community, said Carol was one of the most outspoken women she knew. Maybe she's outspoken in her own circle, but she certainly didn't seem to want to share any of her shocking opinions with me. In fact, she played it straight, circumspect and ho-hum except for a few small glimpses into her personality.

Carol has a clever way of putting herself and Carl down to show you that he's not a supergod or swellhead and they both are just "plain folks." After she's rattled off a few disparaging remarks in a sardonic tone and you've digested it, the message comes off as a compliment. "I could write a book about the things that annoy me about Carl. He's a perfectionist—everything in his life has to be *perfect*. It drives me crazy. [She's proud of it.] Even in a card game he must be perfect . . . he must *win*. We almost kill each other when we play bridge. [They're both good bridge players.] Every time Yazi sneezes he thinks he has a drastic illness. [She should talk to Emmy Cosell.] And his schedules drive me up the wall! [She really doesn't mind.]"

According to Carol, the only thing baseball doesn't interfere with is sex. "Thank God we don't follow a schedule for our sex life like many athletes are forced to do." This is her way of telling you that everything is OK in that department, too.

She can complain all she wants to about that baseball schedule which annoys her, but nevertheless, it has made it possible for her to live on a yearly salary somewhere in the neighborhood of $200,000 and she makes it very clear she has no guilt about having all that money. "I don't want to go down in your book as a wife who's embarrassed by a big salary. I like money. . . .

Money is important!'' As she spoke, I noticed a big diamond flash and sparkle on her left hand. It was the center diamond from Carl's Hickok Award belt, the same one Nancy Seaver removed and now twists on her finger. I wonder if Mr. Hickok knows the fate of his awards?

"Some wives have a complex about their husbands earning so much money in these times," Carol went on. "But I'm worried about *not* having enough . . . when his career is over." At that precise moment the two-level conversation changed. All the manipulatory, deceptive remarks were dropped, and I had the feeling we were, for the first time, on a one-to-one level of communication. Carol looked directly at me and sighed as if she were tired of the whole façade. "I wonder what's to become of us after he gets too old to play well."

So it isn't jock lovers, jealousy, option clauses, replacements, fear of injury, an identity crisis, fans booing, violence, or loneliness that bothers this one—it's the fear of the future. What happens after retirement? Athletes are the only men in the world who are through in their profession by their midthirties. Carl Yastrzemski is thirty-five, he's been a superstar for fifteen years with the Red Sox, and he is coming dangerously close to the day when he will be considered "over the hill."

"Carl is going to have to retire . . . I expect soon I'll feel badly when it happens—it'll be a drastic change. He's looking for a business, something to do, something to get involved in—but *what?* He doesn't know. God, I hope some opportunity will come up!"

Carol and Carl are facing what all these couples will face sooner or later. Some will be forced out by management, others will have to adjust to early retirement because of an injury, and a few will blow the whistle on themselves. Basketball star Jerry West of the Los Angeles Lakers did just that. He didn't think he could live up to his past standards, so he quit. Retirement is not only an emotional adjustment but a financial apocalypse if the player hasn't managed his money, set up a business, or found some way to earn an income. It's extremely difficult to save because most superstars make a tremendous amount of money over a short period of time and get taxed to death. The Yazes are no exception.

"Save? How in God's name can you save? We have to buy what we need now. In a few years Carl may not have an income." Carol frowned and gazed distractedly out the window. "We'll have to get out of the Boston area . . . too expensive. Carl talks about going to a farm in Caribou, Maine, when he retires. Can you imagine? *Me* in Maine?" Suddenly the mask was back, and the old sly grin crept across her face. "Let him go there alone. It's not for me. The Siberia of America? No *way* am I going there. I like tennis, sunshine, night life." Carol poured herself a beer and lit another cigarette.

"Whenever we retire, one thing is for certain: Yazi will have to get there by boat or train. He hates to fly!"

I mentioned that I thought he had to fly with the team. "Yes"—she nodded—"and he hates it! And although he rarely drinks he practically has to knock himself out for courage. If he sees three drops of water on the window, he thinks he's heading into a hurricane. Yazi is an absolute wreck on the plane, so, of course, he only goes on one when it's necessary, which means he only flies for baseball. But I did talk him into going to Japan on a vacation two years ago with Bob Woolf and his wife, two good friends of ours. We knew getting him on the plane would be a major trauma. And it was. In spite of the fact that he was almost out from alcohol. He slept for the longest time and finally woke up screaming that we were going to crash into the ocean. We explained we weren't crashing . . . we were landing in Hawaii. Once we landed and completed a two-day stopover, we had to go through the whole nerve-racking repeat performance of getting that man back on the plane. The next time he thought we were going to crash it was the Tokyo airport. That was the beginning of the Japanese affair!"

The connotation of "affair" has a romantic suggestion. The Japanese affair was anything *but* romantic. As the Yazes and the Woolfs were about to go through customs at the Tokyo airport, Yazi complained of terrible stomach cramps. Meanwhile, a Japanese official, Herman Matsui, from the protocol office was there to greet the baseball star. Yazi's first words to Mr. Matsui were: "Where's the bathroom?" The rest room at the airport was pointed out, and Yazi bolted for it while Mr. Matsui was still bowing. Carol thought her husband looked a little ashen when he came out and noticed that he got in the waiting limousine without answering any of Mr. Matsui's polite questions.

After a few blocks Yazi pressed Carol's arm and whispered, "The cramps are back!" Carol in turn pressed Mr. Matsui's arm and asked him if he wouldn't direct his driver to a rest room. She explained that her husband had a problem. The driver threw up his hands and said the Japanese equivalent of "impossible." They were in rush-hour traffic. Yazi's face became pinched, his eyes staring wide in disbelief at Carol.

"I think we better find a place, Mr. Matsui," Carol said firmly. The driver finally stopped the car alongside the road where down some narrow cement steps there was a public bathroom. Yazi ran down the steps and disappeared into the building. A couple of seconds later he was back, pinched face and all. As the car moved out on the highway, Carol asked, "Is everything OK, honey?"

"No." Carl's voice was barely audible. "I couldn't go. There were no doors . . . and no toilet paper!"

They were back in traffic again, heading for the city.

"Do something!" Carl said in a weak voice.

"Mr. Matsui . . . we'll have to stop at a, uh, *better* bathroom at once."

"Very sorry . . . better?"

"Yes, at once!"

"Better? Ah . . . I see . . . no like?"

"Mr. Matsui, just take us to the closest bathroom . . . at once!"

Herman Matsui's official smile was waning. He looked perplexed but nevertheless told his driver to stop again. Once again they pulled over to the side, and Carl disappeared down the steps of another public bathroom, only to come running right back up again. He got in and slammed the door, and they took off. Mr. Matsui went back to smiling broadly.

"Honey," Carol began, "is everything—"

"No. It's *not* all right! There was no goddamn toilet paper in that place either! Did you hear me, Matsui?" he yelled. "There's no goddamn toilet paper in your *goddamn country!*"

"Ah, so . . . you know! We have paper strike in Japan"—he beamed—"and it affects all paper, even toilet . . . heh, heh, heh. . . . "

Carl took off his jacket and started ripping up his shirt, until he had long strips of cotton in his hand. "*Stop* the car at the next public————house," he ordered. And with his teeth clenched he snarled into Carol's ear, "You worry about what I'm going to do in retirement. . . . Well, I'm going to write a book . . . and the title is going to be: How to survive an attack of diarrhea during a paper strike in Tokyo, Japan!"

"Well, I hope you don't have to go to a farm in Caribou, " I said as she walked me to my car.

"One thing for sure." She laughed in her I'm-not-going-to-mean-what-I-say laugh. "No matter if it's Caribou or Boston, I'm going to have to put up with old perfectionist and his persnickety ways—telling me what to do all day long. God, what luck!" She put her hands to her head in mock dispair. Seconds later we both jumped at the noise of Yazi's tree coming down close by.

"Why didn't you warn us?" Carol screamed.

Yazi threw up his hands in the same old "who knows" gesture.

Several months later when I was passing through the area on my way to (or from) an interview I called Carol to see how things were going.

"Has Carl retired yet?" I asked

"No, he's going strong, but guess what? We've sold our house and we're moving to—do you *have* to know?"

"Well, no, not really—"

"We're moving to Boca Raton, Florida," she went on as if she hadn't heard me. "I'm sooo thrilled! You just have to know, don't you!" Her voice went back and forth between exhilaration and annoyance.

"We bought a lot on the coastal highway, and we're building a gorgeous two-story—it's *none* of your business—"

I finally caught on. "Tell him, Carol, tell him who you're talking to."

The Merry Widow

It's always *been lonely . . . from the very beginning. There has been
spring training, winter ball, trading, moving, being separated. . . . I
got used to it. . . . I've learned how to fill up my life.*

For fourteen years Barbara Ann Cole had no idea that the color of her skin
made a difference. Then she learned it did, but it was too late—she was already strong, confident, and happy. It was too late for the bigotry of a nation
to shrivel her hopes and optimism.

She's only thirty-five now, and there's plenty of time for her to learn disappointment, and the bitter effects of prejudice, but for the present, everything is
cool and looking up. Her husband, Frank Robinson, has a goodly share of
success, but has entertained no illusion about the future. He has broken new
ground, but it took too long, and he's suspicious of his success. He seems to
think his prosperity is a fluke that will evaporate when notice is taken that
good fortune has befallen a black man.

A man as sullen as Frank Robinson needs a wife as merry as Barbara Ann
to temper him. Barbara Robinson* possesses the kind of peace that comes
from lack of fear. She has a positive, joyful spirit that is absolutely contagious. The combination of peace and joy makes her a happy person. She's sat-
isfied with what she has and what she doesn't have. She does not go chasing
after things others consider desirable.

Barbara's husband was a major-league baseball star when she first met him
fifteen years ago, and on October 3, 1974, he became the first black man in
history to manage a major-league team. This accomplishment ranks with that
of another black man of the same surname almost two decades ago.

Our interview took place the day after Frank's appointment as player-
manager of the Cleveland Indians in a hotel suite in New York City. Barbara,
dressed in camel-colored slacks and matching cashmere sweater, was still
flushed with excitement. Friends, manager, and agents drifted in and out of
the room, and I knew at once that we would have no privacy.

---

*Frank Robinson, Manager of the Cleveland Indians, former player for the Cincin-
nati Reds and Baltimore Orioles. In 1956 Frank Robinson won the Rookie of the Year
award in the National League. He went on to become the first and only player to win
the Most Valuable Player (MVP) award in both leagues. In 1966 he became one of
only eleven players to win the Triple Crown (most runs batted in, most home runs,
highest batting average) in one season. His career home run total of 573 ranks fourth
behind Hank Aaron, Babe Ruth, and Willie Mays. Robinson has become the first black
manager in baseball.

"Frank's in the bedroom still asleep," she told me as she poured coffee. "He slept last night—just like nothing ever happened. I turned and twisted all night, but that man, *nothing* ever bothers him. He went out like a light!" Barbara said she was elated over his appointment but realized that when the excitement died down, it would mean she'd see less of him than before—and that was hardly at all. "Our home is in California, and the children are in school there. We're just going to have to adjust to separate lives."

Frank's agent and two secretaries from his office sat in the hotel room that day and listened with stony, unsympathetic faces as Barbara candidly talked about being a baseball widow. "I've never known it any other way," she said. "It's *always* been lonely. There has always been spring training, winter ball, trading, moving, being separated. I am alone! So what? It's made me strong. Frank's been gone so much that I don't know how I'd react to having a man home every night. I'm not used to it."

It has fallen to innumerable generations of wives and mothers to sing the dirge of loneliness and to accommodate the only lives they will ever have to those of their mates in a subservient way. Haven't soldiers, heroes and politicians sold their hearths and wives' privacy for the notoriety that elevated them to the history books and buried their wives in anonymity while requiring them to live beyond reproach as did Caesar's wife, whose name was also not considered worthy of mention. Superstar athletes are only the newest members of the ancient fraternity of superior-class males who teach their wives the female price for male fame. The story is old. The modern wife's reaction is changing as women are changing. Some, like Nancy Seaver, are still wondering how to cope with loneliness, some don't give a damn, like Carol Yastrzemski, or *does* she? and others solve it by doing their own thing, like Karolyn Rose or Julie Swift, absorbed in her law studies. Barbara Robinson is a new woman. She hasn't decided what she's going to do when the children no longer need her, but in the meantime, her mouth is her loudspeaker.

"I figured there was no sense in feeling sorry for myself because I didn't have a husband around like the other wives in our neighborhood. So I just started to learn how to stand on my own two feet—and I like it!"

The long forced separation from her husband, however, does play havoc with her sex life, and she admits it freely. "A normal sex life for me is not very often!" Then she threw back her head and laughed at her own joke. The others in the room twittered nervously.

"Again, it's always been that way—so you don't miss what you don't have!" She didn't appear to be missing a thing, totally lacking in bitterness. Even when Frank is at home, he puts a limit on sexual activities, Barbara revealed in front of Frank's astonished agent. "He won't waste any energy before a game! We never have sex before a game, and it's a rare occasion that he has any energy left after a game!" The thought made her chuckle.

Credit: UPI

A Scotsman by the name of Dr. N. C. Craig Sharp, who served as physiological consultant to the British Olympic team in Munich, has done extensive research on the subject of sex and the athlete. His theories undoubtedly shatter those of coaches like Don Shula of the Dolphins, superstars like Frank Robinson, and many players who believe sex saps their energy before a game. Dr. Sharp says, "I can find no factual evidence that sexual activities in moderation up to and including the night before a game have any detrimental effect on the player. In fact, about half an hour of sexual activity the night before would maximize the onset, quantity, and quality of sleep."

Barbara told me of a book she'd read by a doctor who also insisted that sex does not enervate a player before a game and passed this expert opinion on to Frank. "It didn't seem to convince him," Barbara told me matter-of-factly. "If you *believe* it will sap your energy, it will . . . and I guess Frank must believe it."

As willing as she was to speak candidly about sex, Barbara could offer no authoritative clarification on superstar sexuality. Is a superstar better in bed? How could she know? She'd only tried one. However, she tried to add what little she could on the subject. Barbara believes athletes are better in bed than most other men because they're in better physical condition, are stronger, and have better muscle control. "A strong man with big shoulders can make a difference. That's what I think," she said, while the people in the hotel suite squirmed.

Frank Robinson is strong and broad-shouldered. And no doubt a likely target for jock lovers, as Barbara is well aware. His long absences and the unbridled admiration he inspires in thousands of women make Barbara wonder, but she swears she's not bothered by them.

If she's not, it's not because she has implicit trust in her husband. "He might be tempted," she said with a disarming smile. "After all, he's a man. I certainly wouldn't be smug about it like some wives who say their husbands never do that. I say, 'Don't be too sure.' I think a man will look. Frankly, I might do a little looking myself!" Watch out.

Barbara Ann Cole was born thirty-four years ago on an eighty-acre tract of farmland. Out of convenience and because the Post Office Department insisted, the community was called Bull Creek, Oklahoma. They like to say, down that way, that a strong wind came up one day and blew Bull Creek into the next county. That may be stretching it a little, but it's true Bull Creek no longer exists.

Barbara had eight brothers and sisters, and along with her mother and daddy, they pretty well filled up the small shingled farmhouse that kept them snug together, away from the harsh reality of the rest of the world. Her father and brothers worked the land from dawn to dusk. Barbara remembers how, as a small child, she had the beautiful countryside to marvel at, the weather to worry about, the tall corn where she could hide, the horses to catch and ride bareback. She knew all about sows, mares, cows, and farm life. She knew nothing about slums, poverty, violence, and prejudice. "I often wish my own children had the opportunity to grow up the way I did."

The picture changed abruptly when she was fourteen. Her father died, and the surviving family lost the farm. The children were scattered, Barbara going to Los Angeles to live with an older sister. The change from Willow Spring Country School in Oklahoma to the public school in Los Angeles was drastic. The teenager, who thought everybody loved everybody else, discovered racial prejudice and stuck up her nose at it. She wasn't going to let it bother her.

It was while she was attending Los Angeles City College that an uncle from Oklahoma dropped in for a visit and reversed whatever direction Barbara's life was taking.

The uncle was not a favorite. He was old, forgetful, and demanding. The first demand, made the instant he stepped through the door, was to be taken to the coliseum so he could see the ball game. Cincinnati was playing the Dodgers that day, and he didn't want to be late. Barbara packed him into the car and listened politely as her uncle reeled off the names of all the baseball players he knew and admired. He was still reciting when she let him out in front of the coliseum. She instructed him to return to the exact same spot immediately after the game so she could take him back home.

When the game was over, Barbara was at the appointed place, and so were tens of thousands of fans—not one her wayward uncle. She waited and waited until the place was deserted and it was obvious Uncle had found something better to do. At the moment she started to leave, out of the stadium came a school friend. With him was Frank Robinson.

Barbara recalls the moment vividly. "Frank was the most beautiful man I had ever seen—despite the unfriendly manner and the fact he didn't talk much." He did manage to ask for her telephone number. That's how Barbara got interested in baseball and how she caught hell at home for coming back without her uncle.

Frank was not one to waste time or words. He asked her to marry him shortly after their first date, and Barbara dropped out of school at barely twenty, prepared to take up the life of a wife of a major-league baseball player. She had no idea, at the time, what baseball was about, much less ballplayers. She got into an argument with a school chum over her insistence that her betrothed played left tackle. She swore she remembered that was what Frank had told her—that he played left tackle on his baseball team. The school friend told her she was crazy, and she confronted unsuspecting Frank that evening.

"You shouldn't have lied about your job. You mighta known I'd find out!" she screamed, her nose a hairsbreadth from his.

"Find out what?"

"That you don't play left tackle."

It took Frank two hours and forty-five minutes to persuade her he was a right fielder, always had been a right fielder, and had never claimed, to her or anyone else, to be anything *but* a right fielder.

The wedding took place five months later in Barbara's sister's home. Her uncle didn't show up. (Did he ever return from the ball game?)

That was sixteen years ago, and Barbara has learned a way of life entirely different from anything she had ever known before. In the beginning she followed Frank to spring training and from city to city during the hectic baseball season. But most of the traveling stopped for her with the birth of Frank Kevin, who is now thirteen years old. When her son was three, Nischelle was born, binding her even closer to home.

"I've learned how to fill up my life," she said. "I drive seven car pools and play a lot of tennis." She takes care of herself (she's still a size eight) and has not become a household drudge even though she's aware she has stopped growing to her potential.

When the children are grown I'll do something important with my time. I plan to go back to school, study, be somebody, and build an identity of my very own." She realizes now that she had built her life around her children and husband. "Too much so," she said, "and Frank realizes that, but for now, my children need me."

When Frank is not playing ball, life for the Robinsons in their Bel Air, California, home is quiet. They have few friends and rarely go to parties. "I don't smoke or drink, so there's no use in going to all those parties. We socialize in our home. Frank is quiet, not one for a lot of people. I love people, I love to travel. If I had my way . . . " Her voice trailed off, and sadness crept into her face.

In 1966 Frank hit the peak of his playing career and became a superstar for the first time. The Robinsons decided to rent a house, a show of confidence in Frank's having arrived, and Barbara ran into overt racial prejudice for the first time.

"We'd call about renting and they'd say sure, until they found out we were black," she said. "Never has a player won so many awards as Frank did that year—never in history! And we couldn't rent a house. We tried everywhere. The answer was always no. Finally the owner of the Orioles, Jerry Hoffberger, found us a house. I guess they don't hate Jews as much as blacks. We moved in, and no one in the neighborhood had anything to do with us except for a young couple across the street. When they came to call, no one in the neighborhood spoke to *them* either, but we're still good friends. Later we decided to buy the house we were renting, but the owner wouldn't sell. He said it would devalue the property. A lawyer heard about our trouble, a man we didn't even know. He bought the house and turned around and sold it to us. There are a lot of beautiful people in the world."

As Frank became more firmly established, he moved his family to the Hollywood grandeur of Bel Air, where race was not nearly the obstacle money was. They bought a cream-colored contemporary house and had W & J Sloane do the interiors, except for the den, Barbara's favorite room. The den was the repository for Frank's trophies and awards. There are so many nothing else fits. It almost took a bulldozer to clear space for the pool table. Barbara gave some thought to moving to a house with a bigger den because so many of Frank's 200 or more trophies had to be stuck away in closets. "If Frank had his way, they'd *all* be in the closet," she said. So the den was all her doing. She was proud of her husband and wanted everyone to know why. One friend observed that the room was so loaded with pictures, gold, silver, and brass cups, medals, and statuettes he was afraid to sit down for fear of being goosed by a gold baseball bat.

He'd had it all, Frank had. Everybody thought so. Except Frank and Barbara. Both knew a baseball lifetime was short in years, and the end for Frank was in sight. He wanted something from baseball no other black man had ever had—something to extend his baseball life. He wanted to manage a major-league team. He'd been in line for the job for some while, but each time his hopes had been shattered as he was passed over for somebody else, a white man.

Finally, Frank gave up. "I'm turning my energies in other directions," he told her. Behind his words were frustration and discouragement over the foot dragging of baseball's conservative Establishment, which could not bring itself to permit a black manager.

Barbara found it against her irrepressible nature to accept defeat before the game was over. She kept her hopes. Frank growled, "Don't pay attention to any more rumors." What she didn't pay attention to was Frank's angry words. She'd learned to listen to the hopes in Frank's heart—hopes he hid with his words.

Barbara was lounging in the Frank Robinson memorial den in Bel Air as October arrived in 1974. The phone rang, and it was Frank's agent. "Frank misses you and wants you to fly to Cleveland right away," he said.

"If he misses me all that much, how come *you're* the one calling me on the telephone?" she replied.

"There's a ticket waiting for you at the airport, so be a good girl and come on out."

When her plane landed, the agent met her. Frightened, she thought something had happened to Frank that he was trying to keep from her. Then she realized they were heading for the Cleveland Stadium. They went into the press room, which was mobbed. Frank was busy, said the agent, but would be able to talk to her in a moment. Barbara stared at the sea of reporters and photographers as Phil Seghi, general manager of the Cleveland Indians, announced Frank's appointment as player-manager of the team. Seghi then read a telegram from President Ford congratulating her husband, and she heard the words "This is welcome news for baseball fans across the country . . . and a tribute to you personally, to your athletic skills and your unsurpassed leadership."

My God, everybody, including the President of the United States, knew before she did. She was proud . . . she was angry. She didn't know whether to throw her arms around Frank or a lamp at his head.

Barbara had brought me up to date, and at this point in our talk the Great Frank woke up and came out into the living room of the suite and poured himself some coffee. His entourage moved in quickly. They brought him congratulatory messages from the big names in the sports world, telephone messages from governors, senators, congressmen, business tycoons; they quoted columnists and joked and bantered about public reaction to his appointment. Frank said nothing, and his face showed nothing but suspicion.

Barbara wasn't paying any attention to any of it. She was describing how, in 1966, Frank received a serious head injury. I could tell Frank was more interested in what she was saying than the others.

"Frank was trying to break up a double play," Barbara bubbled, "and he ran right into Al Weiss' knee. God, I was worried, he had a bad head injury and for one year saw two of everything. Imagine, trying to catch a ball and wondering which is the real one?"

"Don't print that!" Frank growled.

Barbara hardly heard the interruption and went on to recount the honors that have been heaped on her husband: The MVP award, the Triple Crown, and the Hickok Award (yes, she was wearing the center stone on her right hand) and how he practically won the World Series by himself, and now: "He's been made manager . . . and they're damn lucky to get him!"

"Don't print that," Frank warned.

"Go ahead. You can print that." Barbara beamed. "This is *my* interview."

It turned out they were lucky to get him and management showed its appreciation by renewing his contract with a raise in '75.

Outsiders believe the Robinsons have a quirky alliance or misalliance. They say she adores him but that he doesn't show much affection. My hunch is that she is absolutely the light and air of his life. I believe she bullies him and charms him, fights and bewitches him, and even though he may not know it, I don't believe he could exist without her any more than he could without sunshine. As for Barbara, her feelings about him are strong. A combination of a clucking mother hen and a delighted child. One intuitively knows she will not capitulate, nor will she be shadowed by his monumental career, and yet there is in her such fierce pride in him, ready to bubble to the surface at a moment's notice, that you have to believe she loves this difficult man, even if he isn't a left tackle.

The Wife of the Poor Man's Plimpton

I'm not taking any chances. Where he goes, I go—even if I have to follow him to Nome, Alaska!

While I was interviewing wives of baseball superstars I began wondering . . . what happens to the superstar who is forced to retire because of injury, dwindling ability, or old age? It can be very sad when the cheering and back-slapping comes to an end, especially if the superathlete has not handled his success in an emotionally and financially mature way that prepares him for the day when he must give up his "place in the sun."

Joe Pepitone is one example of a former superstar who seems to be having difficulties with the transition out of baseball. For years Pepitone was one of the mainstays of the early sixties' world champion Yankees. Now he's out of baseball at thirty-five and rumored to have financial problems. He has gone through several wives, modeled nude for the centerfold of a magazine called *Foxy Lady*, and recently wrote a racy book, *Joe, You Can Make Us Proud*, in which he proudly tells all.

There may be many cases like Joe Pepitone, but one beautiful illustration of the old rule "You can't keep a good man down for long" is Jim Bouton, the superstar pitcher who was traded from the Yankees and after several frustrating seasons shuttling back and forth between the major and minor leagues dropped out of baseball, wrote a bestseller, and began a career in sports broadcasting. Today Jim Bouton is one of the most famous and popular television sportscasters in New York .

I drove up to the Boutons' big white old-fashioned house in Englewood, New Jersey, and had a feeling that the family who lived inside would be warm, loving, nice people. That's usually the kind who like big white old-fashioned houses. And I was right—the Boutons are all those things in a "mod" sort of way.

Twelve-year-old Michael answered the door, and it didn't take long to find out that his interest wasn't baseball—it was ballet. He danced in The New Jersey Classic Ballet Company's *Nutcracker* at Christmastime, and his ambition is to be another Nureyev. Nine-year-old Laurie, whom you'd expect to love ballet, is crazy about baseball—and *her* ambition is to be another Henry Aaron. She was running around the house with her baseball cap on backward, looking for her brother David, an adopted Korean war orphan, who was at the moment among the missing.

Barbara Bouton,* known to her friends as Bobby, a soft, smiling brunette with friendly, intelligent eyes, ushered me into the den with a tray of coffee and the best homemade cookies I've tasted since I left my mother's kitchen. Immediately I felt the warm, cheerful ambience of the household and knew that the den was its center. More than 2,000 books line the shelves on the walls, and they looked as if they had been read. I hadn't seen a book since I left Julie Swift's house in Florida, and to come upon so many in one room was almost overwhelming.

I hit the jackpot that day. Bobby told me Jim was out in the garden, and I was pleased because I knew it would be fun to talk to him about trading, a subject on which he was a personal authority.

"Compared to your lettuce, mine looks like shit," were his first words as he came through the door. Startled, I looked up to see Jim talking to a neighbor who was clutching a head of lettuce that looked like an overgrown bush. The neighbor, Peter Golenbock, who, besides turning out overgrown lettuce, has turned out a book called *Dynasty*, a history of the New York Yankees from 1949 to 1964, sat down and honestly tried to think of one thing in Jim's garden that was worthy of a compliment. Finally, he turned to Jim, who was sprawled in a chair still eyeing his lettuce, and said hopefully, "Your peas look like they're doin' nicely!"

"Oh, sure," Bouton said with a sardonic grin. "They're growin' so goddamn good they're chokin' my trees, but no *pods!*" For the next few minutes I almost choked on my cookie while Jim described his garden. When I asked him to describe trading in baseball, he wasn't quite so funny.

"In baseball the teams own you. A player has no freedom to choose another team if he's unhappy. However, if the team who owns the player is unhappy, *they're* free to trade him, making it possible for one player to be traded as many as ten times a year." He singled out the case of Eddie Brinkman, who signed with the Yankees on June 13, 1975, from the Texas Rangers. The Yankees were the fifth team Brinkman had been with in one year. Five moves! His wife spent most of her 365 days in '75 packing.

The minor leagues move their players around even more rapidly. Those wives probably don't bother to unpack.

Spring flowers and showers must bring out a "rash" on ballplayers because the most frightening period in baseball is spring training! Tension in the training camp's air is enough to run a hydroelectric plant for a week. Only twenty five men play on a big-league team, yet the teams invite seventy-five players to spring training which includes the twenty-five from the season before. Usu-

---

*Jim Bouton, former pitcher for the New York Yankees and Houston Astros. A television sportscaster for CBS in New York City and bestselling author of *Ball Four.*

ally most of the twenty-five make it back, but there are always five to ten new faces every year, and that means five to ten of the original players *won't* make it. The problem is the clubs don't tell you until the last minute who the twenty-five guys are. Whether management can't make up its minds or simply take fiendish delight in making a bunch of guys sweat is pure conjecture. The upshot is that the suspense is almost unbearable. By training camp's end it's been narrowed down, and thirty men and their families are making plans to go North. Some have already rented or bought houses; furniture is put in moving vans; children say good-bye to their friends, and station wagons are loaded. Then at the very last minute management announces the five names. Those five families have to cancel their plans and stay down South until they're traded to the minors.

They waited too late to tell Joe Verbanic (then with the Yankees). It was the last hour of the last day, and Joe's wife and family had already left for New York. Joe called the Florida highway patrol, who in turn called the toll collectors and alerted them to watch for a green station wagon loaded with kids and with four bicycles on top. "Tell the lady who's drivin' to turn around and go back. Her husband didn't make the team."

That's how Mrs. Verbanic found out.

The next stop for these men and their families is the minors, and according to Bouton, relegation to the minors is the most lamentable, disgraceful experience a major-league player can have. *He* ought to know; he went through the whole agonizing ordeal—from the Yankees to the bush league.

"It's really a comedown," Bouton admits, "kinda like being the executive of a big company one day, then having to go back to the mail room the next."

In baseball jargon the people who go from the big leagues down to the minors are called suspects. The ones who go from the minors to the majors are prospects. Jim Bouton was a suspect.

Pulling up roots, changing children's schools, making new friends, only to be traded and lose them again must be more than a frustration for the families. The havoc it causes to households and the heartaches to wives is considerable. Bobby Bouton is one of the few who accompanied her husband on the trip down to the minors with good humor and is still with him now that he's back on top. She'll probably always look on the experience as a reminder of how precarious and illusory fame is.

Thirty-four-year-old Barbara Heister Bouton was born and reared in Allegan, Michigan. From the very beginning she was a baseball nut, becoming official statistician and scorekeeper for her high-school's baseball team and finally choosing a baseball player to marry. At Western Michigan University she met Jim Bouton, who was a pitcher on the freshman team. They dated for four years and a year after graduation decided to get married. Before the wedding Jim invited Bobby to Greensboro, North Carolina, where he'd found an apartment close to the ball park. Bobby didn't accept his cozy invitation to play house; instead she asked for a private room. Jim met a lady who owned a nearby restaurant where all the ballplayers ate, and she told him his girlfriend could stay with her—have her own room at no charge. Jim accepted eagerly. After all, the lady would be company for Bobby when Jim was playing ball, and she seemed nice. Jim knew she was friendly with the ballplayers, but he didn't know *how* friendly. She took on the whole team! When Jim was away on a road trip, the woman asked Bobby if she couldn't help her out, explaining that she had too much traffic for one person to handle. When Jim arrived back in Greensboro, Bobby was already back home in Michigan.

After the wedding they moved East, where Jim had just signed with the Yankees. The year 1963, according to Bobby, was the most fantastic year of their lives. "Jim won twenty-one games pitching for the Yankees, I became pregnant with Michael, and we bought our first home in Ridgewood, New Jersey." And then she was quick to add, "Everything went downhill after that for many years."

The problem? Trading. The worst word in baseball.

In 1968 a friend took Bobby to a seer who told her that her husband, "who was a big star with the Yankees, would be leaving the team in two years." She also prophesied that there would be trouble with his career *after* he left. Bobby shrugged, tucked it in the back of her mind, and forgot it. Two years later, in 1970, at the end of spring training the Yankees had eliminated all but twenty-six men. There remained one left to cut. One of the wives, who was eight months pregnant, rushed into Bobby's apartment sobbing that she was positive it would be her husband. Bobby told her to stop crying. "It's not going to be your husband. Jim is the one who will be cut, and I've already been told." The astonished girl raised her head from her arms where only seconds before she had been in anguish. "You seem to be the only one who's been informed. Jim doesn't know—we've just seen him. Are you certain?"

"Yes," Bobby answered matter-of-factly. "I'm certain."

The Boutons were traded from the Yankees to the Seattle Pilots, and mustering all possible humor, they jauntily said good-bye to their friends and left for the West Coast, battered but unbowed. There was one beautiful thing to look forward to—something that took the edge off their unhappiness. On the day they arrived in Seattle, they were to meet the tiny Korean war orphan they'd adopted. So, instead of talking about what went wrong in spring training and bemoaning their fate, the Boutons practiced their Korean all the way across the country. Having both taken a crash course, they knew how to say such profound things as, "Do you have to go to the bathroom?" "Are you hungry?" and "Are you feeling good?" As they drove and rehearsed, little Michael and Laurie must have wondered if they were in the right car.

When their new four-year-old son, whom they renamed David, stepped off the plane, he asked," "Where's America?" They were relieved he spoke English until they found out that those were the only two words he knew besides "Batman." For weeks David kept asking, "Where's America?" and finally one day, as the Boutons were walking him through the TV section of a big department store, he grinned and said, "Here's America!"

No sooner had the Bouton family adjusted to their new life in Seattle than Jim was traded. This time Bobby read about it in the newspapers. "Golly, Daddy's been traded again," she said to the children, holding back the tears. "Now we'll all have a chance to see Houston." Jim, who was playing out of town, dashed to the phone when he got to the locker room and called her, hoping she hadn't read it in the papers, but she had absorbed the bad news hours before his call and cheerily told him the family was packing.

"One thing you learn is to roll with the punches," Bobby said, summing up the decline and fall of her husband's pitching career. "He was on his way down. He wasn't a big star anymore, but we both kept our sense of humor. That helped more than anything!"

A sense of humor didn't help much that Easter when Bobby found herself in a motel room with three children and her husband playing ball 300 miles away. "We hadn't found a house yet [in Houston], and there I was trying to hide Easter eggs in a tiny motel room. The only thing that saved me from going off the wall was the challenge of figuring out places to hide jelly beans. After you use the shoes, drawers, and the medicine chest, there really aren't many good places left!"

By now Jim felt he had something to say about baseball. The ups and downs, inside and outside the baseball park. He said it all in an exceedingly controversial book, *Ball Four*, a best-seller that caused the entire baseball world to flip-flop. The book was assessed, critiqued, censured, praised, quoted in articles, and discussed on TV talk shows. Bobby remembers it as a wildly frenetic time. "I'd come home with my groceries and could hardly get through the mob of reporters and television camera crews to get in my own front door. The phones never stopped ringing. People were either thrilled with the book or calling to say they wished he hadn't written it. The baseball commissioner wanted Jim to renounce his book publicly. You could go on the air, he told him, and say you didn't mean half the things you said about behind the scenes in baseball!"

Instead, Jim went around the country promoting the book that covered the action in the bullpen, locker room, and night life of the men who play in America's favorite sport. He spoke out about jock lovers, sex, and drugs, divulging that some athletes relied on drugs to help them perform, that greenies (pep pills) were popped automatically by many players, and that after the game it was gropies with the groupies!

In a ripping column about Jim Bouton, one sportswriter quoted Joe Pepitone as saying, "Bouton ought to know. He's the horniest bleep in baseball."

Again Jim was out of town and upset that his wife might read the column. He decided to call and explain before she had a chance. After a long dissertation on what a bastard Pepitone was he was interrupted by Bobby, "Well, I dunno, I read the article and agree with Pepitone—you *are* kinda horny."

Jim hung up with a grin on his face and an enormous sense of relief. Bobby's sense of humor had got them over a tough spot once again.

The public loved *Ball Four*, but baseball wasn't ready for it, and Bouton was traded once again. Just before the final humiliation, however, he was saved by ABC in New York, where management decided that anyone who could write a book like that would make a terrific sportscaster. Two months later the Boutons were back East, and Jim was performing for a camera instead of a baseball crowd. That was in 1970, and he stayed with ABC until 1973, when he switched to WCBS, where he's still performing as sportscaster on the 11 P.M. news.

Once again Bobby had to adjust to a new house and a new neighborhood. This time it was welcome.

"We like it here," Jim said with his eyes on his neighbor's lettuce. "But the soil isn't good for gardening on our side of the street."

"I've been in this house three years, and I still have trouble finding the bathroom, Bobby said with a straight face. "We've moved so many times— lived in so many places—that sometimes I wake up at night and think I'm in Houston and walk right into the wall!"

Jim and Bobby haven't change much since their "gypsy" days. You get the feeling that the same things are important to them today as when they were cruising along the bottom—namely, the children and each other. Money isn't something to flaunt, it's something to have fun with, and the Boutons' favorite story about their priorities when they were with the Yankees still holds today.

During spring training at Fort Lauderdale in 1967 they wanted to live on the beach. The problem was the rentals were way beyond what they could afford. Nevertheless, they decided it was more important to be close to the water than to live within their budget. They'd cut corners and somehow manage it. Jim figured out a splendid way. Instead of renting from a major car rental agency, he'd save money by finding a really cheap rent-a-car. He found a place that should have been called "Rent-a-heap."

"The car I got was so old, so dented and rusty you couldn't even make out the characteristic of the design."

"It was the only car on the street with moss on the right side!" Bobby cracked.

"Yeah," Jim went on. "The only door that worked was wired shut. It looked like one of those cars from the Demolition Derby. When I drove it to the Yankee parking lot, which was full of station wagons and Cadillacs, the guard would stop me, waving his hands and shouting, 'Only ballplayers in here!' I'd have to get out and show him my card. When practice was over, I'd manage to be the last one out of the ball park so none of the other guys would see my car."

"Aw," Bobby teased, "the only thing he lost was his dignity. Living on the beach was worth it."

Another time, in order to stay at the plush Astro World Hotel in Houston they decided to cut corners by eating all their meals in their room. The trouble was it didn't have a kitchen. "We rented a little refrigerator with a freezer and hauled it in by dark of night." One can just imagine Bobby and Jim dragging a refrigerator through the posh lobby of the Astro World at 2 A.M. while a few straggling oilonaires looked on. "It worked quite nicely," Bobby recalled. "While everyone else was drinking planter's punch and eating club sandwiches around the pool, we were having our peanut butter sandwiches and potato chips on the king-sized bed. I think the maid got a little tired of shakin' all those crumbs out of our bed every day, but we saved lots of money."

"We're still the same today"—Jim grinned—"always figurin' ways to save a buck. Someone asked me the other day, *Why*, now that I'm making good bread, do we still pinch the pennies? I told him the truth. My wife is *cheap!*"

"Well, I've had a good teacher," Bobby countered, smiling adoringly at her husband, who was disappearing out the door and into his garden. Bobby doesn't have to say she loves her husband and children and is happy with her life as so many other wives have so carefully explained. It's written on her face—expressed in her eyes when she sends quips flying across the room. It's doubtful Jim's television success will ever alter their relationship. They've made it out of too many sand traps together, experienced too many highs and lows to be frightened or overwhelmed anymore by either.

Bobby is a rare woman. A healthy mixture of intellect and humor—and a rock core loyalty. Her most important asset may be that she takes everything in stride. In fact, the only time she can remember getting annoyed with living with her superstar husband was when they were vacationing in France and had made the usual tourist trip to the Louvre. They were standing among a crowd of about twenty people staring up at the statue of the Venus de Milo. "I was so enthralled," Bobby remembers, "that I was positively speechless. So were the others. All of a sudden a shrill, ear-piercing voice shouted, 'Jesus, look at that! Look at that!' I turned to see a man about ten feet away from us and assumed he was overly excited about the statue, when he shrieked again, 'My God, it's really true. It's Jim Bouton right here in the Louvre!' I turned around and walked out. The man ruined the spell of the Venus for me.''

The recognition factor in television is unreal. There's nothing in the world to compare with television exposure, but outside that there's very little difference between Jim's two careers. Out-of-town games are exchanged for film assignments, and ''Baseball Annies'' are replaced by ''TV Teenas.'' Bobby's sense of humor kinda disappeared when the subject of jock lovers came up. *Here we go,* I thought as she started out by saying, ''You just can't shake those girls. They've been around since the beginning of Jim's baseball career. Once at an out-of-town game a gal got in his hotel room, and when Jim returned and climbed into bed, he found this naked woman lying in it with a rose in her teeth! After he kicked her out, she *still* had the gall to follow him everywhere for weeks. I decided right then and there that my course of action was to be with him, so I traveled with him everywhere. I still do today. The groupies hang around the studio where he works waiting to pounce on him when he comes out of the building. It's the one thing I hate about his success, but he tells me not to worry''—a flicker of a smile crossed her face—''because he'll only leave me for Jennifer O'Neil.'' The grin widened. ''But I'm not taking *any* chances. Where he goes, I go—even if I have to follow him to Nome, Alaska!''

Bobby picked up her needlepoint, which, by the evidence around the house, was her hundred and eightieth pillow cover, and explained that jock lovers don't represent the only threat to wives of some of the well-known men. Sometimes the wives of other athletes or even the wives of friends can be just as big a problem. Then she reminded me of the much publicized case of wife swapping between two Yankee teammates a couple of years ago. The swappers were Fritz and Marilyn Peterson and Susan and Mike Kekich. Jim Bouton roomed with Fritz Peterson at the out-of-town games and was aware of what was going on during the entire imbroglio. The Petersons and the Kekiches were the best of friends and spent all their free time together. Initially they started kidding around about switching partners, but pretty soon it became serious. They decided on a trial run—if things worked out, they would divorce and remarry each other. But before they could experiment, the press got wind of it and they were forced into formal announcements. Fritz Peterson and Susan Kekich got married, and Mike Kekich and Marilyn Peterson didn't. Marilyn lives in Franklin Lakes, New Jersey, and, according to friends, is sorry about the whole mess. The children, who shuttle back and forth between the two sets of parents, may be the sorriest and most confused of them all.

Bobby doesn't hide the fact that she's infinitely happier being the wife of a TV personality than a ballplayer. ''I'm glad he's no longer a jock! It isn't only the trading, the groupies, wife swapping, and drug scene that turn me off. . . . It's the fact that the guys constantly have to prove themselves. Prove they're manly. Most of them believe in their public image and start living that role. It's difficult to say whether it's their fault or the public's, but their image would be shot if you caught them with a book in their hands or even the New York *Times*! However, I'd be lyin' to you if I told you that Jim is completely happy away from the game of baseball. I personally believe these ballplayers *never* adjust. Jim wouldn't say, but I know he'd love to go back to playing ball. If they'd hold his job while he played, he'd run to spring training in a minute." She put her needle and yarn down and looked at me. "It's sad in a way—ballplayers who love the game never want to give it up." Jim proved Bobby's point by going back to the minor leagues in '75 during a three-week vacation from WCBS. He pitched for the Portland Mavericks (four wins and two losses) and said it felt "so great" that he's promised himself another try at it in the spring of '76.

Except for those three weeks, Bouton is making up for not playing ball by getting involved, one way or another, in his reporting. His approach to sportscasting has been to put focus on the minor sports, and he does it by getting into the act. He was fired for this kind of reporting by ABC, but fortunately for his fans, who love it, CBS picked him up and every night during the week New Yorkers can watch him fencing, or sail gliding, or maybe fighting a bull—and not always successfully.

For that last particular assignment, Bobby accompanied him to a bull farm outside Madrid, where she sat safely behind the wall of the bullring with the camera crew while Jim was out in the arena with a professional bullfighter practicing passes with a cape. Just as he was about to try a veronica, Bobby cupped her hands to her mouth and yelled down into the bullring, "Instead of practicing all *that*, why don't you practice climbing this wall?"

It was too late. While Jim was raising his fist to Bobby's remark, the bull took a pass at his cape and knocked him down. Millions of New Yorkers chuckled when they saw it a few nights later.

Bobby's quip about the wall is a good example of her humor. According to their friends, Jim is the professional humorist and can spin one good story after another, but Bobby's humor has bite. Jim admits her one-liners are "deadly," particularly the ones aimed at him.

For Bobby, life with Jim Bouton has just the right amount of insanity to make it interesting. The green yarn dances and the needle flashes as she relates one adventure after another. She tosses bits of sarcasm about, scolding him for trying those dangerous acts in the first place, and when she's finished, a proud little smile creeps over her face, and she gives you an "Isn't he something!" look.

"Would you believe he did the slide for life with a team of auto daredevils?" She looked up to see if I believed, then adjusted her needlepoint and sewed furiously while she explained. "The slide for life is when you stand on the back bumper of a car that gets going around fifty miles per hour, and then you *jump* and *slide. My* husband had to try it in a circle of fire." Her head shook, and her needles flew. "He was supposed to land in the middle of the circle, but his timing was off and he landed *in* the fire! They dragged him out and sprayed him while I was trying to ward off an early coronary. Yeah, it's a thrill a minute living with him . . . I call him the poor man's Plimpton!"

The poor man's Plimpton has a wife who's as vulnerable as the other super-wives in many areas, but her uncommon combination of common sense mixed with a spicy sense of humor is what helps hold the marriage together. And there's something else.

Women's lib may not approve of her housewife role, her submissiveness, her obvious adoration of her husband at the cost of her own identity, and her lack of concern over her own accomplishments, but no one can fail to see that in spite of all this, Bobby Bouton is a happy, fulfilled woman. Perhaps one of the keys to this happiness was exposed when we were discussing the contro-versy over sexual abstinence before a game. "Most baseball players abstain," she told me. "They believe that sex the night before a game will sap their en-ergy." She put her needlepoint down and smiled a wondrous, knowing smile. "But Jim has a *different* theory. He believes in sex before, in between in-nings, and immediately after the game!"

I looked over at this woman who was still smiling at the picture in her mind and thought, *The hell with women's lib!* With Jim Bouton's theory on sex it's no wonder she'd follow him to Nome, Alaska.

When I got back to the other side of the Hudson River, my agent called and wanted to know if I'd like to talk to Jean-Claude Killy's wife? Would I? What a question! This time I *knew* I could bring my skis along with me to Switzer-land.

"Super!" I yelled into the phone. (I use that word a lot now.)

"OK," Jacques said quietly. "I'll make the appointment for tomorrow at your place."

"What's *my* place got to do with it?"

"That's where the interview will take place. The Killys are here in New York . . . he's here to do promotions and she came along. Isn't that a break?"

Some break.

French Fortitude

He wants the children to be like him. A champion! He wants them to excel. I suppose that even if they don't excel, it's a good way to be brought up.

When I first saw Daniele Killy* I was surprised. *Is this the girl,* I thought to myself, *Jean-Claude Killy, the super-looking superstar of the ski world, picked over all others?*

She arrived on my doorstep with an agent who seemed to want to protect her as one would a little girl. Daniele *looked* like a little girl playing "dress-up" in her mother's clothes. A knitted Ali McGraw hat was pulled down over her long silky dark hair, almost covering her eyes. A midi skirt reached well below her knees, and a tight little leather jacket was her only wrap against a cold, windy day. Another look told me she was stylishly dressed. Schoolgirl Frenchified but stylish.

I'd expected someone with the lush beauty of Elizabeth Taylor or the radiance of a Christina Ford. What I saw was a petite, angular woman of olive complexion and dark eyes and a thin, lithe body (which looked as if she had been on a diet of ghost broth and lettuce for most of her life). For an hour I sat talking to her and wondering why Jean-Claude hadn't picked out a ravishing beauty. Then she smiled, and I realized he had! The aurora borealis on a clear night couldn't be brighter. Her smile is positively dazzling!

Daniele speaks four languages: Italian and Spanish perfectly, English with a charming accent, and French fast.

Daniele Gaubert Killy was born twenty-eight years ago in the village of Nuars outside Paris. French all the way down the line, except on her mother's side. Her grandmother was Spanish and probably had something to do with Daniele's olive skin and dark eyes. The Gauberts reared their children in the country but saw to it they got to Paris often. Daniele and her brother attended the theater and opera, visited all the famous museums, and went in for music and ballet lessons twice a week. Mme. Gaubert started her daughter's ballet training early, and by the time Daniele was nine she was a ballet dancer with the Paris Opera company.

---

*Jean-Claude Killy, former Olympic skiing champion, now a professional skier and movie star. In 1965 at the age of twenty-three Killy was the skiing champion of Europe and the next year he became the skiing champion of the world. In 1968 he won three gold medals at the Olympics, a feat accomplished by only one other skier. Jean-Claude retired from skiing and was soon a millionaire, but he missed the competition and in 1972 joined the newly formed professional tour.

One day a scout from a movie company came to the old opera house's rehearsal hall. He was looking for an ingenue, someone to take the part of a young ballerina in a film they were about to make. There was no question Daniele was a competent and graceful dancer, but so were all the other girls in her class. She must have given him that "whammy" smile because she got the part and, at fifteen, went to the Côte d'Azur to make her first motion picture. This cataclysmic event led to a contract, seventeen more films, and a career that put the name of Daniele Gaubert up in lights all over France.

The famous Daniele smile lit up not only the French screen, but also the heart of a suitor named Rhadames Trujillo, the son of the dictator of the Dominican Republic. He courted the actress in the glare of the press, wrapping her in all the luxuries his money could buy. In those days it could buy a lot. In Paris they held hands at the Opéra, dined at Maxims, shopped the expensive boutiques along the Champs Elysées, went riding in the Bois. They also drank the finest wines at the swankiest watering holes of Europe. They were married in a much-publicized ceremony and went to live "happily ever after" in Madrid.

The Trujillos were not like other young couples starting out in married life. Their apartment, furnishings, clothes, jewels, and monthly expenses were not to be compared with their contemporaries'. Their social life was not ordinary either—nor was their circle of friends, consisting mainly of titled émigrés and political exiles from Juan Perón to Daniele's own father-in-law, Rafael Trujillo.

Two children were born: Rhadames, who is now ten, and Maria Daniele, age nine. But the children and the luxuries couldn't hold the marriage together, and after four years Daniele left Rhadames and went back home to Paris. It didn't take her long to find a part in a movie and pick up the threads of her old life.

In the winter of 1963, having just finished a film and finding herself exhausted, Daniele decided to take a vacation in the French Alps with a girlfriend. She had never skied before, her various careers not permitting such a dangerous sport, so she decided to try it—and, like everything else she does, try it in style! She looked over all the ski resorts and picked the impressive Val-d'Isère, and once there, headed straight for the most beautiful chalet hotel in the area. It just happened to belong to the parents of Jean-Claude Killy. And it just happened that she knew it did. She also knew the handsome skier was in residence that week. Her girlfriend introduced them, and Daniele appraised the world's greatest ski champion with a dazzling smile and her computer going a mile a minute. He frightened her.

"He was *too* handsome, *too* sure of himself. The women—they fluttered around him like hundreds of moths to a light. A man like this couldn't possi-

bly be happy with one woman when he has so many. I didn't want to get in the competition, so I stepped back.'' Daniele watched from the sidelines, brooding if he ignored her, smiling secretly to herself when he paid attention, and always cautious—protecting an ego just recovering from an old hurt.

She soon found out that Jean-Claude was as shy as she was. Not the kind of man for small talk or compliments. She was beginning to understand him—to like him—when he left for a ski meet in Austria without a word. Daniele was furious, but when he came back, she was still there. She stayed on at Val-d'Isère in what her agent called the longest vacation ever taken in French history. Hiding, coming out of hiding, lowering her eyes to cut off communication, asserting herself quietly, ignoring him, and then flashing that smile that must have sent him reeling. He took another look at this mouse with the chameleon ability to become a great beauty and was hopelessly caught. Daniele is a true Frenchwoman when it comes to getting her man. Such women seem instinctively to know how to captivate, holding back until the men are conquered, then moving in quietly and getting everything they want without asking for it. They are not liberated when it comes to love. They play the game. And they play it well.

Daniele and Jean-Claude lived together for five years and had a child before they decided to get married. In this sense she was extremely liberated and also extravagantly happy. ''We had such a full and happy life,'' Daniele reminisced. ''It was beautiful. We traveled, exploring foreign countries together, we skied, went on cross-country trips, mountain climbing, picnics. More important we discovered each other. We became 'one,' and soon''—she laughed merrily—''We became three.''

Emilie Killy was born in 1970. Friends used to ask the famous couple when they were going to get married and their answer was, ''When we are ready!'' Now with her baby daughter, Daniele still followed Jean-Claude around the world as he raced or promoted ski equipment.

''Do you not find it very embarrassing to have a baby and not be married?'' she was once asked.

''No'' was her answer. ''Perhaps to others it's embarrassing, but not to us!''

In 1973 when their daughter was almost three, they decided they *were* ready. It wasn't a question of believing the ceremony was so important to their relationship as it was a convenience for their life and for their daughter. ''We were tired of living like gypsies. We needed a home—a home for the children. But after all this time it seemed strange to wake up in bed with the man you've been living with for five years and say, 'This is my wedding day,' I remember thinking this—and then we had a fight. *C'est drôle!* We were bickering about relatives and who was coming to the wedding and who wasn't, and soon it became a fight. I have a temper. It takes awhile to get there, but I can become vereee angry! Finally I screamed at Jean, "OK, I'm finished with you! You can go alone and get married!" Suddenly what I said registered, and we both ended up laughing. Jean says I have a bad temper, but I think it's only a temper. Not a bad temper. If I don't like something I can't live with it, I have to say it!"

They managed to get married before she said any more. The ceremony took place in the courthouse of Daniele's little village outside Paris. Only six people were present, and all six knew the bride and groom were frightened to death at the thought that "marriage" might spoil their beautiful life, their beautiful love, and their beautiful fights.

"It was risky," Daniele will tell you, "but the most wonderful thing happened! Our love grew and grew, and now I am so happy that I am afraid it will go away!"

The Killys settled down in a spacious villa on the shore of Lake Geneva about twenty minutes outside the city with their own daughter and Daniele's two children by her former marriage. Daniele identifies her house as the one next door to Petula Clark's. Petula Clark describes her house as the one next door to the Killys'. There's no question: They both live in the world's most expensive neighborhood. Most houses today on Geneva's shore can't be touched for under $1,000,000. The Killys' villa can scarcely be seen from the road. An immense natural-wood two-story house, it sits on top of a slope looking down over the lake and is completely covered with ivy except for the roof and large bay windows. Flowers grow in abundance around the grounds, and in the spring and summer the villa takes on the look of a huge green garden.

The inside is complemented by the outside. Windows everywhere to bring in the blue and green of the outdoors. Flowers in vases spill color into the rooms and highlight a beautiful, polished antique table, a piano, or a mantel. The fireplace in the forty-five-foot living room was enlarged by the Killys, and you can't see it without envisioning how marvelous a crackling fire must be in that room when the snow is falling softly outside.

But Daniele's favorite room is her own "offeeece," as she calls it, a little room tucked on the balcony over the living room that you get to by climbing a narrow wooden spiral staircase. It's known in the Killy villa as Daniele's room, and it's crammed with pictures, records, paintings, letters, pressed flowers, souvenirs, ballet shoes, recipes, and knickknacks of all sizes and shapes. "This is where I work. In my offeece I handle all the mail—even the letters from the girls, yes? [Referring to Jean-Claude's female fans.] I don't bother to read the silly messages . . . I just send them an autographed picture of him and drop their letters in the waste basket. That is how Daniele Killy handles the problem of jock lovers. But publicly she smiles and asks innocently, "Groupies? What are groupies? We don't have those problems in Europe!"

Like all Frenchwomen, she finds clothes important. Daniele likes casual clothes, but they must be elegant, and she always buys in Paris. "I like classic things. I think the two most important things in fashion are quality of material and classic style. I love furs, but I think like Coco Chanel: Furs are good for linings." Daniele's friends claim she has lots of fur linings! However, she appears at posh ski resorts and ski meets with her furs showing! A fox jacket, a chinchilla hat and muff that make her look like a Russian princess, or a black fur cape. You'll never find her in a conventional mink coat.

With a Spanish couple running the household, Daniele is free to ski, shop in Paris, or travel with her husband. She does very little entertaining at home. "We know a lot of people, but for the moment we are selfish. We are very private, closing the world out. We want it that way for a while. We are enjoying each other—our own little family, our love, our fights, our making up. . . . Just to lie in bed and do nothing is great. It is enough!"

Living with Jean-Claude the superstar is both rewarding and difficult. "It is not hard for me to live in the shadow of his limelight. I was a movie star once, and I hated the lack of privacy. I'm a very shy person and cannot give myself to the public. I let Jean-Claude have the spotlight. I will take the shade and the privacy. In a family you can't have two in the spotlight—it doesn't work. I do my job . . . I am not jealous of his fame. I am a part of it. . . . We become closer and closer as the years go by. But let me say, at the same time, it is *not easy*. It is not easy because he is the *first* in the world in his sport. That takes discipline. I share that discipline, too—I live it with him. Jean demands a great deal of himself, and he also demands a great deal of me and the children. He wants the children to be like him. A champion! He wants them to excel. I suppose," she went on without much conviction, "that even if they *don't* excel, it's a good way to be brought up."

As you might suspect, Daniele is very European in her attitude about the female sex. About the liberation movement. "Equality for women?" Her eyes narrowed, and her voice became defiant at the incredulous thought. "It's impossible! We *can't* be equal. We are *different!* European women understand this. You can't be a woman and live like a man. Perhaps American women are not happy with their men. A woman is a woman only if she is with a *real* man." She looked at her gold Rolex watch and then pulled out a cigarette from her Hermès handbag and lit it. There were no hangnails or rough edges on her perfectly manicured nails. She waved the match out daintily, then settled back languorously into her chair. "American women are curious and enthusiastic. We are more content. They want to work, and we want to keep our man happy while *he* works." She fingered an enormous white jade bauble on the end of a gold chain. "I think you can have your women's lib movement!"

"Perhaps you haven't caught up yet," I heard myself saying, fascinated with the conversation.

"I hope we never do," she said with a pitying look. "I don't think the American woman understands that there is another way of getting what you want without jeopardizing your own sex. I always do what I want to do, but I've learned *how* to do it. It has nothing to do with being aggressive and strong. You never, never win by being aggressive," she said emphatically.

"Never?" I asked, mesmerized.

"Never!" she repeated seriously. "The most important thing to know is to know your place— *Savoir rester à sa place*, find your own place in the world and keep it!"

"But what of your ballet, your acting career . . . the way, uh, you Frenchwomen go after what you want—go after a man. What about sports? Isn't there a time when it's good to be aggressive?"

"Ah, sports. Of *course* there are times," she conceded, "there are times for men. But for a woman, for the most part it is bad. There are ways, of course, to be aggressive. Sometimes, for a woman, not to move is to be aggressive. Like Elizabeth the First of England, *comprenez*?"

Daniele has her own opinions about money, too, and they suit her personality perfectly. "The more money you have, the more problems! You have to find the right place . . . where you have enough . . . and *stay* there!"

"You mean," I said, eyeing her beautiful clothes and jewelry, "set a limit for yourself?"

"Yes, of course! However, if you like something, you shouldn't think of money!" (This last contradictory bit of information was the best advice I received from a total of forty interviews.)

The Killys, however, think about money a great deal, and if there's a limit they've set for themselves, it's the sky. Jean-Claude is so busy pitching, endorsing and promoting products, that it, not skiing, has become a way of life and full-time job. Daniele has been accompanying him for the past few years on this promotional odyssey which has taken him to some pretty remote spots in search of more dollars. I mean, what is a dashing, debonair champion skier and his beautiful wife doing in Slatyfork, West Virginia, if they've set a limit for themselves in earning money? They're earning more, that's what they're doing. Jean-Claude came to America in the spring of '75 to promote a ski resort called Snowshoe in Slatyfork, West Virginia (skiing in West Virginia?), and Daniele tagged along. It wasn't so bad. She got to stop over in New York for a few days and shop at Bergdorf Goodman's, where she picked up a few of those yummy things she *really* liked and therefore didn't have to worry about how much they cost.

I was surprised at how much money a superstar could make commercializing his name. Killy promotes shirts in America (Arrow), ski resorts here and abroad, K-2 skis, a line of Killy clothing worldwide and a separate line of ski clothing in Canada, Rolex watches, which explained the expensive model ($2,500) on Daniele's wrist. He's affiliated with a ski boot company and also a ski binding company (named Navada). His American agent, Michael W. Halstead, said that 80 percent of Killy's six-figure income is earned from promotional work, endorsements, and licensing his name for use on various products. The remaining 20 percent is return on international investments. If he competes in races (he hasn't done any racing since 1973, when he won the world professional ski championship), his income, his agent informed me, is naturally supplemented by his prize money. Naturally.

All this promoting doesn't seem to leave much time for anything else, and that includes their social life. The Killys know all the Beautiful People in the world and socialize with almost none of them. They bump into Jackie and Helen Stewart fairly often since they're neighbors, but Helen is too social-minded for Daniele, who feels more comfortable with her less famous low-keyed friends in Geneva. While everyone imagines that the Killys go from Marie Hélène Rothschild's famous Paris parties to the palace at Monte Carlo, they are more apt to be found in St. Paul, Minnesota, at the home of the Tom Kressbachs, whom they've known and skied with for five years. But their favorite friends are Rod and Mary Laver of the tennis world. There's a great exchange of talent in this foursome. Jean-Claude instructs Mary in skiing, Mary instructs Daniele in golf, Rod instructs Jean-Claude in tennis, and Daniele instructs them all in how not to be aggressive. Once the four of them raced down the mountain, and Daniele, who is an excellent skier, was furious when Jean-Claude won. "Couldn't you have let me finish first just once?" she pouted. Except for these old friends, Daniele claims they've dropped out of the social world for reasons of "love and health."

Heiress-artist Gloria Vanderbilt once said, "Fame you earn has a different taste from the fame that is forced on you." On that subject Daniele is incredibly nonchalant. "I've had both kinds, his and mine, and I have no anxiety about either." She doesn't seem to have much anxiety about anything. This serious, opinionated, sometimes humorless French girl has a confidence that can almost match her smile. It's overwhelming. And nowhere is it more evident than when she speaks of how she feels when she watches her husband compete in a race. "They always ask me am I nervous. Why should I be nervous? I feel he can't lose. I'm confident in him! He made me confident in him, and he can't disappoint me—that is a big responsibility!"

I smiled at her, and she smiled back. She knew I was questioning her answer. Her smile said, "I am different from the other wives, *n'est-ce pas?*"

"I would like to clear something," she said, adjusting her knitted cap, a signal she was ready to leave, "In America, many of the wives who are married to famous athletes are, uh, hopelessly lost in their husbands' strong personalities. They are living *for* a man. I am living *with* a man. That is the basic difference between European and American attitudes. If you live with a man, not for a man, you . . . *vous n'avez pas la sensation d'être dirigée,* you never have the feeling of being under a man's control."

Just then the phone rang. It was her husband calling to tell her to get packin'—they had to go to Slatyfork. She didn't waste any more words telling me how she wasn't under a man's control. She got packin'! *Comprenez?*

Several weeks later, I decided to check out Daniele's good friend Mary Laver in California. I called and was told she'd see me, but only briefly, because she was up to her eyeballs in high finance.

The Brains Behind the Racket

There's a price to pay for everything, and the price I'm paying is high. I'm lonely as hell. I don't see much of Rod. Out of the three hundred sixty-five days of the year, I'm lucky if I see him sixty of those days.

When I got to the house, a slight, sandy-haired man in shorts and sport shirt was watering the lawn. He was more sunburned than tan, and I took him to be the yardman. After Yazi, I should have been wary of this particular mistake.

"I'm Rod Laver," he said, and I thought, *You could have fooled me.*

When I told him who I was and what I wanted, he said, "She's inside in the office. I'll show you."

He left me standing outside the small room, saying, "Please excuse me. I've got work to do."

I went on in and came upon a scene I don't expect you to believe. Mary Laver* was the picture of the "wheeler-dealer" stereotype—with interesting modifications. She was seated at a desk hidden under piles of papers, files, and ledgers. She was talking on the telephone to someone named Sara. "It's only a twenty-five-thousand-dollar investment," she was saying. "I don't want to tie up the whole week with it. . . . It's as good a place for twenty-five thousand dollars as any, interest rates acting so crazy and the market so uncertain. . . . I'm not going to bother Rod with this. Let's just get the thing going and quit horsing around."

She looked up at me for the first time and acted as though we were old friends. She nodded to a chair and shrugged as if to say, "Sorry to burden you with this."

I was in no hurry. I was trying to absorb what I was witnessing, and I needed more time. Mary was deeply tanned over as much of her body as I could see, and I could see plenty because she wore only shorts and a halter. But it would take a while for you to notice because she had a big, unlit cigar in her mouth, chewing it as a big-time wheeler-dealer would.

Well, I said to myself, *this isn't going to be one of your routine interviews, anyway. What I have here is a character.*

As it turned out, she was, but not the kind I thought at first.

*Rod Laver, professional tennis player. Laver is known as one of the greatest tennis players of all time. He is one of only two players to win a grand slam in one year (Wimbledon, Forest Hills, France, Australia). Laver did it twice, once in 1962, when he was still an amateur, and again in 1969. In 1970 Laver won thirteen championships and $204,000. In 1974 he played Jimmy Connors in a $200,000 challenge match over nationwide TV.

The Lavers live in a beautiful house, covering six thousand square feet of floor space, plenty of room for three even if one of them is five (Rickie). It's full of angles, decks, patios, and spacious sunny rooms, all open to the outdoors. Beautiful as the house is, to Mary, it's just their home, nothing worth bragging about. When she hung up and we got through our preliminary greetings, she said in a tone designed to discourage me, "You don't want to see the house, do you?"

She went through the place as though it were on fire and then rushed me immediately out to the patio, where we could see the ocean instead. In this respect I found Mary refreshingly unlike the other wives who took so much pride and time in giving house tours, pointing out special significances of each piece of furniture, painting, and trophy.

Nature bloomed everywhere inside and out. Daisies, dahlias, marigolds, columbines, bougainvilleas and others, and Mary is one of those gardeners who talk to their plants. While I was trying to find out about her, I was charmed and distracted to overhear one of her intimate conversations with a white star jasmine. She clucked over that plant, soothed it, and encouraged it, while plucking dead leaves from its limbs and damning the dry weather.

While she was doing that, I had a chance to observe her closely. My impressions were mixed and cloudy. I wondered whether they would clear before I left. She's not a woman who provokes a second look, but there's an inner beauty that's hard to describe. It makes Mary highly attractive and likable. She's a green-eyed brunette of medium height, somewhere in her late thirties. Her face is not without a few lines. Her intellect has surfaced on her features, but her radiance resides in her spirit. She is merry, outspoken, slightly zany, opinionated, and totally self-possessed. She did not stop growing in deference to her husband's burgeoning fame. She's at least as responsible for the Laver successes as he is, and Rod knows it. He couldn't be out there swinging his racket 300 days a year if he didn't know Mary was keeping watch over everything else. When Rod was preparing himself for the headline match with Jimmy Connors, Mary didn't have to disturb him with irritating, worrisome business problems. She took care of everything so he could train and play, with nothing more to worry about than the match itself.

As we sprawled on deck chairs in the warm sun and sipped iced tea, one of Mary's favorite drinks, she talked about her life.

Mary Benson Laver grew up in Sycamore, Illinois ("a little bitty town where there is absolutely nothing to do"), and Rod Laver was born in the equally tiny town of Gladstone, Queensland, Australia, but they managed to meet, fall in love, and get married. Now they hardly ever see each other anymore.

It's the same old story. He has to travel because he plays tennis for a living, and she, mostly, has to stay home because of Rickie and because she tends to the Laver business empire. That's what it has become. She has made it that, and it's been a full-time job for her.

There's the Laver-Ford Tennis Company, which is currently building a tennis city complex; Laver-Emerson Enterprise, a structured tennis holiday agency for adults; the Laver-Emerson tennis camps, scattered around the country, and all kinds of investments, mainly real estate, but also racket clubs for businessmen and the production of film strips for schools and educational documentaries for television and any other possible moneymakers. Rod's partner is Roy Emerson, another tennis star from Australia. Less than three years after the tennis enterprise began, it was grossing an estimated $2,500,000 a year.

Rod makes the investment capital with his racket (tennis, that is), and she causes it to multiply like the grains of sand on the beach. They each have an end to hold up, and Mary considers her end as heavy as his.

"A tennis career is like summer lightning. A quick, bright flash, and it's gone. We want a good life when it's over." Rod is putting up the lightning. The good life is Mary's department.

She's had some training. She got a job with an accounting firm between marriages (this is her second) and attended Orange Coast College in California, where she majored in business and accounting. She also has help from International Management, the large agency that handles rich people's money. Sara Cheheyl, the Sara that Mary was talking with on the phone when I arrived, is the financial supervisor assigned to the Laver account. But Sara is in Cleveland, and Mary is at Corona Del Mar, California, and Mary is not the type to let others handle her money without supervision, so she keeps the telephone wires hot between them.

Mary does all the creative business work, while Sara offers guidance. Mary doesn't actually run the Laver business enterprises—she's more the executive type. But she gets right in there when she needs to. For instance, when the tennis camps opened in Houston, she went down there for four weeks to make sure the camp managers were on the ball. She kept track of how much financing they'd need for promotions, publicity, and stock for the pro shops. She made sure the ordered merchandise came in on time and was displayed properly. Mary has a reputation for being tough but honest in her business dealings.

She stays on top of the financial situation in the world, studies the market and guides the Laver cash flow. When Rod wins, say $25,000 in a match, she takes the money and decides what to do with it. Rod approves it. Only on really big deals does she consult him in advance, not because she's chicken—she feels, as an equal partner, that he should have a vote once in a while.

She admits she's not much good with figures. "I use a machine like everybody else. Can't add two and two. But my background helps, and I've got a pretty good head for it."

Mary says it's great to have her own career and feel an important part of the team, but it does keep her apart from Rod.

"I go with him when I can, but these past two years I've had to stay home and do my thing, what I'm good at. I can't run our operation, our home and child and be with Rod at the same time. There's a price to pay for everything, and the price I'm paying is high. I'm lonely as hell. I don't see much of Rod. Out of the three hundred sixty-five days in the year, I'm lucky if I see him sixty of those days. He travels all the time. Remember, other sports like basketball and football have seasons. There's a tennis tournament every week of the year."

Mary Laver is nothing if not practical. Take, for instance, the swimming pool. She doesn't have one.

"We've got the Pacific Ocean in our backyard," she explained logically.

Which she has. The Laver house is on the cliffs of Corona Del Mar in southern California, looking down on the surf crashing against the rocks far below. "Anyway, I hate swimming pools," she said.

It's not as though she couldn't have one if she wanted it. There was a pool at the house when the Lavers bought it. She had it filled in and sodded so that Rickie could have someplace to play. And how does Master Rickie show his appreciation?

He complains that all his friends have pools at their homes and why can't he have one, too? Mary tells him, "Look, if you really want a pool, grab a shovel and dig yours up." He thinks his mother is kidding him.

Take, for instance, the tennis court. She doesn't have one of those either. What! Her husband a world tennis champion and no court at home?

"Look at it this way," says Mary with irreproachable pragmatism. "Rod plays tennis for a living. It's his job, and the tennis court is his office. Why would he want to bring his work home with him? And besides, when you live on the ocean, land sells by the inch and a tennis court would cost a couple of million dollars."

That's an exaggeration of course, but the soundness of her argument is unshakable. It wasn't until much later that I realized that others who make a business of tennis have tennis courts at home and I should have asked about that. But it was too late. That's the kind of woman Rod Laver has hanging around the house.

"It's really bugged a lot of people, our not having a court. The funny thing is that Rod has gone from the world's worst court to none at all. In Gladstone, where he grew up, his family was poor, but like everybody else in Australia, they loved tennis. So they cleared away an area, put up chicken wire for a net, and every day they had to shovel out the anthills in order to play. He says he grew up on bad bounces."

Mary went back into the house to get us some more iced tea, and I thought how nice it would feel swimming around in the sea below and how fortunate Mary was to have such a home and how good tennis could be to those who played it well. I wondered whether she'd forgotten what it was like to have nothing and whether she appreciated her good luck.

"I suppose you want to know what it's like being married to Rod," she said when she returned with the icy glasses of tea. "That's your reason for coming out here to talk to me. I can't imagine why else you'd come. First, let me tell you that I'm sick of being asked that, and with that out of the way, I'll tell you."

There was nothing for me to do but listen. *At least she's direct*, I thought, and noted that it would be no fun tangling with her on a business deal.

"A lot of wives I know, married to famous sports figures, go through the perfunctory, glowing propaganda about how beautiful it all is. They tell about how dashing, sexy, loving, family-minded, humble, talented, and super their husbands are, what a superlife it is. I don't live on that level of illusion. I love the man, and we have a good marriage, but it's not a superlife. Let's face it, I'm alone a lot. Tennis interferes with my life."

Maybe it was the way she said it, without rancor. But it sounded as though she didn't mind all that much. She might have if she were sitting at home minding the baby and cleaning house, but she had a real career. So when she said she was lonely, I had the feeling that it was the way Rod would say it if I had asked him about traveling from tournament to tournament almost every day of his life.

"I like being the center of attention myself once in a while," she said, and I reminded her that she had been when Rickie was born and she scoffed.

"No way."

I settled back to listen, but I felt I knew the story before she told it. I was right.

"There was this TV set in the labor room. I wasn't watching because I had a little show of my own going on at the time, but there sat Rod and my obstetrician, ignoring me and my pains, their eyes glued to the screen. Stan Smith was playing Pancho Gonzalez. The doctor was a tennis nut, wouldn't you know it? I'm losing my audience, so I start to groan. Not a tumble do I get. Nothing. So I groan a little louder. They're annoyed because I'm interfering with the sound. 'I think it's going to three sets,' Rod shouts all excited to the doctor. Then he turns to me, cool as ice and has the nerve to ask if I can hold out for one more set. You want to know what it's like being married to a tennis champion? *That's* what it's like."

"Well?" I asked suspensefully.

"Well what?"

"Did you?"

"Did I?"

"Hold out for another set for heaven's sake?"

"Oh. No, of course not. Richard Rodney Laver wasn't taking a backseat to no Stan Smith or Pancho Gonzalez. Neither was I."

Mary and Rod are not at all alike really. Which is not unusual for superstar athletes and their wives, or any married couple. Mary doesn't play tennis much and is not particularly good at it. And as if she and Rod weren't separated enough because of tennis, she had to pick a sport like skiing to keep them even farther apart. You don't play tennis in the snow, and you don't ski in the hot, dry sun. Still, you can't take a woman's skiing away from her if that's what she likes. Mary has been at it for fifteen years and not just fooling around. She's had the benefit of Jean-Claude Killy's coaching. Mary confirmed what Daniele had already told me. Killy just happens to be one of the Lavers' best friends. He and Rod were both sickly weaklings as children, and both were poor. They succeeded against all odds, and Mary says both are charming men.

"For years I just took off while Rod was away and skied alone. Why shouldn't I do my thing? Long ago I decided, you may be the star, baby, but I'm not going to spend my life being impressed. A couple of times when he came home from tournaments I wasn't there. I was in Switzerland or Austria or Aspen. Right? And when we got together with the Killys, Jean-Claude and I would talk about the latest snow conditions or skiing the Hahnenkamm at Kitzbühel. Rod felt out of it, so he decided to take up skiing, too. Now when we can get away, we go skiing together and *I'm* the star, baby."

Mary said that Killy is working on Rod now to help him keep his fanny out of the snow.

Mary admits that Rod may not be an absentee husband much longer because he's slowing down as the gossips claim. She points out that he's thirty-six and "there are new energies, a new generation coming up." She said he's still a tough man to beat, but that they are gradually arranging their affairs so he can retire from the professional ranks "one of these days."

Mary got to thinking back over her husband's career and her part in it. She didn't enter the picture until the summer of 1965, but she talked of Rod's early start in Australia, and she told me something I was to hear again from the wife of another Australian tennis player, John Newcombe: that Australians dominate the game because they play with zest and humor.

"Tennis is so *grim* here," she said.

I had a picture of young Rod stumbling around on his bumpy homemade court in Gladstone, trying to figure out which way the ball was going to bounce and then trying to get it over the chicken wire, and I wondered how this lad from the bottom of the world had arranged to meet and marry the girl from Sycamore.

"Fate. Kismet," explained Mary. "I believe in that. My father owned a grocery store, so we were never hungry, for food that is. But I wanted more than food. I wanted life. I thought I'd found a way to get out of Sycamore by getting married. It got me to California, but in 1959 it also got me a divorce. That wasn't where life was for me."

Then in the summer of 1964 the Jack Bindorffs invited her to the opening of Jack Kramer's new tennis club in Palos Verdes, California. There was to be an exhibition, and Kramer had brought in four Australian players. Rod was one of them. When he finished playing his match, he asked Jack Bindorff who the girl with the aqua dress and deep tan was. A few minutes later Mary went over to Jack and whispered, "Say, is Rod Laver married?" Jack looked in disbelief at Mary's deeply tanned face and at Rod Laver, put down his tennis program, laid his hand over his heart, looked heavenward, and intoned, "Good Lord, this has got to be." It was. They were married a year later. It was Kismet all the way.

Now Mary was thinking about the approaching end to the hectic pro life that would give her back her husband. I'm sure she's looking forward to it, but not without a twinge of sorrow. It's difficult to face the unmistakable signs of age, and age comes calling sooner for athletes who rely on youthful bodies for peak performance. Age falls on a man of action as lightly as snow, but the snow doesn't melt, and suddenly the load grows heavy and the faltering steps are painful.

Mary said that Rod takes care of himself physically. He doesn't drink hard liquor or smoke but he drinks a lot of beer. She was reminded of the time when he was trying to win the grand slam of tennis (the Australian, French, British, and American championships) for the second time. Only two players had ever taken the grand slam: Donald Budge in 1938 and Rod in 1962. No one had ever done it twice. In 1968 Rod thought he would try it.

"I was seven months pregnant," said Mary, "so I didn't travel with him to Australia or France to see him win. But I caught up with him at Wimbledon, where his victory earned him a champagne reception before the Queen's Ball. The press was there from all over the world, pushing and shoving as usual, trying to get his picture or an interview. Outwardly, Rod looked poised with a big smile pasted on his silly face. But inside he was falling apart. He was supposed to give a speech after dinner at the Queen's Ball, and he couldn't remember his lines. Every time he went over them in his head he forgot a little more. So to bolster himself, he gulped down glass after glass of champagne. Now Rod is not a wine drinker, but there was no beer around. I noticed he was starting to act peculiar, but I didn't think too much about it. Then the moment came. He was called to deliver his speech before the royal family and some of the most important dignitaries in Great Britain. I was proud of him. He made no mistakes. Not one flaw. Not once did he stammer or panic. I can still remember it. He said, 'Thank you,' and plopped down in his seat.''

She said the rest of the night was one foggy muddle. Rod, unaccustomed to drinking, dragged her from one bar and discotheque to another trying to route London's entire liquor supply through his digestive tract. She floundered on iced tea, the strongest thing she drinks. Finally, at 6 A.M. he gave up, and they wound up at their hotel.

''He had this crazy notion that cold water would help the searing pain in his head, so he climbed into the bathtub, turned on the water, and promptly went to sleep with his formal evening clothes still on. Just at that moment the phone rang. It was seven o'clock now, and the sun was up. It was a reporter calling all the way from Australia. He wanted an interview with Rod. I told him Rod was out at the moment, which was the truth. The reporter said he had called so early British time to be sure to catch him in. 'How long will he be out?' he wanted to know. He didn't realize how funny it was. I looked over at Rod, crashed out in the tub, and said, 'About six hours I'd say.' ''

Rod recovered sufficiently to swear off champagne for good and go on to win the American championship at Forest Hills and become the first man in history to take the grand slam twice.

Despite the commitments that keep them so much apart, they do manage to socialize on rare occasions—and the parties are rare, to hear Mary tell it. Mostly they have dinner parties, which Mary says are famous but not for the food. For feats of endurance. The parties get started along about 8 P.M. and wind down around 3 A.M. unless somebody still has something left unsaid and voice enough to say it. A lot of dinner parties I know need alcohol as fuel to keep them going past the hors d'oeuvres. But Mary and Rod can keep things exciting for seven hours, about a normal working day, without imbibing. That means they select their dinner guests very carefully, get them very drunk, or there must be something stimulating about the conversation. Liquor is not banned at the parties. Only the Lavers abstain, along with any other teetotalers who might slip into the crowd. What kind of conversation can hold dinner guests until 3 A.M.? Mary was no help there. She gave me topics such as politics, philosophy, sports, and gossip. I noticed she omitted sex, but I'm sure it was an oversight.

I tried to get her to pass along some of the gossip, but she would repeat only her own contributions. Such as:

''Ilie Nastase is unpopular with tennis people, has natural ability, but poor court manners. I find him rude.   .   .   .

"Billie Jean King has done a lot for women's tennis because she's *good*, not because she's a women's libber. She could have done it without all the PR tricks like the Riggs-King match. It took years to bring tennis to its present high level, and in one night she and Bobby Riggs turned it into a circus. Tennis can make it on its own. . . .

"Bobby Riggs is the world's greatest hustler, who has prostituted the game to make a name for himself. . . .

"The woman I admire most today is Jackie Onassis because she has lived in a goldfish bowl and remains strong, with her own convictions. The man I admire most is my husband, as sticky as that may sound."

The Lavers are selective in picking friends. Most are not in the public eye. Not that they don't know a lot of famous people. They simply aren't in the habit of playing them for all they're worth. If they don't like a person, no matter who, that person is not about to get an invitation. If you were to be invited, some of the Lavers' close friends with recognizable names who might be there are Roy and Joy Emerson, Lloyd and Dorothy Bridges, Jim Franciscus, and Charlton Heston. About the latter two, Mary said reverently, "They have really done more for pro tennis than anyone else. They worked to get the pro team going in the days when first prize was three hundred dollars."

Franciscus and Heston have promoted tennis over the years through celebrity matches. Famous showbiz types team up with, or play against, tennis stars, and the fans come out to see their heroes of stage, screen, and TV look silly, get shellacked, or win. It has worked. Tennis has become a respectable sport in this country and now gets an expanded share of the sports pages. No wonder Mary, the business executive, admires those who've put people in the audience and money in the players' pockets.

Mary ranks the celebrity tennis players: "Johhny Carson is playing well; O. J. Simpson is amazing; Bob Evans and Richard Zanuck are competitive. Evans will chew through cement for one more point. Many people think Robert Redford is the best singles player, but my absolute favorite is Bill Cosby. He's the funniest man I've ever met. You wouldn't know it, but he takes the game seriously. Figure it out, at his home he has three courts—grass, clay, and hard. He takes no chances. But to watch him play or, better yet, to play against him, you'd think he was just a clown. All through the game that man will not shut up. I mean he talks a blue streak. Try to beat a guy who has you cracking up most of the time. What a guy! When he plays, he has a big cigar in his mouth, and he keeps doing funny things with it. What a nut!"

"Talk about cigars," I said.

Mary laughed at my shock in seeing her with one in her mouth in her office.

"I chew them when I'm nervous or excited. I don't know why. And the only time I get that way is when I'm handling our businesses or watching Rod play. That's the reason I don't watch him in public anymore. When I do, the television camera or some damned photographer always finds me either pulling at my girdle, tugging at my bra, scratching my nose, or popping a cigar in my mouth. And that's the scene the folks at home see on their television. I dislike the press for that reason. I don't know what people must think of me, so I stay in the hotel when I travel with Rod and watch the match from my bed. There I don't have to be inhibited.

"I'm not superstitious or anything like that, but I own a cowboy hat that's very lucky. I always wear it when Rod plays, whether I'm at the match watching, at home, or in a hotel watching TV. And I'm chewing on my cigar."

A week after our interview Mary Laver went to Las Vegas for the Invitational Tennis Open. The prize was a $21,000 Mercedes-Benz and $30,000 in cash. Mary wanted the Mercedes. She watched the match from her bed at Caesar's Palace, far from the prying eyes of press and cameras, dressed in a nightgown and cowboy hat and the cigar clenched between her teeth, screaming like a banshee, "Sock it to him! Damn! Good shot, Marty [Riessen]! Harder! That's it, Rod!"

I don't know how much the cowboy hat had to do with it, but Mary's driving a new car these days.

Germlish Is Her Language

*Sometimes being married to a professional athlete is fun but mostly no.
. . . There's not a quiet moment. . . . you lose much of your personal life and your privacy . . . you become public property. . . . Oh,
it sounds good when you don't have it . . . but when you do, it's a
pain.*

*I'm insecure about the future. I can never be safe enough. I hate spend-
ing money foolishly.*

One of the few things that really bugs Angelika Newcombe,* tennis star
John Newcombe's wife, is being referred to as tennis star John Newcombe's
wife.

"I'm Angie Newcombe. I make a lot of decisions. Maybe they're small,
but I make them," she said to me in her suite at the Roosevelt Hotel in New
York. It was the ornate presidential suite, and it bothered her because she
doesn't approve of ostentation and wasteful spending. On the contrary, she's
very close with a buck, and she doesn't mind telling you so.

She doesn't need to be, of course, because John makes a very nice living
playing tennis, a living augmented substantially by what envious people like
to describe as "wise investments." But more on that later.

She's strong, this tiny slip of a woman, and darkly beautiful with a wide,
white smile. No fat is permitted to lodge on that body, and the outline of her
bones is clearly visible under the taut skin. She wears her dark hair short, cut
in straight little wisps around her face, testifying to her contempt for hair-
dressers. She wears no makeup, and her enormous green eyes look out on the
world half in amusement and half in apprehension. During the interview she
sat cross-legged in tight, faded jeans and an old T-shirt, hiding behind her
mask, allowing only those eyes alternately to express warmth, reserve, curiosity, fear, and humor.

She's outspoken: "Ilie Nastase is shy or stupid, lacks confidence, or is just
plain dumb. I think he's dumb. He's also a pain. He yells, swears, and complains, trying to throw his opponent off-balance. Instead of doing it with foot-
work, he does it with his mouth.

*John Newcombe, professional tennis player. John Newcombe was ranked first in
the world in 1970 and 1971 and second in the world in 1973 and 1974. Newcombe has
won at Wimbledon three times and at Forest Hills twice. He won the 1974 World
Champion Tennis Singles title and was the third leading money winner in 1974 with
$273,299.

"Bobby Riggs is too much. An old man putting people on, but he's clever with a buck."

Angie is also secure (except when it comes to money), independent, and apparently respected and loved by her husband. Yet she wants no part of Billie Jean King's women's lib movement.

"I don't like her language. It's quite filthy. And I don't like the way she behaves in public. She doesn't behave like a champion," she said.

That's how Angie talks. With her, you always know where you are. And talk about chips, they fly everywhere like sparks from a welder's torch.

In her relationship with husband John, she owns at least 50 percent of the stock and maybe more. John's fame overshadows her as far as the public knows, but she and John and the three children know better. "We are both strong. I don't crawl around in his shadow. I am not impressed with fame, but I *am* proud of John's accomplishments." That's it. What he takes from life does not come out of her portion. She protects her territorial imperative with the ardor of a lioness with cubs.

She's not so independent that she dislikes being married to a star of John's caliber, though, because it is glamorous. What she disapproves of is paying the price of glory. Her parsimony won't permit her to accept what others might consider a fair bargain. In return for the fun and glamor, she says, she must give up peace and privacy. "There's not a quiet moment," she says, echoing the plaint of all other superstar wives. "It sounds good when you don't have it, but when you do, it's a pain."

It's the kind of remark that usually demands a pinch of salt, but Angie looked serious when she said she has had to learn *not* to believe "all that glamour. I never particularly thought of John as glamorous. I'm not in awe of him. He's just my husband, a nice guy who hasn't changed."

I got the distinct feeling that if he ever did decide to change, a common procedure among sports celebrities suffering from rocketlike upward mobility, he'd have one tough tangle with tiny Angie, the *Fräulein* who makes small decisions but makes them stick.

"Why should he change just because he can play tennis well?" she asked. "I think the wife of a great athlete [and despite her insistence that John walk the earth as mortal, she does consider him great] can get crushed when she starts believing that her man is some sort of supergod. When you're famous, you're supposed to be superhuman. That's silly." If she feeds John doses of that philosophy regularly, she is helping relieve the pressure on him, as well as securing her own self-worth, something he probably understands.

After having watched John in action on the court, I realized how accurately Angie analyzed her husband's talents. Angie is one of the few superstar wives who can view their husbands objectively. She says other tennis players have

more natural ability than John but not his concentration. "I think he's the best thinker in tennis. John is using his head all the time." And probably using hers, too, except when he goes on a spending spree.

So far Angie is also one of the few wives who have defeated loneliness. She has a simple solution, temporary though it is and one which won't work for all. She travels with John wherever he goes and takes the kids, too, because the eldest is only six, a condition which is bound to change and cause complications. But for the moment, she lives in two hemispheres and loves it. They spend five months of the year, from November to March, in Australia where it's summer, and then follow the season to a condominium on their tennis ranch in New Braunfels, a German community three miles out of San Antonio, Texas, for the other seven. And of course, they move from one tournament to another. But *dammit!* she has to shell out for this luxury, too. She has to travel, poor thing, and that means packing, flying, and jet lag.

"I never know if it's tomorrow or yesterday. One thing I do know it's *never* today. The kids are up in the middle of the night screaming for breakfast, and often John and I end up sitting in bed playing Scrabble until dawn, and when everyone else gets up to go to work, we're exhausted." Too much!

When she complains of the inconveniences of living and working at opposite ends of the world, it sounds a little like Jackie "O" complaining that her sunglasses are too heavy for the bridge of her nose.

What really worries her, though, is the near future, when the children become too old to pick up and haul from one continent to another, a problem all young sports mothers share. Traveling is bad, but staying home while hubby travels is worse.

"When that happens," she mused, "I suppose I'll be lonely and sex-starved." But that was as far as she was prepared to go on the subject except to pooh-pooh the widely held notion that superathletes are also super bed partners, which should also take a big load off John's mind. As I was to hear again and again, Angie said, "They're just like everybody else. I don't believe in getting into open conversations about our private sex life. It's bad to talk about it because there's a danger of making it artificial when you publicize it."

She wasn't keen on publicizing her pungent attitude toward jock lovers either. Her comments were tight-lipped and pouty. "They don't bother me. I think they're obnoxious." They aren't likely to bother her, not as long as she dogs John's trail and shares his consuming interest in tennis.

Angie has a distinct advantage over nonathletic wives. She met John on the tennis tournament circuit, not as a jock lover but as a performer. Her prowess on the courts had earned her more than passing notice from the aficionados. As a matter of fact, it was while she was competing (and losing) in the International Open Championship of Germany that she was introduced to John, at his insistence. It was 1963, and she'd won a singular honor in her homeland. She was the first junior ever allowed to enter the International Open, where she was competing, for the first time, with the top pros.

At age twelve and string thin, she had been picked by the Tennis Association of Hamburg (her hometown) as the most promising young player in the city. Her prize was free lessons. She would have preferred money, but she wound up on the junior circuit. By the time she was eighteen she was ranked second among juniors in all Germany. She was a long way from being just a pretty *Fräulein* in training to become a *Hausfrau*.

The story of how she met John is ho-hum. After she had lost her match, the captain of the Australian team, having no-telling-what-in-mind, invited her to tea, cakes, and conversation. It was a rainy afternoon, the kind screenwriters are partial to as a setting for romance. John happened along and spoiled the whole thing. He approved of her dark young beauty but disapproved of the boy-girl arrangement, so he shouldered his way into an introduction. Screenwriters have drawn theater-wide yawns with that old B movie chestnut, too. But John and Angie found the plot original and exciting at the time. Nothing happened to foreshadow the love and marriage that would follow, but the two kept bumping into each other on the tennis circuit, and a romance was budding. Not that Angie was aware of it. John was the strong, silent type, and she was young and shy. The proposal came later that year. And that *was* unusual.

They weren't even in the same country. Angie was playing in the Junior Davis Cup matches in Salzburg, Austria. She received a long-distance telephone call. Not from John. From her father, Kurt Pfannenberg, in Hamburg. According to Angie, her father said, "There's a picture of John Newcombe in our local newspaper."

Puzzled, Angie said, "Yes, so what? He's a famous player, known throughout the world."

But her father had all the best lines and knew it and milked his part for all it was worth. "There's a picure of you in his hand."

"Oh?" she breathed, trying to conceal growing fascination.

"Underneath the picture, it says something interesting."

"So what does it say? Tell me, for heaven's sake!"

"It says, 'This German girl is the girl I intend to marry,'" crowed her father triumphantly. Angie was stopped cold. Words stuck in her throat, and her heart was rattling her chest cage. Her father played along with the dramatic pause for as long as he could, then threw in, "Well, this is all news to me."

Angie had caught up with the runaway excitement now. "It's news to me, too," she said, trying to sound thoroughly disinterested. She calmly hung up the phone, and the shriek of delight was heard clearly, much to the alarm of everyone in the tennis club.

The rest is predictable. John and Angie were married in Sydney, Australia, in 1966, in the chapel where John had gone to school. Poor Herr Pfannenberg! He read about that in the newspapers, too.

Angie still plays tennis, and she doesn't mind telling you she's still good enough to make life fairly interesting for John on the courts at home from time to time. Tennis, instead of breaking up this home so far is holding it together in an ever-strengthening bond. It's made to order for families. You bang away at tennis balls, not each other. Not only does it work for the Newcombes, but it is widely recognized. In June, 1975, she and John were named official hosts of Family Tennis Week, a national promotion that achieved gilt-edged respectability despite the official endorsement of the President's Council on Physical Fitness. The purpose of the event was to promote tennis as a family sport, and the Newcombes were chosen as its symbols. John told interviewers at that time that he frequently takes on his son, Clint, who is six years old, and rather than try to badger him into improvement, he simply concentrates on keeping the ball in play, making it as easy as possible for Clint to keep hitting it. John said he misses often enough to encourage the boy and sometimes arranges to lose. "The idea is to keep it fun," he said. Not a bad kind of old man to have. No mystique of indestructability, just a man who happens to play tennis better than most. To Clint, a decent kind of chap who's hard to beat though not unbeatable. To three-year-old Tanya and the infant, Gi-Gi (Jeanette), life is a merry-go-round which has not gotten rocky yet.

Although they spend less than half the year there, home to the Newcombes is a secluded house they built thirty minutes outside Sydney.

"I like Australia best," she said. "The people are real. Life is real. Australians have the best sense of humor and are probably much like the early settlers in America; they work hard and play hard. They're not the most fashionable, but then, American men are the world's worst dressers. Such baggy pants. And the women all look like they've just come from the hairdresser's." I couldn't divine from her inscrutable face whether I was the inspiration for that remark, and I decided it would not be profitable to pursue it.

Angie describes the house as "bastard Spanish." It has white stucco walls, iron grillwork, a tile roof, dart boards, Ping-Pong tables, a billiard table, a football game, backgammon, checkers, one entire wall reserved for bat ball, a popular Australian game, trophies (his *and* hers), a sauna, and a few straggly pieces of furniture apologetically scattered about as an afterthought. That's inside.

Outside, the grounds are primitive and overgrown with undergrowth and gum trees, except for the inevitable swimming pool and tennis court.

Guests seeking country peace and quiet could find more of it in a steel mill. When the Newcombes are at home, the place is usually crawling with friends and neighbors, all shouting, laughing, and competing. All those games are going on at once, and not a willing loser in the place. Each has the kind of self-confidence that requires a little something on the outcome to support it.

"Australians are big on betting," says Angie as though they had discovered it. "Not in large amounts, mind you, but always something."

And to be fair, handicaps are administered. For instance, when Archie, a neighbor, plays John at tennis, which he does often, John plays left-handed, and to keep the game interesting, they bet lottery tickets which sell for fifty cents apiece. John has a trunkful of lottery tickets and blisters on his left hand.

Because of this national proclivity for gambling, says Angie, Australian athletes learn how to play hard and to win and lose gracefully. I know a few incurable American gamblers, and most of them have learned to be graceful part of the time—when they win. So gambling alone would not explain good sportsmanship but might clear up the emphasis on playing to win. It goes without saying that when John plays in serious competition, he is not shooting for second place. And in the stands, Angie puts on a Sphinx face but seethes inside.

"I can tell you I have cramps inside. I'm in a knot! My concentration, every cell in my body, is with him when he plays."

The stakes these days are high; winning can mean thousands of dollars in the bank—and for Angie there's no such thing as enough dollars in the bank. She insists, however, that the money is not uppermost in John's mind when he plays. "A champion thinks only of winning, being the best. He gives the same concentration to a game whether the stakes are a fifty-cent lottery ticket or $100,000."

Skepticism must have registered on my face because she hurried to clarify her statement. "Tennis is John's living, of course, and he must win the prizes to survive as a professional, so money is enticing. Tennis players are not different from anyone else."

Now my face must have said, "That's more like it," because she plunged into: "But when you're out there in front of a massive audience, playing someone who's your equal, maybe better, your concentration would be the same no matter what the prize. Pride is also at stake."

As she talked, she fingered a choker made of Indian beads and fishing swivels around her throat. She said it was a good-luck charm and she always wore it. It was given to her by the young son of a friend.

"It's the only piece of jewelry I ever wear," she said.

Athletes, like sailors and gamblers, are wildly superstitious. Scholars denigrate superstition as the product of ignorance, fear of faithlessness, foolishness, weakness, and melancholy. Yet, to a greater or lesser degree, we all are heir to it. Sailors and gamblers are superstitious because they routinely deal with forces that defy control and reason—the wind, sea, the toss of the dice.

Athletes are not so helpless in their sports but have a healthy respect for chance. In John's case, says Angie confidentially, it's baked beans. "He always eats them before he plays. He loves them hot or cold and sometimes for breakfast."

She swears it's how he gets his energy to withstand the grueling challenge of a tough competitor in the murderous afternoon sun.

Angie has a Buster Keaton straight face. What she said could be true: John Newcombe wouldn't be the first jock with crazy notions. She was waiting for the obvious question which every unwary sucker apparently couldn't resist; I fell just like the rest. Don't beans release gas during the digestive process? She was so delighted to have the fish rise to the bait, it was worth the humiliation to see it.

"But of course," she fairly shouted. "Why do you think he's so fast on the court? Jet propulsion!"

And why do you think he always wears pink shirts when he plays? she went on. "It's his lucky color!"

She told how he came to the U.S. Open Tournament in Forest Hills once, and as was his practice, he brought along a dozen pink shirts. Enough, he figured, to get him through the tournament successfully, if he should win. Of course, he was counting on Angie to see to their laundering as he sweated and soiled them up. She was happy enough to contribute to the cause of victory and the Newcombe exchequer that she retained a laundry service.

"It was the language barrier," she explained, referring to her proclivity for mixing up the English language. "Before he got to the semifinals, I had the maid take them out to be laundered, and they were due back that morning. So, when John asked me where his pink shirts were, I said 'gone' meaning out being laundered. John didn't get a little edgy—he freaked out. After yelling at me a lot, he bolted out of the hotel to a store and came back with a dozen new pink shirts. By the time he and his anger and twelve new shirts returned the twelve original pinks were back all fresh and clean. He ended up with twenty-four pink shirts for one match!"

If you see John Newcombe playing without a pink shirt on, you know that Angie's in a lot of trouble!

Angie has no real problem with English. Anyone who wants to understand her can. She and her children speak what she calls "Germlish." It's a mixture of German, Australian-Engish, and Texan (the New Braunsfels influence). It's only entirely accessible in New Braunsfels, where Germlish is the native tongue.

The German influence on Angie's personality remains strong despite years of Australian and American orientation. It goes back to her birth and early years in post World War II Germany.

Magdeburg had the unparalleled ill luck to be bombed in quick succession by the RAF and the U.S. Air Force toward the last days of the war in the spring of 1945 and, also, to be in East Germany.

Two months later Frau Elizabeth Pfannenberg gave birth to a daughter whom she symbolically named "Angelika" in bomb-shattered Magdeburg Hospital's only room that remained intact. Kurt Pfannenberg, the father, was a German officer, held prisoner by the Russians at the time, and knew nothing of it.

At the war's end Germany was divided, and Magdeburg fell into the Soviet Zone, where living was hard, especially in the winter. Short of food, money, medicine, and adequate shelter, the frantic mother and small daughter left the city and joined friends who had a little house in the country. What living they had was eked out of the soil. Finally, when Kurt's release was imminent, a cunning plot was devised for the Pfannenbergs to escape to West Germany. Frau Pfannenberg and her imprisoned husband worked out the details through the use of a secret code transmitted via the mails that baffled the censors. When Kurt was released, he made his way to a predetermined point on the German border where his family joined him. With the help of experienced friends a daring plan—the kind that often ended in failure and even death for many German families—was executed, and the Pfannenbergs were slipped safely across the border and made their way to Hamburg.

The first home Angie can remember was an apartment house in Hamburg with no doors. "The whole building was made from the remains of a bombed-out building, so the bricks and materials were scorched and ugly. We slept on mattresses on a cement floor."

Now she has more than she needs, much more, but her values were determined in those perilous childhood years and haven't changed. They are not those of typically nouveau riche sports skyrockets. Glamor is not Angie's style. She has succeeded in weeding it out of the Newcombes' life with only casual transgressions by John, who is by nature a spendthrift. (World War II wasn't a big deal in Australia.)

She wouldn't go into detail, but times improved slowly for the Pfannenbergs, and they joined the Hamburg Tennis Club, where the whole family played together. The seeds of a lifetime and life-style were sown.

Angie is the worrying kind. Even when money is rolling in from John's winnings, investments in profitable tennis camps, and the promotion of tennis rackets and clothing, she broods about inflation getting so bad that people may not have enough money left to spend on tennis.

"I guess I'm just that way because I'm German, insecure about the future. I can never be safe enough. I hate spending money foolishly." Her definition of foolish spending, girls, is on fancy clothes, makeup, jewels, and household furnishings. "I think the prices in America are ridiculous. I still think in German marks—four marks to the dollar—so, to find out what I'm *really* paying for something here, I multiply it by four, and it always comes out too expensive!"

Angie Newcombe and Mary Laver have something in common besides both being married to world-famous tennis stars. They both are concerned about money. Mary's worries drive her to fulltime investment counseling for the Laver-Emerson empire, and Angie's worries make her keep tight rein on Newcombe overspending, a disease many celebrities seem afflicted by. I don't know if this is a common trait among tennis pro wives because I spoke with only two—most of the big stars being single or unavailable. And I didn't think Larry King would fit the category, though it's interesting to note that he too is very preoccupied with Billie Jean's earnings.

Unfortunately for Angie's heightened sense of thrift, John "spends money like crazy if something strikes him." She said they don't buy gifts for each other very often, but every now and then, "when he remembers," she'll get an expensive handbag or something she wouldn't *think* of buying for herself. Apparently, it's all right as long as the cash doesn't actually pass through her hands to the sales clerk. "One Christmas I got a solid mahogany baby grand piano. You want to know why? The only store open at eight P.M. on Christmas Eve was a music store. John had been playing a tennis match, and by the time it was over [he had won, of course] it was eight o'clock at night. He'd forgotten it was Christmas until almost too late. . . . He had also forgotten that no one in the family plays the piano!"

At this point in our interview Angie revealed that John and his agent made most of the financial decisions, and unlike Mary Laver, who is the brains behind the Laver operation, she didn't interfere. "When it comes to money, I am the saver, not the spender, but I make a lot of other decisions. Maybe they're small, but I make them just the same!"

"I make the decisions! You are a follower!" John mimicked in a heavy German accent from the other room. "I am your leader. You Chur-mans were made to follow!" He came out of a door, tennis racket in hand and took a couple of playful swipes at her. This was followed by a pillow-throwing contest and squeals of laughter. I was reminded of a couple of bear cubs while I watched them.

And the comparison wasn't all that wide of the mark. During the 1974 U.S. Open at Forest Hills, John almost killed Angie. By accident, of course. One rainy afternoon the match was postponed and the Newcombes made their way back to their suite at the Roosevelt Hotel in New York. Angie decided to take a shower. She undressed and ran the water, only to discover it was cold. She left it running, closed the door, and went into the kitchen to fix a cup of tea until it got hot.

Meanwhile, John also stripped in preparation for a shower and went to the bathroom. Through the closed door he could hear the water running and assumed his wife had beaten him to it. Not bothering to put on a robe, he wandered into the living room to read a magazine. As he passed the kitchen, he heard noises inside. What normally would have been taken for innocent kitchen-type sounds became suspicious and menacing—New York can do that. Quickly he picked up one of the heavy chairs that belonged to the baroque presidential suite and crashed through the swinging kitchen door, counting heavily on the surprise factor to give him the edge.

Angie says she'll never forget looking up over her teacup and seeing this naked madman coming at her with murder in his eye. She said she saw the vicious expression on his face slowly change to recognition, disaster narrowly averted. Between the two of them, the only sign of decorum was Angie's little finger daintily hooked over the teacup. The shock over, they collapsed on the floor in gales of laughter while the shower water, now hot, continued to flow unheeded.

Three days later, in that same suite, our interview was interrupted by phone calls from all over the world. Angie talked to her callers in German, Aussie, American slang, and Germlish. John was in the bedroom throughout, and although he only came in once to tease Angie, there was a lot of yelling back and forth between the bedroom and living room.

"It's a phony world here," she said. "People in America don't say what they mean. 'You must come and spend a weekend with us in the country,' someone will say to me. They don't mean it. You're never invited. For instance, *you* invited me to lunch today. You said, 'We'll have lunch while we talk.' Well, here it is four o'clock in the afternoon, and no lunch!"

Startled, I looked at my watch. "Gosh, I forgot," I apologized. Angie grinned at my discomfort.

"But don't you remember," I said, "you asked me if I would like a cup of coffee when I first arrived and I said yes. That was hours ago and no coffee."

"Oh, my God," she wailed. "I *knew* I had water boiling for some reason."

"You were boiling water? Why didn't you call room service?"

"Too expensive," she said. "I've brought along instant coffee. It saves a lot of money."

Tennis wives, if Mary Laver and Angie Newcombe were typical, seemed a happier lot than football, race car, or baseball wives. Now it was time to find out how the golf wives fared, and my first call was to the wife of the Golden Bear.

"Come on down," said the surprisingly warm and friendly voice of Barbara Nicklaus. "I'd be happy to see you if you don't mind a minor interruption now and then."

Probably the only fabrication Barbara has ever uttered in her whole life was that the interruption was going to be minor.

The Organization Girl

Golf? It just never grabbed me. I really don't enjoy it. For me, tennis is a better game.

Jack has said to me, "For God's sake, come out on the eighteenth green and show you care." I do care, but I can't show it in public.

Lost Tree Village is a carefully manicured private community at the north end of Lake Worth in North Palm Beach, Florida. If you don't like golf, you probably wouldn't want to live there.

Luxurious homes and condominiums are tucked in and around the Lost Tree Golf Course, and the putting green grass covers everything but the water. Somehow it seems appropriate that Jack and Barbara Nicklaus* live there. It also seems appropriate that they bought the next-door lot and turned it into a private putting green with a bunker for Jack to practice his sand shots.

Lost Tree Village's claim to fame is Jack Nicklaus. The guard at the gate (it's extremely well protected) can't remember where anyone else lives without referring to his chart, but he points with pride to the Nicklaus home: "It's the big one . . . straight ahead!" It's a big one all right—a sprawling white stone contemporary with six bedrooms, six baths, numerous dens, playrooms, family rooms, a swimming pool, a whirlpool, sauna, dock and motor yacht, a garage full of wine (a hobby), go-carts, bicycles, baseball bats and golf clubs, and the *pièce de résistance*—a huge convertible grass tennis court which becomes a golf course or football field by simply pushing aside the mobile net.

Their house is a community within a community. There's Momma and Poppa Bear and five children under twelve: Jackie, Jr., who's an excellent golfer; Steven Charles, baseball is his game; Nancy Jean, a T ball star; Gary Thomas, who is five and into everything; and Michael Scott, the ten-month-old baby, who likes to drink the dog's water.

Life in and around the house is forever changing and moving like a current. People flow in and out. Day help comes and goes; gardeners work on the lawn; a repairman fiddles with the air-conditioning. In the game room two young black girls fold diapers and stack them on a nearby billiard table.

---

*Jack Nicklaus, professional golfer. By winning the 1975 Masters and PGA tournaments Nicklaus has accumulated the incredible total of 16 major tournament wins (five Masters, two British Open, 3 U.S. Open, four PGA victories and two U.S. Amateurs), which is more than any other golfer has managed, and he has won more money than anyone in the game ($2,243,623) and came in first in golf winnings again in 1975. The Golden Bear is the odds-on favorite to win every tournament that he enters.

Someone is always just waking up or going to sleep or coming home from school. The kitchen is the busiest place in the house, with the Nicklaus kids and their friends hitting the cookie jar every five minutes. The reason I noticed was I was hitting the cookie jar myself, after sampling the one Barb gave me with my coffee. I was on my fourth when someone yelled that the baby was in the dog's dish. I looked down on the floor, and sure enough, Michael Scott was slurping up the dog's water. One of the maids appeared and swooped him up as the poodle barked ferociously at its dwindling water supply.

In a moment of calm I had a chance to examine the bulletin board and review the various schedules for schools, Cub Scouts, Girl Scouts, gymnastics, PTA, golf tournaments, and the driving pool for three different little leagues. It's hard to say whether Barbara should get a gold star for mothering or chauffeuring, but her schedule would kill the strongest athlete.

It nearly killed me. Trying to have a discussion with Barbara any time is difficult, but after 3 P.M. it's sheer madness. Nan goes to gymnastics at 3:30 P.M. then it's back to the house to pick up Gary and take him to swimming lessons at 4. There's not really time enough to go home because Nan has to be picked up at the gym at 4:30 and taken to the ball park, where she has T ball practice.

By now you can't help feeling weak. One minute you're freezing to death in an air-conditioned car and the next, panting under the sweltering Florida sun. However, no need to mop your brow—it's time to go back and pick up Gary, because after swimming lessons he, too, has T ball practice, but at a different ball park. "He belongs to a different league," his mother explained as we continued on our frantic course. I thought of asking her why they didn't join the same league, but it seemed futile. It also seemed a trifle inane to ask Barbara what kind of life *she* leads—a question I crossed off my list. Anyway, there wasn't time, because we still had to get over to the golf club and pick up Jackie, Jr., and then get back to the ball parks and pick up the T ball players. And then she had to rush home and feed the baby and be prepared for a call from Jack which might end the day with ten people coming for dinner. Wild. Every day four children going in four different directions at four different times and the fifth child at home drinking the dog's water.

Barb's image might be that of "Little Mother," but her looks belie it. Only thirty-four years old and a size eight after five children, she looks as if she belonged to that sporty set of millionaires who live and play in Palm Beach because it's famous for parties and golf. Her casual clothes have that expensive air (her ash-blond hair is streaked from the Florida sun, nothing about Barbara comes from the bottle), and she can find a car in their driveway to go with every outfit if she wants. But she's a different breed from the rich and superrich women at the other end of Lake Worth. She's a super homemaker with a sunny disposition and a chatty, easy way about her.

At first I thought the only thing I was going to get out of this interview was a Little League schedule and a migraine, but Barbara turned out to be a real, live person—a side she showed when she wasn't busy chauffeuring kids. "One thing about my past—we didn't have anything in the way of material luxuries"—she waved her arms as if to encompass the Nicklaus compound—"and I was never aware of it as a child."

Barbara was born and brought up in Columbus, Ohio, where her family was poor, but only in terms of money. Her father, Stanley Bash, was a mathematics teacher at South High School, and he taught his daughter, at an early age, the benefits of a neat, orderly mind, a head for figures, and a love of teaching that remains with her today. She was majoring in elementary education, with ambitions to become a teacher like her dad, when she met Jack Nicklaus in her first year at Ohio State. Jack was already a well-known amateur golfer but not doing well in mathematics.

Jack loves to tell the story of how math brought them together. "I had no chance for escape after what her father did for me on the eve of my final exam in Math 401 [an algebra-trigonometry course]. My professor was a German with a heavy accent, and I was going into my final without a clue to what he'd been talking about all year. The night before the exam Barb's father showed me an easy way to solve every type of problem. I got one-hundred on the exam, an A in the course and a new father-in-law!"

On their honeymoon Jack discovered Barbara's peculiar predilection for shoes. "The first thing on her agenda when we reached New York," Jack remembers, "wasn't to go to a nightclub, the theater, Tiffany's, a ride through Central Park, or even one of the great restaurants for dinner. The first thing she wanted to do was buy a new pair of shoes. This surprised me since she'd brought along more shoes than she could have worn in a lifetime. Nevertheless she wanted a new pair. OK, so I bought her two pairs, and told her that that was enough for at least a year, little knowing at the time that I was married to a woman who *never* stops buying shoes. Compared to her, Doug Sanders is a barefoot boy!"

Barbara won't comment on the number of shoes she has. When I asked to see the collection, she refused at first, and then finally escorted me back to the shoe vault to show me a "kookie pair of sandals." They were kookie all right. It was also obvious they'd never been worn, a condition probably shared by the shoes in the other boxes lining the walls of her dressing room and closet. How many shoes does she have? is a question I was asked many times by other wives. My guess would be over 200 pairs, but I know for sure that Barb's closet would put the back rooms at I. Miller to shame. The collection is staggering.

Not all people who collect large quantities of things are compulsive shoppers, but Barbara Newman, psychologist on the staff of Marymount Manhattan College, claims there are some who compulsively buy things they'll never use, as a substitute way of dealing with enormous amounts of daily anxiety which they don't understand. Sometimes buying things makes a person feel better because of the sense of accomplishment. In Barbara's case I have a hunch that it's the only way she can compensate for holding back on her own potential.

But back to the honeymoon. The new Mrs. Nicklaus got some eye-openers, too. New York City was their destination, but the route through Pennsylvania took them so close to the Hershey Country Club that Jack just *had* to stop and play a little golf. Driving through New York, they were so close to Winged Foot it would have been *criminal* to pass it up. Unfortunately, it was raining. Even so, Jack managed to play a very wet eighteen holes. Barb walked the whole way in the rain. Romantic! When they were packing their bags in the hotel room after a few days in New York City, Jack said, "Say, hon, wouldn't it be terrific if on our way home to Columbus I stopped off and played Pine Valley?" She didn't think it ranked as an inspiration.

Pine Valley was great except it's strictly a man's club. Women aren't even permitted to step onto the course. Never mind, Jack fixed that up. A friend of his drove Barbara around on the club's private roads so she could see him play. He shot a disappointing 74, but he told her he didn't think it was a fair test having to play Pine Valley under such strange conditions with her tagging along like that. When they got back to Columbus, he told everyone what a good sport she'd been on their honeymoon—how she never complained—and added, "She probably realized how lucky she was to see three such famous courses such as Hershey, Winged Foot, and Pine Valley!"

I guess if Barbara *hadn't* been such a good sport, he would never have taken her on a second honeymoon that following August, and then she never would have had the chance to see the America's Cup Match and another fine golf course, the Ottowa Hunt Club.

Jack turned pro at the end of 1961 and entered his first big tournament in Florida in March 1962. Barbara had just given birth to their first, Jackie, Jr., and decided to fly to Florida with the new baby for the big event. Jack had gone ahead to warm up for the tournament, and on the day Barbara arrived he drove to the airport in a small rented car to pick her up. He should have hired a truck. Barb got off the plane with her new baby, her new baby's crib, basinet, bathinette, playpen, sheets, towels, pillows, diapers, toys, and a suitcaseful of clothes. Jack came out of shock long enough to ask how much she'd paid in overweight. "Ninety dollars" was her reply. "Ninety dollars!" he exploded. "We don't have ninety dollars. You'll have to find a better way to travel or stay home!"

Barbara found a better way. She left the children at home until the money started rolling in, and today, when they're not in school she takes all five along. Even though these days they could buy the plane if they wanted to, each member of the family is allowed only one suitcase. That includes Barbara. The Golden Bear does rule.

The Nicklauses avoid the socially swinging life of Palm Beach and entertain at home informally and usually with old friends like John and Beth Havlicek (friends since Ohio State days); the Putnam Piermans (Jack's partner in all his financial ventures), Ohio State football player Pandel Savic and his wife; Gary and Vivian Player; and the Tom Weiskopfs.

When couples become rich and famous, they usually drop their old friends and look for bigger and better circles to travel in. In Westchester County it's called "better dealing." Jack isn't above a little better dealing and counts many celebrities, including Bob Hope and Jim Garner, among his close friends. Barbara, however, has said, "It's OK for Jack, but as for me, the people I grew up with I like best." It's difficult to determine from this remark whether she's loyal, discriminating, or simply narrow-minded and unchangeable.

Certainly, her eating habits haven't changed. With all their millions, lunch is still in the kitchen, and it ain't smoked salmon and cloudberries from Denmark. It's tuna fish on white bread from the A&P. Of course, the kitchen would make Betty Crocker weep with envy—air-conditioned, huge, with every conceivable electrical gimmick known to man and, as I mentioned before, the finest cookie jar in town. As we sat in this Spartan-clean, push-button, temperature-controlled room eating our tuna sandwiches, I gazed out the window and wondered why we couldn't have had lunch by the gorgeous aquamarine swimming pool or on the motor yacht tied to the dock, bobbing around the waters of Lake Worth unused. But Barb had to eat in a hurry, because there was more chauffeuring to do, and besides, I don't think she ever has time to play. Glancing at her calendar on the wall a few feet away confirmed it. I wondered if Jack had to make an appointment to see her, and somehow could hear her say, "In between Gary's swimming and Nan's T ball practice I can fit you in for five minutes, darling!"

But friends, and later Barbara herself, straightened me out on the order of her priorities. This efficient little mother, who is as organized as the Strategic Air Command, only *appears* to put her children and household first. The person who is really first, who has always been first, and who knows he is first is Jack. She's smart enough to drop whatever pressing thing she's doing for him, if need be. The Golden Bear is the golden center of the Nicklaus house, and it's Barbara in her infinite wisdom who has made him king. She realized long ago that if she wanted to make her marriage work, Jack, not the children, would have to come first. If it's a matter of staying home because they need her or going on the golf tour with Jack because he does, there's never any question about choice. She always goes with Jack. She's not about to let him get lonely and fall prey to the she-wolves out there in jock land. Not for one minute! Not even at the risk of Nancy missing T ball practice.

Barbara is the high priestess of the anti-jock-lover cult. She wouldn't demean herself to condemn these women publicly, but her philosophy is well known throughout the golf world. She once told newly married Linda Miller, "Stick with your husband. Don't send him off alone. Remember he doesn't have to look for these women—*they'll* find him!" Linda took her advice. Boy, does she stick (as you'll soon find out)! Barb has passed this advice on to more than one golf pro's wife and has continued to practice what she preaches.

All in all, there've been very few times when she's said no to Jack, but there was one celebrated case a few years ago when he was on a duck-hunting trip with his father and eight male friends. The night before the duck hunters were to return there was an accident at the Nicklaus house. Jackie, Jr., who was four at the time, cut his finger off (that's off, folks) in the ice crusher. Barb never lost her cool. She wrapped Jackie's hand in a towel and raced to the children's hospital, where a plastic surgeon worked feverishly on the severed tendons to save the hand. After spending the night in the hospital with Jackie, she brought him, minus a finger, home the following day. The phone was ringing as they came in the door. It was Jack, elated over the success of his hunting trip. "We'll all be there in four hours with enough ducks for a *great* dinner party! Call the other wives and tell everyone to—"

"No!" she interrupted.

"What did you say?"

"I said *no*, Jack."

"What do you mean no?" said the astonished Golden Bear. In all their married life she'd never turned him down when he called late about bringing friends for dinner. It didn't matter if it was ten or forty, Barb always managed. "What's the matter with you?" he growled.

"Nothing is the matter with *me*," Barbara said in an exasperated voice. "But something's the matter with Jackie—he cut his finger off!"

There was dead silence on the other end of the line. Twenty seconds later Jack's father's voice demanded to know what she'd told him.

"Why?" Barbara asked, puzzled to find herself speaking to her father-in-law.

"Because Jack has just passed out cold!"

Jack, who appears to be cool, grim, and Teutonic (at least on TV), is warm, emotional, and all-American. Barbara, who appears to be warm, emotional, and all-American, is cool, unemotional, and Teutonic. This is especially evident at a golf tournament where she always shows up but never shows any emotion. Other wives cheer their husbands on excitedly or fall back on one of a dozen little nervous gestures—frowns, hand-wringing, eye covering, nail chewing or jumping up and down in delight. Barbara remains perfectly calm and stays well back in the crowd, seldom venturing a word of praise or a visible sign she's pleased Jack won. People in the golf world have been puzzled by what they call her "peculiar attitude." "It just isn't *natural*," one golf pro's wife remarked. "Barb walks around the course like she's at a tea instead of a tournament, always wearing a pleasant smile and never changing her expression." Jack has scolded her about this and once after a difficult game angrily accused her of never showing any emotion. "Make an effort!" he told her. "For God's sake, come out on the eighteenth green and show you care."

Her answer was: "I do care, but I can't show it in public or share your success in the limelight."

But she *was* coaxed out of the crowd after one match, and the hug of congratulations, which was caught by a photographer, is probably one of the great pictures of a man and wife flushed with happiness and success.

I never would have guessed it, but Barb, the paramount pragmatist, believes in luck—luck in the shape of a small gold bear pin. When the Australian press ran the headlines THE GOLDEN BEAR ARRIVES FROM THE U. S. FOR THE '62 AUSTRALIAN OPEN, the name Golden Bear stuck. Jack has used the nickname for a trademark ever since and Barb has worn her gold bear pin with superstitious regularity. "I wear it with every outfit and wouldn't even consider going on the golf course without it!"

It's interesting she has never taken up golf personally. It's rather like living in the Caribbean and not liking warm weather. Golf is all around her, yet it's definitely not her sport. "It just never grabbed me. I don't really enjoy it. For me, tennis is a better game."

The people she admires most, however, are in the golf world, and the woman who heads the list is Winnie Palmer. "She's the greatest! Arnold can be, uh, difficult, but Winnie handles him and their life together beautifully!" (Winnie doesn't like golf either. She likes to read.)

Not only are her favorite people in the golf world, but so is her favorite moment: The supreme elation, Camelot encountered—what some describe as a spiritual rush—came to Barbara in England on a golf course. After winning the Masters and U.S. Open at Pebble Beach, Jack was playing the British Open, the third leg of the grand slam in 1972, and the pressure was terrific. It wasn't rotten luck; it was just that he had played the first six holes badly. However, by the time he was walking up to the eleventh fairway, his grim face had broken into a confident grin and his whole game had turned around. While Barb quietly watched from the sidelines, Jack birdied nine and ten and came from six shots behind to tie for the lead. Then Barb, with her sweet, placid smile and heart hammering, watched the shot that put him ahead at the eleventh hole. Suddenly there was an explosion as thousands of fans joined in with thunderous cheering and clapping.

"In all my life I've never heard or seen anything like it," Barb recalls. "I was so overwhelmed tears came to my eyes [Now that's something for Barbara!], and then I looked over at Jack and saw that his eyes were misty, too."

It was really Jack's moment, but Barbara has borrowed it for her own. When it comes to who she is, what she feels and wants, much is borrowed, transferred, or doesn't show. Women's liberation might go into shock, but she admits to putting aside all personal interests for her family at this time. This confirms what friends say: that she is a good wife, good mother, and good person. That's a lot of "good," but the order is peculiar. After Jack and the five little Nicklauses comes Barbara . . . last. Maybe that's why she buys so many shoes.

The kitchen was swarming with children again, the cookie jar was rattling, and Barb was looking for the car keys so she could go pick up Jackie, Jr., at the country club. "Jackie," she informed me as she went through her purse, "is an excellent golfer! He got an eighty-three in the same tournament his father won twenty-three years ago with a score of one hundred twenty-six." She came up with her car keys and a beatific expression on her face. "I think we're going to have another pro in the family!"

I just couldn't resist asking her if there wasn't something she wanted to do besides chauffeuring, guiding, and watching others reach their goals.

"Well, someday, when the . . ." She never finished. Her voice trailed off, then resumed in a high-pitched "No, *no*, don't *do* that!"

Michael was in the dog's water again. This is where I came in.

I wondered as I drove to meet the woman Barbara admires most, Winnie Palmer, if I'd get tuna fish for lunch.

The Queen

I deeply regret that we haven't had more time to enjoy Arnie's success. His golf and business ventures consume him. He works ridiculous hours—no one would believe his schedule . . . I'm hard pressed to think of a vacation or even a weekend we've had on our own.

It was a cold spring day in Latrobe, Pennsylvania. A small dark-haired matron in her thirties entered a supermarket and started pushing a grocery cart up and down the aisles. She resembled the other housewives in the store except for a deep tan and a camel-hair coat that was threadbare and a trifle too tight. It was the kind of coat young girls wore to school twenty years ago.

When the woman reached the bakery department, a clerk thought she recognized who she was and asked a customer. The customer, covering her mouth discreetly, whispered the name.

"*That's* Arnold Palmer's wife? The famous golfer?" blurted the clerk incredulously. "That woman in the old coat?" Heads turned. Eyes stared. How dare a celebrity's wife turn up in an old coat? Couldn't she afford anything better? Now everyone in the bakery department knew the awful truth, including Winnie Palmer's mother-in-law, who was waiting near the check-out counter. It was Arnold Palmer's wife in the old coat. Should they pass a hat?

Of course one thing Winnie Palmer* didn't need at the time (ten years ago) was financial help. Not then and not now. Gerry Eskenazi in an article for *Sport* magazine entitled "Who Is the Richest Athlete in the World?" said, "Judging by net worth, the criterion being used here to determine the richest active athletes, golfer Arnold Palmer has gotten the biggest share of all. Palmer is the world's richest athlete."† His net worth exceeds $10,000,000, and his annual gross income is $2,000,000. Only a mere $200,000 comes in from golf tournaments. The other $1,800,000 is in royalties from the sale of golf

---

*Arnold Palmer, professional golfer. It has been said that Arnold Palmer has made the game the popular spectator sport it is today. Famous for his charismatic grin and his exciting "charges" from far back in the field to win tournaments, he generated enormous fan interest in golf. Palmer is reputed to be the richest athlete in the world but is second to Nicklaus in winnings on the tour. He has seven major tournament victories (four Master's, two British Open, one U.S. Open). In 1975 Palmer won the Spanish Open and the British PGA Championship, the 78th and 79th victories of his 21-year professional career.

†As this book went to press, the Washington *Post* broke a story that the Jack Nicklaus business interests are estimated at $200,000,000, which would make him richer than Palmer.

clubs and gloves that bear his name, TV commercials, and a hefty annuity set up as part of an $8,000,000 deal he worked out when he sold Arnold Palmer Enterprises to NBC. Some people think that Pele, the soccer star, is the richest athlete in the world. But according to Eskenazi, who made a survey for this article, Pele's net worth is *only* $8,000,000.

Anyway, back to the supermarket. It isn't that Arnold is stingy and won't buy his wife new clothes. He wants her to have designer clothes, jewels, and all the luxuries other rich women have. It's Winnie herself who's tight with a buck. She doesn't care about any of those things, and besides, she *likes* her old coat. She has to put up with Arnold buying her emeralds. He's been doing it ever since they hit it rich, a new ring or pin on her birthdays. But she doesn't flaunt her jewelry collection. As a matter of fact, she stashes the emeralds away in little velvet boxes.

When she and her mother-in-law got home after the supermarket incident, the elder Mrs. Palmer, half amused and half embarrassed, complained to Arnold, who jumped up decisively, tore one of the sleeves off the coat, and threw the remains in the trash can. It was a nice little act, but a waste of time. Winnie retrieved the coat, took it down to the tailor, had it repaired, and went on wearing it—and to hell with everybody.

Attractive, calm, and intelligent, Winnie Palmer has a quiet, unpretentious way about her, and at forty-two she's not about to change and wear emeralds to the supermarket. She prefers a life that is as simple and modest as multimillions of dollars will allow: a home on twenty acres near Latrobe Country Club (which Palmer also owns), a plush penthouse condominium at the Bay Hill Club in Orlando, Florida, for when it gets cold up North, and a $750,000 Lear jet to make the trip between the two residences more palatable and quick. The plane is only for business, Arnold's administrative assistant, Doc Giffin, insists. Sure.

But with all this, the Palmers do manage to live simply and quietly when they're not entertaining Presidents, tycoons, or astronauts. And they do live in the same house they built twenty years ago, when they were first married. The lot cost $600 at the time (it was smaller then) and the three-bedroom house cost $18,000 to build. It was later, when the ball started going into the hole better, that the Palmers put four additions on the house and purchased twenty additional acres to make room for two beloved daughters and an assortment of animals.

The location for their home was picked because Arnie's father, M. J. Palmer, had been golf pro at this particular club for some fifty years, and Arnie had grown up and learned to play there. Now he owns the club. That's what golf can do for a man if he's on good terms with it. "We've come a long way."

Winnie sighs. "My favorite room is the library in our home in Latrobe. It's a charming room, I think, and reading is my passion, so I almost look forward to Arnie going away so I can get some reading done in my beautiful library." The room has rich red gumwood paneling, a polished dark wood floor, a claret-colored rug, deep sofas and chairs with squashy, down-filled cushions covered in a red and green Mount Vernon print—all reflecting Winnie's quiet good taste.

One unique table says more about their years together than anything else in the room. It's inlaid with Arnold's gold medals won in golf tournaments, and they're considerable. Like everything else the Palmers have touched, the medals have tripled in value over the years because of the escalating price of gold. Certainly the table is one of the reasons for putting in an elaborate security system. The bigger price of success.

The penthouse in Florida is reported by those who've seen it to be nothing short of gorgeous, with a view out over the lake and Bay Hill golf course. There neighbors frequently see Winnie hanging out a wash on a clothesline strung across the penthouse deck or standing between flapping pillowcases ironing in a swimsuit to take advantage of the sunshine. The neighbors may think it unseemly for the wife of such a rich and famous man to do her own laundry, but Winnie doesn't live her life according to what other people expect of her, except for Arnold. She likes doing her own work, just as she likes wearing certain clothes that perhaps aren't high fashion. She dresses like a Peck and Peck girl and couldn't give a fig about what *Women's Wear Daily* says or about a spot on the Best Dressed List. "It's not for me," says the modest millionairess. "Neat I am. Well dressed I'm not."

Winnie is conservative, solid, family-minded, and dependable. She was brought up that way in Bethlehem, Pennsylvania. Her father owned a successful food company that catered to hotels and restaurants. He educated her at Moravian Seminary for Young Ladies and at Pembroke, the women's college at Brown University. It would have been impossible for Winnie to turn out any other way since Mr. Walzer himself sprang from conservative German stock and believed in hard work and frugality. "We must earn our way in life" was his favorite maxim. He also believed in the acceptance of responsibility, to God and his family, if not to less fortunate minorities. In Winnie's own words: "One thing Daddy had been was a bit prejudiced and thought if you stuck to your own religion and race, you wouldn't have any problems, so I was never allowed to date Jewish boys in college, and Catholics were frowned on, too." Winnie's father was more typical of that generation than not, and "what Daddy might think" was to crop up and bother Winnie on the very day she met Arnold Palmer, whom she was immediately attracted to, but uncertain whether he belonged to the right religion.

Daddy also taught Winnie to count her pennies. The early training proved advantageous in the Palmers' first year of marriage, though it became irrelevant later. Arnie was just starting out as a golf pro making the rounds but not being able to accept any money. That was the way it was in those days. When you turned pro, you had to serve a sort of six-month golf apprenticeship, and the only income the Palmers had was a sporting goods contract. Winnie remembered it as somewhere in the neighborhood of $3,000 a year, plus golf equipment. *That was it!*

They lived and traveled in a trailer, and while Arnie played, Winnie kept the books, ever alert for tax-deductible items like gas mileage. "We always had to be careful," she recalls, "but because of my early training, penny-pinching came easy. I still handle the household money and can't get used to the idea that we're rich."

Being economical was one thing but living in a trailer was another. She couldn't bring herself to approve of it. "Trailers and trailer parks had a wrong-side-of-the-tracks connotation for me," she said. "*Nice* people didn't live in them. I thought it was beneath me. But Arnie decided it was the only way to go on the golf circuit, so we bought one in Phoenix and drove it to a trailer park near the course."

And that's where she learned that her new husband was painfully short on patience. "The first morning we woke up in our new home it was freezing outside. I got up to cook breakfast for Arnie and went to turn the heat on. *No heat.* Went to turn the stove on. *No gas.* Went to crack an egg in the frying pan, it slid onto the floor. Turned the water on to wipe up the egg. *No water.* The pipes were frozen. I was easily reduced to tears in those days. I was young, and this was *not* my idea of a honeymoon. I sat down and cried. Arnie was furious and rushed out in a terrible temper and kicked the frozen pipe. It burst. Water rushed out in a torrent, spilling all over the campgrounds. Arnie announced we were going to the clubhouse for breakfast, so we just walked off and left the mess. Later on he went off to play golf, and guess who had to return to the trailer camp and explain the broken pipe and do all the dirty work—as usual."

The truth is Winnie knew very little about Arnold when they married. He proposed seven days after they met, and vows were exchanged three months later. It happened this way: Winnie had left Pembroke after three years to go to New York to business school and to seek her fortune. She found it but not in New York—it was in Shawnee, Pennsylvania, on the Delaware. One of her school chums was Dixie Waring, daughter of Fred Waring, the musician. Every summer the Fred Waring Four Ball Tournament was held at the Shawnee Country Club, and Dixie always invited Winnie. For one solid week in 1954 the two young ladies planned the social events. On the first day of the tournament they were arranging place cards around the luncheon table, and Winnie came across the card for Arnold Palmer and asked Dixie who he was.

"Oh, he's a new one, very attractive. I've had my eye on him, so put him next to me."

So of course, Winnie put the card next to her own. What are friends for? That sealed her fate. At lunch she learned he had recently been discharged from the Coast Guard and had a job with a paint manufacturer who'd invited him to be his partner in the Fred Waring Tournament. When he wasn't on the course winning, he was romancing Winnie Walzer, who didn't mind his attentions one bit. So when Friday came, she went through the buffet line with Arnold, holding her breath and praying that he did not select the fish. No problem, he loaded up on roast beef. The next day Arnold won first place in the tournament and that evening asked her to marry him. She said yes, and Fred Waring made the announcement that Arnold's prize for taking first place in the contest was Winnie Walzer. Not the nimblest of witticisms but suitable and well received at Shawnee that year.

Originally the wedding was to take place in six months to please both families, who were understandably shaken by the precipitousness of the development. It turned out there really was no point in delaying the nuptials if the reason for the delay was to give the young lovers a chance to get to know each other. Arnold was in Florida playing in his first pro tournament and would be on tour most of the time. Also, he was playing so badly in Florida that his exasperated father growled, "If you're going to act like a sick cat, you may as *well* marry the girl. It might improve your game."

That certainly made good sense to Arnold, and he rushed back, picked up his bride, and they eloped before Christmas, leaving Winnie's parents to nurture their resentment while the newlyweds took their honeymoon on the golf circuit, where Winnie started discovering the man she married.

What she found was that they could not have been more unlike. He was outgoing and aggressive, she was a passive introvert; he was domineering and often selfish, she was submissive and considerate of others; he read the sports pages, she read books; he loved the country, hunting and fishing, she loved the city, opera, theater, and museums. And on top of everything else she was not interested in sports.

"It's funny," she said, "we're not compatible, but our marriage works." She has twenty years of it behind her as proof. She must be doing something right because he hasn't helped much. He's tended mostly to business, and that took him to the top of his profession and to wealth, which, significantly, impresses Winnie the least. But it has put them on a first-name basis with celebrities of all kinds.

Golf is the kind of a game that attracts the rich and powerful. For one thing it preserves the caste system. For another, it's a challenge that must be faced individually as well as in competition with others. Just what plenipotentiaries like. They didn't get where they are by fooling around. They admire superior players and shrewdly seek them out, hoping to improve their games. So it's not surprising that over the years the Palmers have hobnobbed with board chairmen, Presidents, and kings.

Especially Dwight Eisenhower, a golf nut, if there ever was one. Winnie's favorite story is about Eisenhower during his last term in the White House. He did something that probably no President of the United States will ever be able to do again.

"One year," Winnie recalls, "I decided to give Arnie a surprise birthday party. I wanted just a small group of his favorite people. I called Mamie and asked her if she and the President could somehow get to our home in Latrobe without the world knowing about the surprise." After many phone calls back and forth between Winnie and Mamie, they finally decided to send Arnie's private jet for the President and his Secret Service men,* and Mamie, who doesn't like to fly, was to come by car.

Winnie remembers the surprise party took place in the late fifties, when Ike was President, because "the Secret Service men were all over the place and had set up an office in their den."

She had arranged a dinner party, which included the Mellons, George Allens, George Loves, several generals and business friends of Ike's. It was scheduled for 8 P.M. at the Rolling Rock Country Club. Earlier in the evening the doorbell rang, and Winnie, who was in her room dressing, said, "Arnie, will you see who that could be?" He went downstairs, opened the front door, and almost collapsed. He couldn't say a word. There stood the President of the United States with a duffel bag and that great grin of his. "Could you put up an old friend for the night?"

You don't get surprises like that anymore.

For a birthday gift the President presented Arnie with one of his original oil paintings, a farm scene. It's one of their most treasured possessions. Later they all went back to the Palmers' house for after-dinner drinks and the men wanted to watch an important football game. Mamie wanted to see the Miss America Contest. So guess who won? That's right. All those prestigious men filed upstairs to watch football on a small set in the bedroom while Mamie and the girls watched the Miss America pageant in color on the big set in the den.

Winnie has warm recollections of Eisenhower. "Ike was such a regular guy. Genuine, honest, so down-to-earth—they don't come like that any-

---

*Arnold disagrees with Winnie's version and remembers the Eisenhower incident taking place when Ike was out of office.

more.'' The morning after Arnie's party the Eisenhowers and the Palmers sat around the kitchen table in their bathrobes, eating oatmeal and exchanging golf stories.

"He was the most lovable man, but after he left the White House, that was the end of our trips there for a while, though,'' Winnie said, biting her lip, "Arnie turned down an invitation when Johnson was President. I said, 'You can't turn down a presidential invitation! But Arnie wouldn't go!'' One has to assume Democrats weren't his favorite golf partners. The next time the Palmers went to the White House was in 1969 during the Nixon administration. President and Mrs. Nixon gave the dinner party in honor of the Duke and Duchess of Windsor on their wedding anniversary.

"It was beautiful!'' said Winnie. "Tricia looked like a fairy princess, Anne and Charles Lindbergh, so shy and intelligent, Vice President and Mrs. Agnew, we knew them well and entertained them often when he was in office, and many friends of the duke and duchess. The duke and Arnie were great friends, of course. He loved golf and would come anytime he was in the country to be in Arnie's gallery. I've always found him charming, but I'd never met the duchess before, and I was disappointed. I didn't care for her. She was always pulling at his arm, trying to steer him away from Arnie to the socially prominent people at the party. But the duke loved to talk golf, and he kept slipping back to chat with my husband, and then she'd come over and pull him away again. She was beautifully dressed and groomed. The duke got up to toast his wife and never took his eyes off her. It was so moving that when he lifted his glass, every lady in that room had tears in her eyes. I don't really know why, but there was no question he adored her.''

Winnie flies to Augusta, Georgia, every year to spend a weekend with Mamie, and they continue to be great friends.

The Palmers are not name-droppers. Winnie insists they accept the famous "if they are warm, good friends just like we do ordinary people down the street.'' Ordinary people down the street, of course, are not likely to be you or me. She talked of influential friends only when specifically asked. There's a drawer in the library stuffed full of pictures and letters from celebrities. Once Prince Bertold of Sweden caddied for Arnold in a charity tournament in Europe. The prince sent a letter thanking Arnold for the privilege. It's one of the many letters carelessly thrown in the drawer and mixed in with pictures of Arnold and Sinatra, Arnold with astronauts, Arnold with Kissinger and, most recently, Arnold with President Ford, who also likes a game now and then.

Fame and fortune come more easily to some than to others but doesn't come easily. Skill alone did not do it for Arnold Palmer. It took hard work and all the time he had to give, time he had to steal from his wife and two daughters. All four are paying off that mortgage.

It was a hasty marriage, and according to the adage, the Palmers should be repenting at leisure. Winnie admits that all is not perfect, but she has few regrets looking back over two decades. As she got to know her husband and the usual post-honeymoon disillusionment set in, she learned that survival hinged on her pliability, because there was only rigidity in Arnold, as is typical of men with a singleness of purpose. So it was no accident that the marriage held together. Winnie saw to it, and only she knows how difficult that was. Others can only guess and they do not always approve of her methods, not in this era of women's liberation.

One golf wife in Florida says, "Everyone knows Arnold is difficult, but Winnie knows how to handle him."

Winnie admits she is primarily a good mother and wife. "Why should I be difficult and demand equal time? That would be ridiculous and self-defeating. My job is to make it easier for Arnie, not more difficult. I want him to play golf well. The tension on the circuit is so intense that only a golf wife really understands. It's hard to keep an easy climate for these men. If I succeed with Arnie, it's because I put my problems on a hold button."

Another golfer's wife bridles at this. "It's a neurotic way to live. She has no right to give him that control over her. She's not a golf club to swing around. Wail until all those problems mount up; she'll take herself off Hold and put Arnie on the Off button."

Other friends argue that there's a difference between handling and holding. Winnie solves her problems like any other intelligent person, they claim, but by putting them temporarily on Hold, she finds it easier to live with Arnold. I don't know who controls whom in that family. Their friends and acquaintances don't agree, and chances are the Palmers don't know either. But everyone agrees on one thing—Winnie has raised their daughters.

Margaret Ann (Peggy), twenty, and Amy Lynn, seventeen, have been extremely close to their mother because Arnold was always so distant. Winnie is candid about it. "He has always been wildly busy, compulsively busy, and just never made time for the girls. To this day he rarely has time to spend with them. Consequently they were primarily raised by me. However, Arnie expects a lot from them. He expects them to excel in everything, to be perfect ladies, but he won't hear their problems. The girls resent this. They resent the fact that they could never do things with their father like other girls because he was so busy building his empire. Now don't get me wrong: They love him and are very proud of him, but they are not close."

She looked down at her clasped hands and added sorrowfully, "There's the frustrating feeling that they can never, never do enough to make him feel proud of them."

Winnie felt her daughters' bitterness when they were still young, and she

compensated by becoming friend as well as parent. However, she still felt the
the need to spend more time with her husband and tried to put the girls in a
boarding school. Arnold said no, that children belonged at home and reared
by the mother, but eventually she convinced him it was important for their
growth, and they went away to school. The Palmer women were separated for
the first time.

Later, when Peggy went away to college, she had new problems. She wanted to Make It on Her Own, but her name was linked to her famous father, and
it was thrown up to her constantly. If she got a good grade, it was because Arnold Palmer's daughter had pull. If she got a bad one, she thought it was back-
lash. She told her mother she needed her own identity. The Palmer girls are
still seeking identities, Peggy as a sophomore at William and Mary College
and Amy at Masters Prep School in Dobbs Ferry, New York.

Winnie spends more time with her husband now, and "just in time, too,"
she says. "Arnold needs me. His peak period is over. There are other golfers
on the horizon. His game isn't what it used to be. He—needs ego boosting.
The cheering section is dwindling, and it's my job to help him through this period."

Winnie Palmer, the queen of the wives because her husband has been a superstar for twenty years, has passed over more hurdles than any of the other
wives of famous athletes. Now added to them she has the problems that go
with the aging of a superstar. Arnold is financially secure with his vast business interests, and he will always be an institution in the golf world, but he is
no longer the best, and money can't make up for that. Winnie said one of the
few regrets she has is that the family hasn't spent more time together to enjoy
his success. Golf giveth and golf taketh away time to enjoy it all.

"Arnie's golf and business consume him. He works ridiculous hours—no
one would believe his schedule." Then without a trace of bitterness she added, "Jack Nicklaus has made time to enjoy his family, he doesn't care what
business has to be canceled, he takes time off with his family and goes to
Mexico, fishing. . . . Arnie doesn't do that. He feels committed. He's all
work and no play! I feel it's too bad he hasn't had the time to enjoy the things
he's worked so hard to achieve. I think that of all the golfers Arnie has taken
the least and given the most of his time. Billy Casper has his religion, Johnny
Miller has his family and enjoys fun, Jack Nicklaus thoroughly enjoys his life,
Gary Player has a farm and home in South Africa and is always there for the
holidays. . . . I would have to say, I would be hard pressed to think of a vacation Arnie and I have had together over the past twenty years."

Winnie isn't idle just because Arnie is up to his ears in business. She takes
care of both households, has been a deacon in the Presbyterian Church in Latrobe for three years. "Religion has played a very influential role in my life,"

she says. And she devours books with passion. "I can be perfectly happy all by myself reading." There's a difference between being lonely and being alone. Winnie likes being alone. "I'm a very private person, and living with Arnie has been good for me. I'm sorry we don't have more fun together but being alone so much gives me a chance to build my own ego. I like myself. Probably the secret to our successful twenty-two-year-old marriage is that we've been apart a lot. Getting together again has always been just great. It keeps the marriage fresh."

The last time I saw Winnie Palmer was in New York. She had just brought a seventy-pound sheepdog named Shog up on their private jet from Florida. How many dogs do you know that get to fly in a private jet to Latrobe because the weather didn't agree with it in Florida? Winnie stopped in New York to see her daughter in school, and I was able to talk to her for a few hours before she flew back to Orlando.

"I don't have much time," she said, anxiously looking at her watch. "Arnie wants me home tonight."

"He's very demanding," I suggested, thinking how a schedule defeats the purpose of a private jet.

"Yes," she said, not the least apologetic, "and I'm grateful that he's the one I want to give my time to."

He should be, too. Friends say that Arnold Palmer could not have made it without his wife. It is she, they say, who has steered him into good business ventures and saved him from losing a fortune, that she is the mastermind behind the empire. Winnie will only say, "I like to think I had a share of the business of his life. I have been actively interested in his investments over the twenty years."

Winnie admits Arnie is difficult but never with her.

"Is it because you handle him?" I asked.

"That's my secret." She smiled.

Barbara Nicklaus claims it's because Winnie knows how to handle Arnie that their marriage has been such a long and happy one. Winnie's prescription is simple: "There's ups and downs in this golf life. It's a roller coaster. When the husband isn't playing well, you're down. When he plays well, you're up. Most women, over a long period of time, can't stand the emotional ride, up, down, up, down. I can because I set my thermostat at sixty-eight degrees and keep it there. It makes the thrills less thrilling, but it makes the down times easier to bear." Upon which, with her mouth set in a faint smile and her thermostat set at 68 degrees, Winnie boarded her jet alone and took off for Florida and her waiting husband.

After Winnie left for Florida, I boarded a commercial plane (the last seat in the economy section) and headed for the West Coast again. This time my appointment was with Linda Miller at the 1975 Bob Hope Golf Classic in Palm Desert, California.

I was anxious to meet the wife of the man who had come up so fast (he had already made $100,000 that year, and it was only February) and with such cool (he didn't bother to practice because it took time away from his family).

Palm Springs! Such an indecently, flashy, affluent oasis where everyone wears a copper tan and Gucci shoes and drives a Mercedes. I had a vision of sipping Château Beychevelle under a cool beach umbrella by the pool of some plush country club while one of the world's most enigmatic (she doesn't talk to the press) superwives confessed to me that her husband wouldn't practice golf because they spent all their time in bed. Was *I* in for a surprise!

The Picture Book Life

There have been no tragedies in our lives. Why? I keep asking myself, Why do we have it all? There's so much sadness around us, it's such a tragic world—and we have a picture book story life!

The Roadrunner is a dusty little motel on the edge of Palm Desert, California. It's the kind of place you'd pass by if you had more than $18 to spend on a room. The rich roar by on their way to the posh Thunderbird or the El Dorado. On this particular early February morning the Roadrunner parking lot was filled with a lot of station wagons and rented cars. A few men were practicing their golf swings on a small patch of grass. Inside the walled motel, people were beginning to drift out of their rooms onto the concrete apron around the kidney-shaped swimming pool. Most of them were children, and within an hour it looked like a nursery school. There were dozens of little ones playing with their plastic toys, sucking on pacifiers, drooling in their toast, splashing in the pool, being bounced on mothers' laps, crying, laughing, screaming, and whining.

Inside one of the crowded suites that consisted of two connecting bedrooms and a minute kitchenette, a family of five and a nursemaid from Ireland were stumbling over one another in an effort to start their day. They had just finished their morning prayers with the young, blond, Germanic-looking husband reading a psalm to the assembled family. The nursemaid poured cereal into two bowls for two small children in swimsuits. The dark-haired mother, who was nursing the baby, signaled to her husband that the child was wet. He put down the prayer book, disappeared into the bathroom, came back with two clean diapers, took the baby out of the mother's arms, and expertly changed the diapers.

Outside, two well-dressed men were waiting, drinking hot coffee and impatiently tapping manicured fingernails on a white and orange metal table. The dark-haired mother, her blouse now neatly tucked into her blue jeans, walked out of the motel room and smiled at them. "I have a favor to ask," she said, shielding her eyes from the bright morning sun. "Could you schedule me a day with my husband next week?"

"It'll cost you ten thousand dollars!" one of the men said good-naturedly.

"*No.*" The other one shook his head. "The price has gone up. . . . It'll cost you fifteen thousand dollars! That's the new price for a day with Johnny Miller."

This is not exactly the life-style one would envision with a million-dollar-a-year income from golf and a multitude of contracts for endorsements, but then, Linda Miller* would be the first to tell you that their life isn't glamorous to begin with. They are family people and both deeply religious. Put two religious homebodies on the golf tour and you not only have two fish out of water, you have two fish in the Mojave Desert. It takes talent to find Palm Springs a dull place to visit, but it's dull to the Millers, whose way of life is the antithesis of everything the desert resort stands for.

They stay in cramped little efficiency suites around the country because it's convenient for everybody. They can pull out the cereal without having to dress up and go to the dining room. There are no elevators or steps to contend with, the motels are usually close to the golf course for John, and since Linda has to wash every day (hasn't she heard of room service?), she doesn't want to have to truck through the lobby of some snazzy hotel with stacks of diapers. All very good reasons, but not if you're earning a million dollars a year. I think what Linda enjoys most about going second class is that she likes to be around other Mormon golf families, like the Billy Caspers, who usually stay at the same motel and keep each other company. It's a sort of Mormon communal living golf camp.

The morning I interviewed Linda at the Roadrunner she was dressed in the uniform of the day, faded blue jeans and a crisp tailored blouse. Her long dark hair was pulled severely back in a ponytail and tied with a bright ribbon, a hairstyle that seemed to stretch her already taut, clear skin even tighter, giving her a restrained, almost Spartan look. It went very well with her cool, detached gray-blue eyes. Linda is attractive but misses being beautiful. Her features aren't at fault—it's a lack of vitality and sparkle. She is extremely passive.

I'd asked an old friend of mine, Nancy Dreher, to join me in Palm Desert because she lives in nearby La Jolla, is crazy about golf, is madly infatuated with Johnny Miller, and promised to take some pictures of the shy Mrs. Miller with her new German camera. (She took twenty pictures. Not one turned out. The last I heard she was planning a trip to Germany to return the camera.) That morning Nancy and I chatted with Linda under an umbrella just as I'd imagined, except it wasn't exactly a yellow and pink cotton Marimekko first-class umbrella. It was a plastic-coated second-class orange job that matched

---

*Johnny Miller, professional golfer. In 1974, at the age of twenty-seven, Johnny Miller set a new money-winning record for a single PGA season of $351,321. His eight victories in 1974 climaxed a sensational year of golf, which began in 1973 with the U.S. Open victory, where he shot a record 63 in the final round to win the tournament. Miller continued to play exceptional golf in 1975 by winning several tournaments in the early season, finished second to Jack Nicklaus at the '75 Masters, and came in second to Nicklaus in money earnings for the year.

the orange paint on the metal tables and chairs; the soft breeze from the San Jacinto Mountains was laden with the yelps of children, and we weren't exactly drinking Château Beychevelle either. In fact, for a while we weren't drinking anything, since everything you can think of—coffee, tea, wine, Coke, et cetera—is against Linda's religion. But finally, Nancy got up and brought back some coffee they were serving in the lobby. Two weak cups of instant coffee-colored hot water. Linda looked at us as if we were about to drink poison. We probably were.

"Johnny is really playing well!" Nancy started the conversation enthusiastically.

"Uh-huh," Linda said sluggishly.

"If he wins today, that'll be it!"

"Uh-huh," Linda repeated.

"I'll bet you're all on edge," Nancy went on, oblivious to the response she wasn't getting.

"Uh-huh."

"In fact," Nancy said, brightly turning to me, "you could do your interviewing while following him around the course today, and I could get some great pictures!"

"You can if you want to, but it's confusing out there . . . too crowded. I really don't feel like it," Linda said in her flat, nasal voice.

"Well"—Nancy faltered—"maybe we could watch the match on TV since today is the big—"

"Go ahead if you want to," Linda said without moving. "There's a TV inside."

This incredible lack of interest on Linda's part was confirmed by Johnny at a press conference when a reporter asked why they never saw Linda watch him play. "That's not all," the blond superstar cracked. "When I come home, she never even bothers to ask me what I shot that day!"

Linda neither confirms nor denies this. If their agent calls and tells her it's an important match, she might run over to watch the last few minutes and be on hand to give a congratulatory kiss to the old man to appease the photographers. But it's strictly for show and John's sake, and when they're at home, they never discuss the game. "Some golfers will come home and replay their game shot by shot," Linda told me, "but our life doesn't depend on golf!" It does depend on religion. Religion is the most important thing in the Millers' life, next to their immediate family, and it's impossible to separate the two. It is ingrained in John from his past and acquired for Linda—but for both, it is the fundamental substance, soul and spirit of their life together. John brought his wife into the Mormon way of thinking shortly after he met her, and today she is a devout convert.

Linda Strause Miller was born in Hulmeville, Pennsylvania. Her father is a general practitioner who still lives and practices there. Protestant, proper, and placid Linda finally left home for C. W. Post College on Long Island, New York, and immediately decided she didn't like it. A girlfriend, attending Brigham Young University, wrote a glowing report of life on the Utah campus, and it didn't take Linda an hour to pack her bags and transfer to BYU. It was there on a warm May day that she met her future husband and religion.

After seeing each other on campus a few times, John asked Linda to go skiing. She remembers it as a complete disaster. John, it seems, was a ski instructor, an excellent skier who could have given Killy competition if he hadn't decided to bug Nicklaus. What's more, he brought a lot of friends along who were equally proficient. Linda couldn't keep up with the rest and was cautiously picking her way down the slope. John, much to her irritation, had long since skied off and left her to her own devices. By the end of the afternoon she'd worked up a lot of resentment and, shaking from exhaustion, she took off her skis and propped them up against John's car while she started to unbuckle her boots. John, who has always had a passion for cars, keeping them spotless and waxed, shouted at her to get her skis off his car! And then, because she didn't move fast enough, the old fussbudget grabbed her skis and threw them on the ground. It was months before she braved another date, and to this day everyone in the family stays away from Johnny's cars.

A year later, when John's sister got married, Linda flew to San Francisco for the ceremony. John picked her up at the airport, and on the way to the wedding he reached over, put a tiny box in her hand, and said something sweet and profound: "Here."

She opened the box, found a diamond engagement ring, gasped, and blurted out, "It's beautiful! But you're not very romantic . . . aren't you going to put it on my finger?"

"Well, that would be pretty stupid," our Romeo said, "since I'm driving."

But it was an improvement from the ski trip, and for the rest of the year John switched from romance to religion, quietly explaining the wisdom and laws of the Mormon church. Eventually Linda joined the church, and John, who'd been her teacher, baptized her with his family looking on. Within a few months they were married in the Mormon Temple in Oakland, California, where John was brought up, in a private ceremony with only church members present. Since the Strauses weren't Mormons, they weren't included at their own daughter's wedding. For them it must have been hard to appreciate the "church's wisdom."

In Mormon tradition the young Millers set out at once to have a family. There's five-year-old John, Jr., three-year-old Kelly, and baby Casi, who was six months old when I visited them. When they're not on a pro tour and living in a dusty motel, the Millers live at the Silverado Country Club in Napa, California, while they're waiting for their $300,000 house to be completed on the eleventh green of the north golf course at the same club.

Some members of the Mormon Church and a few golf fans have expressed shock over the price of the new home, considering it a little ostentatious for a couple in their twenties who are supposed to be leading a simple, wholesome, religious life. Perhaps the Millers hope their Maker can understand what some of their public cannot. Since the talk and criticism about the money they're spending on the house, Linda has capitulated and canceled the copper roof that would have brought the price up to $400,000. "Who needs a copper roof?" she asks languidly, closing the subject. Certainly, in every other way, Linda and John are practicing Mormons. They don't drink coffee or tea, smoke or serve liquor in their home. They contribute 10 percent of their income to the church—and that's right off the top. It's called tithing.

"To read about us," Linda complains, "you'd think we never had any fun—that fun is against our religion—but that straitlaced portrait just isn't true. We really don't lead such a terrible life. We don't drink, but it's fine with us if our friends do. We're not out to convert the world. The press makes it seem like the whole focus of our religion is on avoiding smoking and drinking. Actually, it's a minor part. We live by the word of wisdom, but it's just a health code that guides us so we don't take in things that are bad for our bodies." As she said that, I pushed my coffee cup away and was aware that Nancy had crushed out her cigarette.

A woman drifted by our table and said that Johnny was winning. Nancy got up and raced inside to the television. Linda never moved or betrayed any sign of interest. Amazing! I remembered Winnie Palmer telling me that it was hard to judge who was the cooler: Linda or John? But Linda isn't cool; she's just detached. John is the cool cat, at least on the course. Out there he shows no sign of emotion. The fact that he doesn't tinker with his swing or bother to practice before a tournament has been the talk of the golf world, and his much-publicized statement in '74 that he never bothers to practice because he knows from the beginning that he's going to win has annoyed other golfers and his critics, whose ranks are gradually swelling. "John is exactly like his mother," Linda divulged. "His mother is a stoic about everything. The only emotion she ever showed in her entire life was when she watched John lose a tournament by making a bad putt on the eighteenth green. She blinked."

Johnny Miller's father makes up for every member of the family when it comes to reacting. A good amateur golfer himself, he taught young John how to play and has coached him ever since. When others question his son's seemingly arrogant remark about not having to practice, Mr. Miller always says,

"Johnny's been practicin' for twenty-two years!" The elder Miller, unlike the other phlegmatic members of his family, is about as cool as a lobster in a pot of boiling water. He lives and dies with every shot. The other stoics pretend they don't know him if Johnny's playing poorly in a match because he's sure to act up. He's been known to shout, cry real tears, moan, throw his hat down and stamp on it, and make himself sick with anxiety. Strangely enough, he can often be found hiding behind a tree or bush when Johnny is trailing behind by a few or even a great many points. One day a friend of the family saw him crouching down behind an azalea bush as Johnny was about to sink a putt and went over to ask why he was hiding. "Because," the old man rasped, "I can't stand to see him miss another shot!" During the 1966 Open at the Olympic Country Club in San Francisco, Johnny chipped one into the bunker, and his father, who was standing nearby, got so angry he walked over and punched a tree with his fist, breaking his wrist.

When Linda and John came back from their honeymoon, John's father, who resented the intrusion of a wife into the life of the son he was training to become a professional golfer, took Linda aside and told her, "John has to practice eight hours a day if he's going to be a great golfer. He can't be frit-terin' away his time." Linda thought about it. Eight hours for golf, eight hours for sleep—when would there be time for Linda? Maybe that's when Johnny Miller stopped practicing.

Although she seldom reveals her feelings to others, a reporter from the Los Angeles *Times* was present one day when domestic boredom triggered pent-up anger, completely unexpected and un-Linda-like: "There are times when everyone thinks John has played great golf and that he's the most talented human alive . . . and I think, here *I* am trying to run my family in a cramped little motel and nobody's ever going to put me on the cover of *Newsweek* and say I did a tremendous job of being a mother!" The outburst was like a cathar-sis, and now she can talk about it without anger. "Sometimes I feel that John has everything and nobody pays any attention to me, but most of the time I resent the fact that so many people take up his time. I'm jealous of that. I feel I have to share him with so many others, and I don't want to."

She may be jealous of sharing John with his public, but she doesn't have to waste any energy on jealousy where jock lovers are concerned. Thanks to Barbara Nicklaus! Barbara gave Linda that eminently sound advice when they were first married: "Stick with your husband! Remember, if you don't go along, he won't have to to go looking for those girls—they'll find him!"

She took Barb's advice. Now you know why she's spending her days at the Roadrunner instead of supervising the decoration of her $300,000 home in Napa.

Besides protecting her good-looking young husband from jock lovers, Linda has an almost neurotic need to be with him. "Once John went on the road without me for two weeks, and I almost died of loneliness. We're very close. . . . Separation is extremely painful. I can't even *think* about the day when I won't be able to go with him. . . . It's too tormenting!" This growing apprehension almost spoils the time when she *is* traveling with him. Ah, the elusive bluebird. But besides the fear of loneliness, which isn't very real in her life right now, Linda has another. This one, I believe, is the spookiest I've come across in all my interviews. You say to yourself, *What could bother a woman who has so much of everything—health, love, religion, money, recognition, success, beautiful children, a gorgeous home, good friends, and both sets of parents alive and well? All* those things bother her! The guilt of having too much and the fear of having to pay the price some dark day in the future. Linda simply cannot enjoy the present because her fears keep nibbling away at the future.

"There have been no tragedies in our lives. Why? I keep asking myself, *Why do we have it all? There's so much sadness around us, it's such a tragic world—and we have a picture book life!* Sometimes I can't sleep at night just thinking about it. I lie awake and try to figure it out. Why do we have so much? Will it be taken away from us? When I ask John, all he will say is, 'Let's handle it well.' I worry, though; maybe our turn will come later." Strange. Maybe this is the paradoxical reward for obtaining all our goals, the fear that all will be wrested away.

The match was over, and the warriors were returning from battle. Some smiling, some grim, and the victor, although we didn't know it at the time, Johnny Miller, among them. Johnny set his golf bag down and walked over to us with the faintest of smiles on his handsome face. Linda smiled back at him and handed over the baby, whom he immediately threw up in the air, caught, and kissed. Then he turned and kissed the top of Linda's head and disappeared into the motel room. There were no words exchanged. My friend, Nan Dreher, was noticeably astonished with the nonchalance of the homecoming scene, and her eyes were wild with curiosity. We had chatted right through the afternoon and had no idea how the Bob Hope Classic turned out. "Did he win?" Nan asked helplessly several seconds later.

Linda didn't answer. Not because she didn't know, which I'm sure she didn't, but because she was still caught up in explaining her fear of the future.

"I have thought that having so *much* is perhaps our . . . adversity. Success is a form of adversity—adversity turned inside out. Much is given. Much is expected." And then in a low voice she added, "And there is that much more that can be taken away."

Another prominent golf pro, Billy Casper, was playing in the Bob Hope

Classic, but his wife, Shirley, was difficult to pin down because she'd walked eighteen holes with her husband every day, even though she was six months pregnant, and spent the evenings talking long-distance to her kids at the family farm in Utah. It seems an exaggeration, but if she gave each child a couple of minutes, she'd be talkin' til midnight.

Adoption, Anyone?

It's the power and force of the Mormon Church that hold us together. I believe it's because of our faith that we have such a happy life. We are super-close!

Shirley Casper* gets up in the morning and cooks twenty eggs and three pounds of bacon, toasts two loaves of homemade bread, pours out a gallon of orange juice, and then sits down with her family and housekeeper to breakfast. She might as well be running a hotel.

The Billy Casper household has so many members it's hard, even for them, to keep all the names straight. Shirley must set one of the largest home breakfast tables, on a consistent basis, in America and a considerable part of the Western world.

At the outset, there were William Earl Casper and Shirley Franklin, Chula Vista High School sweethearts in San Diego, California. They were duly married, as everyone knew they would be, in 1952, and by 1961 they had three children. So far they were an unremarkable family except that Billy was already making a fair-sized splash in the professional golf world. And typically, they were chugging along but not particularly happy. Billy recognized the disunity, brought on at least partially by his devotion to the golf circuit rather than to family life. The Caspers recognized it was a crisis, and Shirley decided the family was worth holding together and prescribed finding a common bond. No one expected Billy to give up golf; that would have been a negative solution. He loved to play, and it gave them an excellent living. So the decision was made to add something. That something was religion. Mormonism. They adopted it in 1966. The entire family, Billy and Shirley, daughter Linda and sons Billy, Jr., and Bobby, were converted and baptized. Life hasn't been the same since. Mostly because, as is frequently the case among converts, they took their new religion more seriously than others.

Life immediately assumed new perspectives and dimensions for the Caspers. The church emphasized family life and large families, and they took its exhortations to heart. But they thought their baby-having days were over. No problem. Determination conquered all. Billy had learned that from golf. They

---

*Billy Casper, professional golfer. By the end of the 1974 PGA tour Billy Casper had become the third leading career money winner in the history of golf. He had won $1,479,330 in a career that included two U.S. Open wins ('59 and '66) and a victory at the Masters Tournament at Augusta, Georgia, in 1970. He came in fourteenth ($102,275) in money earnings for 1975.

started adopting. First it was a little boy, Byron, then twin girls, Judy and Jeni. Charlies proved irresistible, and they no sooner brought him home than the agency called and they trotted down to pick up little David. Two months later a friend called. There was a tiny baby girl who needed a good home. And Julie made eight. The Caspers seemed to be trying to solve the problem of unwanted children single-handedly. Fortunately, Billy earned enough money from golf to support the venture.

With six instant children added to the fold, the Caspers decided a country environment was called for. They picked Utah, the home of the Mormon Church, not only because they had friends there but because they found a beautiful piece of property that was ideal: a hundred acres of farmland, meadows, orchards, and trout streams all backed up by the National Forest in Mapleton.

It took two weeks just to pack. Two more days were needed for the movers to load two moving vans. Finally, the Caspers divided up into expedient groups, each getting a fair share of the animal population, filled up five cars, and set out, caravan-style, for their new home.

While they unpacked in Mapleton, a friend called. This couple was in the midst of divorce, and a sixteen-year-old boy was left over somehow after the property settlement. By any chance. . . ? Sure, why not? And Tom was added to the collection, making it ten.

Their newly adopted life-style must have met with the approval of "Somebody Up There" who must have thought these good people were trying to gain a corner on the child market. As a reward, six months after Tom was adopted, Shirly noticed a slight irregularity she hadn't experienced in years. *It couldn't be*, she thought, *not at forty-two, not after adopting seven kids*. It took nine months to convince her.

So now, sitting around the huge breakfast table is twenty-year-old Linda, eighteen-year-old Billy, Jr., fourteen-year-old Bobby, six-year-old Byron, six-year-old twins Jeni and Judy, five-year-old Charlie, three-year-old David, one-year-old Julie, sixteen-year-old foster son Tom, and now the infant, Sarah Beth. Add to that an occasional friend or two, a live-in maid, a cleaning woman, a handyman, and Shirley and Billy. About a dozen and a half. Hovering nearby and under the table, looking for handouts, are two poodles, Precious and Puppy, two black retrievers, Blackjack and Poker, a huge white shepherd, Jigstrike, a German shepherd, Noname, and four cats. Outside, waiting to be fed are two pigs, a goat, and a few cows. By the end of the summer of 1975, they moved into a new house. They built a new barn for the animals. Now they raise all their own food and have become self-sustaining. They certainly have enough hands to keep it that way for a long time.

Since Billy's away a lot of the time, most of the responsibility for making

this thing work falls to Shirley. She is a phenomenon. She's not beautiful in the conventional sense, but she has boundless energy, patience, and will. A natural blonde with a ruddy, freckled complexion, she has a wide, friendly smile and an overall look of maturity, which was accentuated by her recent pregnancy. She has a flat, nasal voice that belies a happy, gentle nature. Five minutes with this woman is enough to reveal a kind, loving temperament.

She was six months pregnant when I first met her. She'd just come in from the eighteenth green on the last day of the Bob Hope Classic. Every day for three weeks she had walked a total 234 holes, her six-year-old twin girls in tow, as she watched her husband play in three tournaments. Win or lose, rain or shine, Billy can look up and invariably spot his wife's comforting, encouraging face and one or more of their children (they take turns). If she's not there, he knows there's a darned good reason.

"I get so involved with this game I may as well be playing," Shirley said. "I'm mentally exhausted by the end of the tournament. I wish I could be more like Barbara [Nicklaus] or Winnie [Palmer]. They are so cool. Not at all emotional like I am. I'm a nervous wreck when I watch. I pray, mumble to myself, chew my nails, stamp my foot, and go through all kinds of contortions when he's not playing well.

"I know Billy's movement. I can tell when his swing is wrong. I also know what's going on in his mind [something that must give him pause]. Just the other day a plane few overhead and my little daughter said, 'Where is the pilot flying that plane?' I said, 'How should I know?' And she said, 'You always know what Daddy is thinking.' And I do."

Unlike Linda Miller, who can't tolerate her husband's replaying golf games, Shirley dotes on it if she can't see the match itself. Billy calls and goes through the entire game hole by hole, while she listens raptly on the other end of the line, visualizing the game in her mind's eye. But nothing short of an emergency can keep her home.

"I love to watch and hate to wait," she declared.

The fans know Billy, but she's not so recognizable in the gallery, so she hears things that, more often than not, amuse her but can sometimes irritate her, too.

"When Billy was heavy a few years ago, I used to hear people call him names like Mr. Fats and a few less complimentary." Her Mormon teachings kept her from being more explicit. "One time in Phoenix a man standing next to me watched Bill's shot and then nudged me and said, 'Old jelly-belly really laid into that one.' He didn't know who I was. Bill lost a lot of weight after I told him about that remark. But people in the gallery really don't think. Once I heard a lady tell her friend what a prima donna Billy was, that he demanded breakfast in bed every morning. Well, I laughed out loud. He's never had breakfast in bed in the twenty years we've been married.

"Another time in England, when Bill was playing in the Piccadilly Tournament, there were two men discussing his religion. You know how stuffy the British sound, with that accent. Well one man said to the other, 'He's a Mormon,' and the other one said, 'Oh, I've heard about those people. Very sexy, I believe. I wonder how many wives he has?' I set them straight. 'One. Me,' I said. They turned and gaped. 'But I have ten children,' I said to make up for their obvious disappointment. 'Well,' one of the men said, 'I don't know whether to congratulate you or offer condolences.'

"You can't blame everyone for thinking we're freaks. Like the buffalo meat business."

I told Shirley I hadn't heard about *that* but looked forward to it.

"For a long time Bill was allergic to all domestic meats, beef, pork, lamb, ham, and even poultry. All he could eat was wild game. Well, he got tired of turkey and duck after a few years, so we looked around for variety. I found a meat-packing company in Chicago that supplied us with bear, moose, elk, venison, wild turkey, and buffalo. I didn't know what to do with that stuff, but a friend gave me a cookbook that helped. I fried, broiled, stewed, and casseroled buffalo meat for four years. It was bound to leak out to the press eventually, and when it did, Bill was nicknamed—you guessed it—Buffalo Bill."

Naturally.

The allergy departed as mysteriously as it had come, and the strange diet with it.

The farm has brought joy to the Casper family, but no one claims it's all fun and games. It's a tight ship with each member having a job to do. With ten children and two maids, the work gets done fast and efficiently. Shirley probably has less to do in her house than most women because of the help she has, but the cooking is her exclusive territory. With that mob to feed no one would fault her for putting a lot of hamburger and pizza on the table, but rack of lamb, escargots, and artichokes appear more often. Every other day she bakes six loaves of bread. From scratch. I mean she buys wheat in hundred-pound sacks and grinds it to make her own whole wheat flour to bake into bread. The delicious smell permeating the house on baking day is enough to induce a perfect stranger to consider being put up for adoption.

However, anyone entering the Casper household would have to like the religion to get along. They pray all the time—at the start of each day, after breakfast (a family devotional period at which the older children take turns reading Scripture or thoughts for the day), after school (religious classes at church), mealtimes, and before going to bed. On Sundays they go to church twice, Sunday school in the morning and devotional service in the afternoon.

"It's the power and force of the Mormon Church that hold us together," Shirley insists. "I believe it's because of our faith that we have such a happy life. We are super close. We don't have a problem child in the bunch. 'Course, we've had to work at it every minute. It's hard to raise them to be good human beings. It doesn't just happen, you know. Many a night we've sat up late with one of our teenagers, talking, exploring, trying to reason, trying to firm up that moral fiber. But they're all OK. Children in America are begging for discipline. Bill and I are very strict, but at the same time we show our love for them and for each other."

During the Los Angeles Open in 1974 the police put Billy on twenty-four-hour guard because his name was on a Symbionese Liberation Army list discovered shortly after the Patty Hearst kidnapping. Billy immediately arranged for extended police protection around his house and warned Shirley of the danger. Two days later four-year-old Charlie had breakfast as usual but failed to show up for his sister's birthday party. That meant he was missing. The family searched for him calmly and methodically in the meadow and orchard. After an hour the police and security men, who were sure Charlie hadn't slipped through their line, grew uneasy, and the hunt became more intensive. Soon word got out, and neighbors joined in. The besetting fear that haunts superstars and their wives—fear of their families' vulnerability—seemed about to come true for the Caspers. By 6 P.M. the family was frantic, and a citywide alarm went out. Shirley had put off telling Billy because she didn't want to worry him needlessly during his match. Mapleton's citizens, 85 percent Mormon and 100 percent concerned, turned out, and within an hour hundreds of people, young and old, were combing the countryside, yelling Charlie's name. There was no answer.

Shirley turned the barn inside out and finally, tears streaming down her cheeks, rushed into the house to call her husband in Los Angeles. On her way to the telephone she passed a closet in the back hallway and thought she heard a giggle. She tiptoed back and jerked open the door. There stood the missing Charlie with a big, embarrassed grin on his face. He'd been there all the time. He said that when the police searched the closet, he'd simply hidden inside a box until they had left. Most of the time he had stood with the door ajar so he could watch all the people looking for him.

"He was trying to get attention," Shirley said, "and almost got more than he bargained for."

With so many children individual attention is impossible, but as a group they get plenty. Billy takes the boys hunting, fishing, and camping. Shirley teaches the girls to sew and bake. This will come as a disappointment to the anti-sex-discrimination crowd, but no one in the Casper family complains of stereotyping. Monday night is reserved for family activities. Everyone stays home to do things together.

"The activities aren't so important," says Shirley. "The important thing is being together. Sometimes we sing or play games. Sometimes we read Scriptures."

According to another golf wife, "Mostly, they pray."

But it isn't all a "down-on-the-farm" kind of existence. Twice a year the Caspers fly to Africa to see their good friends King Hassan of Morocco and his wife. When the men are not playing golf, the king puts his private jet at their disposal so they can get around his kingdom with ease.

The Caspers were at a tournament in Scotland, planning to leave for Morocco the following day, when they heard the palace had been bombed in an attempt on the king's life. They flew to Washington to await the coup's end, and one week later they were walking through the palace gardens with King Hassan and his family.

"Everything seemed normal and relaxed, but you couldn't help noticing the increased security. Guards were everywhere."

Shirley said they were not anxious being there during such unsettled times. "The king wouldn't have let us come if there was any danger. We all mean too much to each other."

I asked Shirley how people from two such divergent cultures could become so friendly, and she explained that the king is extremely religious, "a direct descendant of Mohammed the prophet and spiritual leader of Morocco." Then I began to understand the kinship. "I doubt we'll ever be able to convert *him,*" said Shirley with a straight face.

It all started as a business relationship, which became warmly personal because of the mutual love for golf shared by Billy and the king.

Shirley has simmered down a bit since she left California, where she was Mothers' March Chairwoman for Muscular Dystrophy in San Diego for three years, on the Republican State Committee for two years, California Young Mother of the Year, and finally National Young Mother of the Year in 1972.

Today, if you were invited to the Caspers' farm in Utah, you would be greeted by eleven children and an assortment of pets, the aroma of baking bread and rolls would make you salivate, and you *might* get a glimpse of Shirley—if she weren't cooking a gourmet meal, grinding wheat, hugging a child or planning a family party or adopting somebody or working at the church or teaching Sunday school or singing in the choir or solo at a friend's wedding or doing five different kinds of charity work or going to a PTA meeting or tending to her duties as president of the Quarterback Club at Billy, Jr.'s school or following her husband around the links or (if it's spring) planting or (if it's July and August) canning with the older girls.

The last time I saw Shirley was in the early spring of '75. She was still six months pregnant and apologizing to someone on the phone because she couldn't take on another committee assignment.

"I don't think I'm going to have time to be chairman of anything," she said.

I reminded her, as I left, not to forget to schedule time out in May to have her baby.* She gave me one of her wide, sunny smiles to indulge me in my little joke, and I walked away, thinking that if they could only find some way to harness her energy they wouldn't need that new generator down on the farm.

---

*Shirley didn't forget to schedule her baby. Sarah Beth Casper was born on May 3, 1975, checking in at seven pounds.

The Pacesetter

I'm a pacesetter. . . . I've brought the jockey out of the stable. . . .

*I can feel people's curiosity . . . their eyes are like tape measures and
they're saying to themselves, "Wonder how those two people make it in
bed?"*

It may be difficult to catch up with whirlwind Shirley Casper, the thoroughly domesticated practitioner of the housewifely virtues, but as for creamy,
curvy, knockout Babbs Shoemaker,* you can almost always find her home in
the Truesdale Estates section of Beverly Hills, California—at least until early
afternoon. You wouldn't be able to talk to her, though, because she sleeps till
noon and it takes two hours for her to decorate, ornament, spangle, bedeck,
emblazon, primp, preen, perfume, brush, comb, and otherwise get herself
together to meet the adventures of the new day. "I'm a night person," she
says.

Whatever needs to be done along domestic lines is taken care of by a crew
of obedient Oriental servants. Babbs concentrates on the social calendar
(jammed) and the procurement of luxuries (endless) because, you see, she has
always wanted to be rich, accepted by society, a lady of leisure, and live the
"good life" as she defines it. And she has succeeded. She swirls through life
as though time had stood still for her. Linda Edwards, actor Vince Edwards'
wife, describes her best friend as "expensive."

All this is possible because a tiny man of ninety-three pounds rides horses.
He encourages them to run faster than other horses and to win millions of dollars in prize money for their owners and himself. His skill has put him on the
list of the ten richest athletes in the world. With a wife like Babbs, he needs to
be.

"I'll spend up to five thousand dollars on a piece of jewelry without asking.
If it's more than that, I ask William." She calls him William because it's
more dignified. To the rest of the world he's Willie.

"I'm a pacesetter in my group," she discloses immodestly. By that she
means she swaddles herself in St. Laurent and Galanos and condescends to
accept the offerings of Halston if he behaves himself. Her handbag is Hermès;
her address book is Gucci; her pearls are real.

*Willie Shoemaker, who turned forty-four in August, 1975, is the winningest jock-
ey in history. He has been riding thoroughbred horses professionally since 1949, and
his career marks entering the '76 season show 7,000 victories and more
than $20,000,000 in winnings.

"I don't feel comfortable in beads, only gold and diamonds. I was wearing those chains before Tiffany's came out with them." She's a sable-lined raincoat sort of girl.

"I don't like fads, trendy things. I'm not a fashion pioneer like Betsy Bloomingdale or Mary Lazar, but I'm together," she said as she checked approvingly over her outfit. "It may not be the 'in' look, but it's right for me."

The stable and its tenants, which provide these riches, are of no interest to Babbs. She cares not for horses (indeed, she's *allergic* to them), nor will she set foot on a racetrack except for unusual social occasions. The whole scene bores her, and she feels no guilt about it. "If my husband were an attorney, would I be interested in every damned case?" she said by way of clarification.

Anyway, because of her allergy, Babbs has a good excuse for staying away from the track. She discovered the allergy when she and Willie were dating. They went riding together once, and she broke out in giant hives. Her eyes were swollen shut, and breathing was difficult. She was rushed to the hospital for a shot of adrenaline. After they married, Dr. Bob Reed, head of the Allergy Department at the Scripps Clinic, told her she shouldn't have married a man so intimately associated with horses. It would cause her an infinite amount of trouble. Dr. Reed was right on one score and wrong on the other. It's an infinite amount of trouble, but not to Babbs. To Willie. The solution was simple and effective. Before Willie comes home from the track, he scrubs like a surgeon—from head to toe and from skin out. If he's halfway home and has to return to the stable for something he forgot, he has to endure the pasteurization process all over again. Once in the house, he hits the shower again just to be sure. He's got to be the cleanest man in town!

On her rare appearances at the track, Babbs quarantines herself inside the airtight air-conditioned Turf Club and watches through the heavy plate glass windows.

"Even then," she says seriously, "just looking at horses makes me feel sick."

Over the last twenty-five years Willie has kicked home horses like these paying the owners $55,000,000 in prize money, of which he retained 10 percent or $5,500,000. In good years Shoemaker has earned about $450,000. More recently, because of an injury, he's cut down on his activities and has been taking home around $200,000. But experts will tell you there's no way to estimate exactly *what* Willie earns, because there are "over the table, under the table, and around the table" deals in horse racing.

Horses and racing may mean nothing to Babbs, but "My poker club means a lot to me. I wouldn't miss it for the world." The club meets at least once a week, and she's the only woman in it. Lee J. Cobb, the actor, claims she's the best player in the bunch.

Credit: *Ellen Graham*

"She doesn't perform when she plays," he said. "She watches the cards, while the rest of us compete for laughs."

Dr. Robert Kerlan of Beverly Hills started the club. He wanted to gather the best poker players in town, socially acceptable, of course, and he got Fred Astaire, Walter Matthau, Cobb, Marty Ritt, and a guest ringer—all people who would not blanch at the $500 ante.

Once the game moved to the Shoemaker house, but Willie had to knock off early because he had a race the next day. Babbs substituted and cleaned out the game. She wanted permanent membership, but Doc Kerlan said no. He could have saved his breath because nobody says no to Babbs for long once she's made up her mind. She was finally inducted, Kerlan said, "because she was so persistent in applying for membership."

That's how Babbs gets things, determination.

For instance: "A few days after returning from our honeymoon, I got my first shock. The most devastating thing happened. My membership at the Turf Club was turned down. In those days [fourteen years ago] they did not accept jockeys and their wives into the social world of racing. I heard that when they brought my name up at the meeting, someone said, 'A jockey's wife? She has a lot of nerve applying for a membership here.' Well, I had some wealthy friends. I mean I *had* lived in the social world in Dallas. They spoke up for me. The board of directors called a special meeting, and I was approved. It was a good thing for both sides."

She paused in search of the modest thing to say and decided against it.

"I've brought the jockey out of the stable not only by joining the Turf Club but by setting an example. I always try to look well dressed, to entertain lavishly and live with great style."

The Shoemakers' is one of the most beautiful of all superstar homes. When I first drove up to the low, sprawling Moroccan mansion, dodging the sprinkler system watering the perfectly kept lawn, I classified it as Linda Edwards had its owner—expensive.

The Oriental butler let me in and mumbled something about "Mrs. still in bed. Come in and have some coffee."

A voice boomed from another room. I followed the echo and found myself in a cavernous formal dining room. Sitting at the long dining table, amid newspapers and coffee cups, were a large, corpulent man who obviously owned the voice and a tiny man at the head of the table whose shoulders barely cleared the tabletop. They both nodded to me in a friendly way, waved me to a seat, and retreated behind their newspapers.

I decided to take a look around the house. There was not a sign of primary colors. The large rooms had white walls, white furniture, and white tile floors with touches of chamois, brown, beige, and black. A zebra rug here, an Ethiopian rug there. African tapestry, Indian baskets, and everywhere, great tropical plants the size of trees. The effect was simple and sumptuous.

Finally, Babbs came in. She was dressed all in white cashmere and wool with touches of gold and diamonds. Her hair and make up were perfectly done.

"You'll have to excuse me. I just couldn't get myself together," she said. It was 2 P.M.

We sank down in one of the deep, luxurious sofas. It felt like falling into a sea of goosedown.

"Aren't you early?" she asked. "It seems a bit early to talk about my life. Let's have a bloody mary." She picked up a white telephone and gave the order, like room service.

I walked over to the window and gazed out on a green tropical garden, swimming pool, and tennis court and told Babbs what I thought she'd want most to hear.

"It's a beautiful house."

"Yes? Well, it would have been, but a business deal I'd counted on didn't go through, and I had to work on a budget." She made "budget" sound like a dirty word. "*Never* try to decorate a house on a budget," she advised, and I agreed.

I looked for signs of economy in the room and figured, finally, that it must be the Indian baskets.

Babbs stretched and yawned.

"Let's start out by saying that William calls me a night prowler. I feel guilty about it because I often crawl into bed pretty late, but he never says a word. I guess he has to get his sleep"—yawn—"so he can ride. A lot of our friends tease us and say we never see each other. In bed, I mean."

From the beginning of their marriage, friends have been teasing Willie and Babbs about their sex life.

"What's sex like with an Amazon, Willie?" they'd ask.

"Everyone is the same lying down," is Willie's stock answer.

"What does it feel like to be so small?" a movie star asked him once.

"Hard to tell," he had replied. "How does it feel being tall?"

"I hear you're married to an Amazon?" a fan once remarked at the track.

"Everyone looks like an Amazon to me," he said, "even you."

"I can feel people's curiosity," Babbs said. "Their eyes are like tape measures, and they're saying to themselves, 'Wonder how those two make it in bed? He's short-legged and she's long-legged [she's 5 feet 7 inches, 125 pounds; he's 4 feet 10 inches and 93 pounds]. If she rolled over, she'd squash him flat as a pancake.' The truth is," she went on candidly, "William is right. There's no difference when you're lying down. Anyway, it's *when* you make it more than how you make it. With athletes"—she paused, chewing on a huge pear-shaped diamond hanging on a fragile chain around her neck—"I have a theory that athletes are not sensual, just physical. They live in a physical world, taking care of their bodies for their sport, but I don't think they're very sexual. There are times when William's *not* riding—a six-week period or vacation time—and (William will hate this if you print it in your book, but it's true) his sex drive doesn't become any greater than when he's riding. He doesn't have a strong sex drive, but if I should complain to him about it, 'Hey, let's make an appointment. I haven't seen you in a while,' he'll say, 'I don't have my head into *that* right now.' "

She reached for a cigarette. Her long, slim fingers with gleaming pink-frosted nails gracefully held it to her mouth while an Oriental maid materialized out of nowhere to light it. Babbs was expecting the gesture and was waiting for it.

"When we were first married, William didn't know if it would be a good idea to have sex the night before a race. Our doctor settled it. He told the story about a patient, who happens to be a friend of ours, who had a severe heart attack. Before he left the hospital, the doctor asked him how many times he had intercourse. The man answered, 'Every day and sometimes twice a day.' The doctor gulped and asked him how long the act lasted, and he said, 'One to three minutes.' 'Continue your sex life,' the doctor told him."

Babbs roared with laughter. "Can you imagine? Now I don't know if the doctor thought ours only lasts a few minutes or not, but he did tell us that sex before a race wouldn't make any difference to William the next day. In fact," she said, chuckling, "he said it might help him sleep better." (Shades of that canny Scot Dr. N. C. Craig Sharp.)

She squashed her cigarette out in a crystal ashtray and sipped her bloody mary.

"Many of the owners seem to think sex is enervating. William was riding Gallant Man for Ralph Lowe, and Ralph didn't want us to stay together the night before the race. He pretended he was kidding, but he was on the square. He even suggested that Willie solo at his guest cottage. Well, William spent the night with me, and the next day he won five races at the track, including Gallant Man. I told Ralph *I* was responsible for his big purse."

Babbs will be the first to tell you her husband doesn't always understand her sense of humor and doesn't like her outspoken manner. By way of defense, she says, "I'm affectionate, loving, and tactile. Willie is aloof. He has said to me, 'Babbs, you're so aggressive that some morning you're going to wake up and find male appendages.' But"—she sniffed—"we both know I'm feminine, and I'm not bothered by his remarks."

If Willie-the-Shoe is King of the Turf, Babbs is Queen of Truesdale Estates, and her home is a haven for movie stars. Babbs fondly calls it Café Society, and Easterners call it That Hollywood Crowd. You'll see anyone from Cary Grant to Frank Sinatra around the sunken bar at night, but during the day the tennis court is the most popular place in town. And like everything else, it matches the decor.

"I hate green, so I ordered a chocolate and vanilla tennis court to go with the house."

Babbs never knows until she looks outside who might be there.

"Johnny Carson cut his teeth on our court, and now he's out there playing doubles a lot. Some of the regulars are O. J. Simpson, Burt Bacharach, Bob Seagren, there's always *someone* playing. Sometimes we have to wait until evening to get on our own court. We'll rush home from a dinner party, change clothes, and play until two in the morning. William is a good player and often joins us if he doesn't have a race the next day."

When William is racing the next day, he retires early, but not Babbs. She always stays up until at least 2 A.M. When Willie doesn't have a race and they go out, they make a striking couple. Physically they're as different as Macedon and Monmouth, and when they walk into a fashionable restaurant, like Chasen's, Babbs will rivet the attention of the room in her Oscar de la Renta pants and matching black satin blazer, beautifully cut, simple and smashing, diamonds shimmering against muted satin, sparkling on her fingers and flashing from her ears.

Willie, who barely comes to her shoulder, looks like an elf in a tuxedo. He stands shyly in the background while kisses and affectionate greetings are exchanged. The headwaiter will be one of the few who will cater to him because headwaiters earn their living by recognizing the important people in a party, the ones who pay the check.

Babbs knows they'll attract attention so she pays extra heed to her appearance.

"I know I always have to look good because wherever we go, people will be looking at us."

She's one of the few wives of superstar athletes who have not only learned to live with fame and financial success but to wallow in it. She feels no guilt about having more money than most people. On the contrary, she has an "If you've got it, flaunt it" attitude. Babbs loves being rich.

Babbs Bayer Shoemaker is forty-two years old and one of five children born in Houston, Texas, to Mr. and Mrs. Henry Bayer.

"My childhood was uneventful," Babbs recollects. "Dad was an upholsterer, and we lived a nice, quiet, dull life. No luxuries."

And luxuries are what Babbs wanted more than anything else. She first got them by taking a business course and going to work as a secretary for the richest man she could find, an oilman-rancher, whom she married within the year. The marriage failed, but the luxuries survived through a generous settlement and alimony. And they've been piling up ever since.

In 1958, while waiting for her divorce, Babbs received an invitation from one of her friends to Derby Day in Dallas. The invitation read: "Our friend, Willie Shoemaker, the great jockey, is going to ride Silky Sullivan in the Derby. Come and meet him. Willie, not Silky."

"I'll never forget my feelings when I saw William for the first time," Babbs says. "I looked at him and thought, *My God he's small. I've never seen anyone so small and fragile.* I didn't know anything about racing. I thought jockeys were like grooms and wondered if it wasn't a little gauche to have him at the cocktail party with all the wealthy Dallas crowd. I decided not to pay any attention to him. I mean, why would I want to waste my time? But he wouldn't leave me alone. He kept gazing up at me like I was the Venus de Milo come alive. Since he was a houseguest, too, I had to be moderately pleasant. Later in the weekend, he pulled up a chair to watch me play cards. I looked at him, eye to eye, and thought, *He's really very nice-looking, quiet, and sweet.* And before the weekend was over, I was strangely fascinated by this little man."

Willie was more than fascinated. Six months after meeting Babbs, he separated from his wife. Three years later, after a difficult divorce and a long-distance courtship, they were married. And she's been holding court ever since.

If there is any fear in Babbs' life, it's that her husband might be injured.

"I've only been bugged by it recently. Seven jockeys were killed either on the track or by an overdose of drugs and one a suicide in 1974."

She says the suicide rate among jockeys is high because of weight problems. According to her observations, they rely heavily on diet pills that lead them to other drugs.

"Eating habits can alter the body chemistry. You can't be a very up person if you're always starving yourself to death to keep your weight down. Some racetracks have vomitoria for those who *must* eat to satisfy a craving and then throw it up before a race. A lot of jockeys have drug problems," she said.

The death of Alvaro Pineda, who was killed in the winter of 1975, after a freak accident in the starting gate, brought Babbs' fears to the surface. She claims she isn't neurotic about her fear but is spooked by the fact that her famous husband had two bad accidents in a row after twenty years without a scratch. Three months after a serious leg injury he received a crushed pelvis and punctured bladder when his horse reared and fell up against him in the starting gate. It was an accident similar to Pineda's. Willie was on the critical list for five days. Toots Shor wired him: IF YOU WERE A HORSE, THEY'D SHOOT YOU.

Many wonder why Willie goes on risking life and limb at an age when most jockeys retire and get high marks for pushing a lawn mower, but forty-four-year-old Willie-the-Shoe always answers, "What else could I do with myself?"

Most of their friends believe he still races because he has no other interests. The rest believe he races to pay Babbs' bills.

"I do have a fear that William may be pushing things," she said distractedly. She looked at her watch and added, "You'll have to come with me into the kitchen. The Freddy de Cordovas are coming here for dinner, and I have to show my cook how to make lemon graham cracker pie."

I followed after her into the kitchen, protesting that I had to leave anyway, and noticed that the room was full of people. The Oriental couple worked separately. She was arranging the flowers, and he was standing next to a butcher-block table piled high with canned goods and mixing bowls.

A hairdresser from Beverly Hills had taken a brush, comb, and hair spray out of a Gucci shopping bag and set up shop on the countertop. Babbs mixed another drink and sat down on a white cane kitchen stool so the hairdresser could tease her hair. With a drink in one hand and a cigarette in a long gold holder in the other, she started to instruct the Oriental cook.

"Take one can of condensed milk and put it in the big bowl," she recited.

"Very well," said the cook running for the can opener.

"Now open a can of frozen lemonade and put that in with the milk."

"Very well."

"Darling, hold still," scolded the hairdresser.

"I think I'd better be off," I said. "But before I go, may I ask one more question?"

Babbs looked up from a tangle of teased hair. "Yes?"

"Do you have an identity problem being married to the most famous jockey in the world? Does his fame overshadow you in any way?"

She looked at me as though she didn't understand the question. The Orientals and the hairdresser suddenly stopped working as though frozen. A rose dropped from the maid's nerveless fingers to the floor.

"That's two questions," Babbs said. "But to answer you, no, I've never been threatened by an identity crisis because my husband is famous."

The workers nodded in agreement.

"I'm *Babbs* Shoemaker," she declared emphatically. "It says so on my credit card."

They all resumed ministering to memsahib and never even noticed that I had left.

The Lady and the Puck

They can replace his teeth . . . sew up his ears and his face, mend broken bones—but they can't replace his eyes. . . . I'm always relieved after every game when I see his eyes are OK. . . .

Everyone wants to know what it's like being married to a great athlete. Is it super? Is he super? Not any more or less then the guy down the street.

Three women sat in the first row at the Chicago Stadium completely oblivious to the noisy hockey game going on in front of them. They were carrying on a rapid, animated conversation interrupted by squeals of delight when the woman in the middle, Jill Cerny, waved her hand in front of them, flashing a huge diamond engagement ring. While they exclaimed over the diamond, the spectators cheered at the flashing skates, screaming when the pucks slammed into goal, and groaning vicariously at the crunching body blows. Suddenly, the puck flew up and hit Jill Cerny in the head, just as she was turning from showing the woman on the right her sparkling new possession. The thud was sickening. Her eyes were first dazed, then rolled back into her head. Blood trickled down her face and onto her fur coat. The two other women, speechless at first, began to scream. "My God, she's been hit!" Pandemonium hit the stands as a stretcher from the stadium hospital arrived.

One of Stan Mikita's teammates skated up to him, pointing at the scene. "You see that dumb broad up there who was talkin' and not watchin' the game? Well, your puck hit her!"

"Oh, my God," Stan cried, straining to see up in the crowd. "That dumb broad happens to be the girl I'm going to marry!"

This random shot—with less than a million to one chance of hitting the head of Stan's future bride—was an unexpectedly direct sampling for Jill Cerny Mikita* of one of the most violent contact sports in the world. From that time on she knew, when Stan picked up his skating socks and left for the stadium, that the price he paid for money and fame was a broken, beaten, bruised, pulverized body. And as for Jill, she never took her eye off the puck from that time on.

*Stan Mikita, professional hockey player for the Chicago Black Hawks. Mikita is the only player in National Hockey League (NHL) history to have won the three major hockey awards in the same season (scoring leader, Most Valuable, Best Sportsman). He won all three in the 1966–67 season and again in the 1967–68 season. He has played on the NHL All-Star team eight times and is in tenth place on the NHL's all-time scoring list.

I remember taking my son and ten of his little friends to a hockey game on his birthday at Madison Square Garden. The little monsters were cheering wildly as two hockey players started beating each other up. I'd never been to a hockey match before and was appalled that no one seemed to stop them. Suddenly the ice rink became an arena for a battle instead of a game. *Everyone* was fighting—sticks were flying, blood was spilling on the ice, and the body blows could be heard in the back row. My news instinct prompted me to leave the kids, who were yelling for blood, and go to the nearest pay phone and call the CBS newsroom. Breathlessly, I reported the incident to Frank Gifford (who was with CBS at the time). "Frank," I said excitedly, "you've *got* to get right over with a camera crew. . . . There's a major riot going on here on the ice rink."

"Good!" he said in a ho-hum voice. "Go back and enjoy it."

The brawling battles on ice are enough to make you wonder why the NHL hasn't tried to stop some of the violence through fines or suspensions. Gordie Howe suffered a near-fatal brain concussion when a player sent him crashing headfirst into the sideboards. Red Sullivan never played again after a stick was jabbed into his stomach, rupturing his spleen. But there've been so many skulls crushed and so many spleens ruptured in hockey that it's not worth mentioning isolated cases. Comas and concussions are as common as broken teeth. People come to watch the violence, as well as the game. It's as much a part of hockey as tackling is of football. Tone down the violence, the experts say, and you tone down the box office.

The women who are married to the men who play this incredibly fast, dangerous sport are conditioned to their husbands' going to work, getting beaten up, and coming home with new scars. Most pray their hockey-playing husbands will get hit anywhere *but* the mouth because dental work has become outrageously expensive. Jill Mikita doesn't worry about Stan's teeth—he lost them long ago. She worries about his eyes—they're about the only thing left that he can call his own.

Stan Mikita, superstar center forward for the Chicago Black Hawks, is a clean-shaven, thin, not particularly muscular-looking, surprisingly short, attractive young man. His front teeth, which are false, have been replaced many times, one ear has been sliced off and stitched back on again, his jaw has been broken and wired together, his shoulder broken, and if you look very closely at his face, you'll see hundreds of fine little lines—scars from more than 400 stitches.

A plastic surgeon moved into the house across the street from the Mikitas in the suburb of Oak Brook, Illinois, and was introduced to Jill and Stan at a neighborhood cocktail party. Long after the introduction the good doctor stood mesmerized, gazing into Stan Mikita's face. "It made us uneasy," Jill recalls. "He stared at Stan with cold eyes, and you could tell he was mentally reconstructing his face."

Before all the scars got there, Stan Mikita was desperately trying to get over some emotional scars brought about by his parents' being forced to send him away from home as the Communists took over Czechoslovakia. He arrived at the home of his aunt in St. Catharines, Ontario, when he was nine years old, frightened, lonely, and unable to understand a word of English. The first thing he did was learn how to play street hockey, Canada's alternative to hide-and-seek, and by the time he was seventeen he spoke perfect English and was one of Canada's best hockey players, already under contract to the Black Hawks.

During this time, Jill Cerney was living a quiet, uneventful life in Oak Park, Illinois, consisting of school, family, and the Catholic Church. After attending the University of Illinois, where she was a physical ed major, Jill took off for Washington, D.C., and had a brief career as secretary to Harold Collier, Congressman from Illinois. On a trip back to Chicago to run Congressman Collier's testimonial dinner, she met Stan. He and handsome Dollard St. Laurent showed up at the dinner with a friend of Jill's, who whispered, "The short one is yours." The short one wasn't the one she wanted, and she spent most of the evening ignoring Stan, obviously disappointed that Stan wasn't Dollard.

Stan wasn't disappointed in Jill, though. He pursued her for months and finally flew to Washington with a diamond in his pocket and a three-page proposal he had memorized. He never had a chance to deliver it. He called on Jill at eight, and by midnight he was still pushed up against the wall of her small Georgetown apartment while dozens of friends smoked, drank, and talked politics. When the last one went out the door and he found himself alone with the woman he loved, he was too exhausted to give the speech he'd almost forgotten anyway. He walked over to the bar and threw the diamond ring down. "If you want it," he said wearily, "put it on. If you don't, I'll just put it back in my pocket and go home." Jill put the ring on her finger, and they were married the following April.

Today the Mikitas and their four children, two boys and two girls, ages three to ten, live in a white pillared two-story Colonial house in a new and expensive section of Oak Brook. It may be Middle America's dream come true, but when asked about her life, Jill almost yawns. "It's dullsville," she states flatly. She didn't say, but I got the feeling she would rather be back in Washington working for the Congressman than decorating her $150,000 dream house in the suburbs.

We decided over the phone to meet for lunch at the hotel where I was staying. "How will I know you?" I asked.

"Just go up to the woman who looks like a raccoon, and it'll be me." I stood in the lobby for fifteen minutes looking for a raccoon, and then one walked in the door. A small, piquant face peered out of a gigantic raccoon coat, smiling at me. "Hi, I'm sorry I'm late—chauffeuring the kids, you know?"

Boy, another one! How did kids get around for all those centuries when there *weren't* automobiles? I couldn't believe the transformation that took place when she removed her coat, revealing a slim size eight figure in a dark-green Halston pantsuit. Jill isn't beautiful, but she has her own special style of looks, rather like a grown-up Gigi, with her upturned nose, small dark head with its boyish Sassoon haircut and wide brown eyes. The pixie quality isn't French; it's a combination of Irish and Bohemian, and the eyes are not co-quettish, they're quizzical and seem to be saying, "OK, what's next?" Per-haps it's a special look that wives of hockey players wear.

The food was terrible and the conversation worse. Jill did a lot of sighing and apologizing for not having very much to say. Answers to questions were short—"I can't remember," "Nothing special," and "It's dullsville around here." By the time we were on dessert she'd settled on the subject that occu-pies most of her thoughts—the violence and injury factor in hockey. "I'm not exactly a nervous wreck over worrying about Stan being injured. You can't constantly worry for sixteen years, but I'll tell you, back in the corner of my mind, perhaps even in my subconscious, I have a deep anxiety about his eyes. They can replace his teeth and, God knows, they have many times. They can sew up his ears and face, mend broken bones—but they can't replace his eyes. Doug Barkley lost an eye, and just recently Henry Boucha had to have an op-eration to save his sight." Jill shuddered visibly. "I'm always relieved after every game when I see his eyes are OK, that he still has his sight!"

When she was first married, Jill used to go to games and sit with her hands over her eyes, peeking out through her fingers and groaning over every jab Stan got. After having been hit in the head, her fear of the puck was almost neurotic, and to make matters worse, her husband was very chippy in those days, fighting in almost every game. "He was a runt who went against the big guys!" Jill told me. "And I spent my early married years watching him get beat up!" It's probably not very romantic to go to bed with someone who groans at the slightest touch to his bruised and battered body. One can envi-sion a soft, loving Jill climbing into bed and getting an "*Ouch*, don't touch me!" It would make a marriage "dullsville," to use Jill's favorite word.

At a game in Montreal, Stan got in a fight with Claude La Rose, and a two-minute penalty was given each one. They went to the penalty box, where a policeman stood in between the two quarreling players. They weren't in the box three seconds when Stan called La Rose a name, and while the policeman looked on helplessly, the two men started shouting obscenities at each other. Finally, La Rose pushed the officer aside and lunged at Stan, who turned and ran for the stands. Jill was at home watching the game on television. When she went to the kitchen for coffee, Stan was in the penalty box; when she came back to the set, he was being chased through the stands by La Rose, both of them yelling and cursing as they climbed over people and seats with their skates on, taking vicious swipes at each other.

Jill spent a good deal of her married life cringing while Stan got into one fight after another, and then one day their eight-year-old daughter Meg asked a very grown-up question: "How can you score a goal when you're in the penalty box all the time, Daddy?" From that moment on, Jill recalls, Stan wised up. His energy went into playing well instead of fighting well, and he started winning all kinds of awards—the Most Valuable Player of the year and the Triple Crown for two years in a row, just to name a few, and all thanks to little Meg.

Now that Stan doesn't get in so many fights life could become almost normal if it wasn't for the fact that he's away from home 60 percent of the time. That gives hockey an edge over Jill. There's a requirement in the National Hockey League that the players have to be in the city they're playing in for twenty-four hours before game time. Add that to their out-of-town schedule, and you have a lot of hours away from home. Gee, now that she's got him in bed without those lumps and bruises, it turns out that he's only a part-time partner. When he's away, Jill admits to lying awake at night alone in her bed, wondering if he's alone in *his* bed. "I'm jealous. It's a normal emotion. I'm aware that the minute those fellows get off the plane the groupies are waiting. It's stupid to say your husband would never play around—of course, he would. I often wonder, *Is Stan playing around?* I don't think so because he's happy at home, but I wonder." Her eyes narrowed, and her mouth became a crafty grin. "If I ever caught him, I'd kill him. Get a divorce, get seventy percent of his income, and make him take care of the kids!" (Watch out, Stan.)

"How is he, by the way, with the kids?" I asked.

"Absent!" she snapped.

Having a part-time bed partner doesn't seem to frustrate Jill half as much as having a part-time father for the children. "These guys may be superstars on the ice, but they sure aren't super-daddies when it comes to raising children. How in hell can they be a father when they're *gone* all the time? I have my career cut out for me right now. It's that of mother *and* father. It's so amusing when reporters ask, 'Are you going through an identity crisis since Stan has all the glory?' and 'Why don't you get out and have a career of your own?' Hogwash! I have the toughest job of all."

Babbs Shoemaker may have brought the jockeys out of the stable, but Jill claims it's impossible to bring the hockey player off the rink. Once they exchange their skates for shoes like other mortals, they lose their glamor.

"They're really not very sophisticated—in fact, most of them are horns! I like the theater, politics, am vitally interested in what's going on in the world and thrive on a provocative dinner table conversation, but with hockey horns?" Her voice took on an exaggerated tone of disbelief. "No way! Only a few are intellectual. You see, hockey players are a breed apart from men of any group you can think of. They're rugged individuals who are able to withstand intense pain and insurmountable obstacles. Unless an injury puts them in the hospital, they're on the ice—sometimes in a cast, almost always in pain, but they're out there! Courageous, yes. But not intellectual."

It's hard to tell *who* she is. I think she's smoldering from the frustrations of suburbia under a Jill Mikita mask and would really like to be Jill Cerny again, dashing around Washington. Many of her friends are still there, including President Ford and his wife, Betty, whom the Mikitas have known since the old days when the President was a Congressman. Jill sees to it that tickets are always sent to the White House when the Black Hawks play in D.C. In Chicago her life is ho-hum, and she doesn't try to hide her boredom. She puts up with "horns," being lonely, rearing her children by herself, envy among the other hockey players' wives—"I'm surrounded by envy"—and the lack of good dinner-table conversation. "What can you expect when you're eating dinner by yourself most of the time?"She plays bridge with the girls when she'd rather be planning a political campaign, and she goes to mass every Sunday and prays that her husband will get out of hockey in one piece before he's forced to retire because he's too old to skate. Of all the frustrations that beset Jill, the worry over whether or not Stan will get out of hockey intact is the most overwhelming and certainly a candid answer to what it's like being married to a hockey star.

"If a woman wants a peaceful life, a life free from worry, it would be better to be married to a superlawyer or a doctor. A hockey star's life may be exciting on the ice—but peaceful it isn't. Once in Pittsburgh a puck shot whizzed through the air and caught Stan as he turned and shirred off half his ear. He skated back and picked up the ear, and they sewed it on at the stadium hospital. When he came home that night, he was dizzy and weak from loss of blood and collapsed on the bed. The doctor called and warned me Stan couldn't play hockey for at least two weeks, as any *kind* of a knock would be dangerous to the ear. I assured the doctor I'd keep the old boy home, quiet and away from his skates, if I had to *sit* on him. The very next day I went upstairs and found Stan cutting out a big round circle from a piece of foam rubber. Naturally I inquired if he'd found a new game to keep him busy. He told me to stop being sarcastic and mumbled something about the team's needing him. I knew he'd decided to play that evening and was horrified. I watched him improvise a cast for his ear with a jockstrap and the foam-rubber circle, which he placed in the cup of the jockstrap, then taped the ridiculous-looking bandage over his ear. He drove to the stadium with me raging at him all the way, put on his skates, and went out on the ice. Now I was in the first row that evening, not to cheer on the Black Hawks but to watch my husband closely—and to hope that no one would bump into him, to pray that his ear wouldn't fall off and then be mistaken for a puck as it went swirling down the ice. That's what it's like being married to a superstar hockey player.''

I left the windy city for New York to talk to Judy Gilbert, wife of the Rangers' Rod Gilbert, who hasn't spent five minutes worrying about injury in this rough sport. Fact is, Judy hasn't spent five minutes worrying.

Flyin' High

I tricked Rod one night, and he scored two goals the next day. Still he refuses sex before a game . . . and afterwards he's too exhausted.

Summers are just great. Rod changes. I change. We play more. . . . Once the season starts, though, he's another man. It's like turning off a switch.

The setting is a dark, narrow, smoke-filled room. Leroy Nieman's lithographs of prominent sports figures and events line the wall. Bill Halsey is at his piano, where he's been for fifty-two years, playing "Harlem Nocturne" with soul, suddenly switching to "Fly Me to the Moon" as Buzz Aldrin passes by. Derek Sanderson's at the bar swapping stories with Bill Swain and Steve Thurlow, former Giant football players. Howard Cosell is trying hard to ignore *Daily News* reporter Dick Young (they're not speaking to each other these days), who is sitting directly across from him. Bill Russell and Frank Gifford look up from their dinner to watch a young, opulently endowed redhead go by their table.

The place is Duncan's, on Manhattan's East Side. It's where the jocks hang out. Where the action is! No one knows why a place becomes a hangout for a certain crowd, but in Duncan's case it probably has a lot to do with the owners. Duncan MacCalman,* a low-keyed, likable British merchant seaman who jumped ship in '59, and two former New York Giant football players, Frederick Tuckerman and Bill Mathis, bought the place in the mid-sixties, invited all their friends to the opening, and have been packin' 'em in ever since.

It's the Elaine's of the sports world. Sportswriters come for extra newsy tidbits, announcers and reporters flock to the place in hopes of a good story or to set up a future interview, the superstars come to see and be seen, and jocks and ex-jocks come to ogle the girls who come to ogle the jocks. It's the kind of vicious circle that keeps Duncan and his partners happy and also perpetuates business, news business, monkey business, romance, marriage, and divorce. Duncan's has been the mating place for many sports figures. Johnny Bench talked Tuckerman into giving him Vickie Chesser's phone number one night, and two months later they were married. Duncan's was also the setting for the Judy Preston-Rod Gilbert meeting.

---

*Duncan sold his Duncan's as this book goes to print. The crowd now goes to his new place (Suydam's).

Judy Preston Gilbert* is a five-foot-eight-inch green-eyed blonde, who looks as if she belonged in an embroidered smock, milking a cow on a farm outside Kristiansund, Norway. Actually she's a thirty-one-year-old bottled blond professional model from Miami, Florida. She doesn't wear embroidered smocks: she wears jeans and pantsuits, and instead of a Scandinavian accent, she speaks in a high-pitched Middle America voice with her words coming out almost as fast as her husband skates—in a breathy "isn't it wonderful?" tone. It's been that way—wonderful, that is—for most of her life. Wonderful, carefree, and fun. Fun should be Judy's middle name, but her parents didn't have the foresight.

A Tallahassee girl, graduate of Leon High School, she attended college for two years, dividing her time between Georgia State and the University of Colorado, where she collected a record number of fraternity pins. But school was a bore, and Judy was a high flier, and it doesn't take much imagination to guess what she turned to next. Being an airline stewardess was fun. The hardest work she had to do was pass out hot towels on a DC-10. Those hot towels, she remembers, confused the passengers when they first started the custom. They simply didn't know what to do with the piping hot bloody things and used them to clean their trays, briefcases, shoes, help change the baby's diapers—one bald man even used his to wipe his head. Outside of a little inconvenience here and there, the New York to Miami run was a ball! Jill went from the beach to Duncan's, from Duncan's to the beach—blond, tan, and gorgeous. Suddenly a whole new career popped up quite by accident (everything in Judy's life happens by accident).

National Airlines went on strike, and she was marooned in Miami—no Duncan's—nothing to do. She was discovered, pouting on a beach, and asked to do a Coppertone commercial. Soon Judy's copper-tanned body was languorously draped on full-page ads and billboards across America. Her own airline discovered her picture and asked, "This sexy creature is working for *us*?"

No sooner said than screen-tested, and Judy became the first "Fly Me" girl who was a real-live stewardess instead of a mere model. The stewardess-turned-Coppertone girl now became the sex symbol of the airways when she shed her blue jeans on TV, revealing a form-fitting bikini and with a breathless little smile told Americans everywhere (including some indignant old ladies), *"Hi, I'm Judy, and I was born to fly!"*

*Rod Gilbert, right wing for the New York Rangers of the National Hockey League. In his fourteen-year career with New York Gilbert has set practically every important individual record for the team. He has played in 900 games, the second most ever, and is the all-time leading goal and point scorer for the Rangers. The New York fans voted him the most popular player in New York in 1975. Gilbert has been named to the NHL All-Star team twice and played on the original Team Canada against Russia in 1974.

Judy *was* born to fly. She's been flying for years. The only time she was ever grounded was during the period when I met her, when she was pregnant. Shortly after her television debut, and still deftly balancing two careers, she walked into Duncan's one night and hit the jackpot. Rod Gilbert was there.

Duncan, who was sitting with Toots Shor and his wife, clearly remembers the occasion. Toots had just acknowledged how well Duncan was doing and Duncan thanked him but reminded Toots that there were no more "saloon-keepers" like himself.

"There's no more *drinkers* like me either!" Toots moaned modestly, "They don't drink booze anymore. . . . I've wrung more outta my socks than they drink today!" In the middle of his laughter Duncan was suddenly aware of a major shock electrifying the room. The "Fly Me" girl, Copper-tone and gorgeous in a white pantsuit, had just sauntered in from Miami. Duncan heard a deep intake of air coming from the next table, as Rod Gilbert gasped his last breath of bachelorhood before he seized the bait.

Rod Gilbert, the handsome superstar hockey player, was in those days called the Joe Namath of the ice. Canadian by birth, he had started playing the national sport very early, become famous, and left a trail of broken hearts across Canada and the United States. Rod almost *didn't* make it. When he was twenty-one, an accident just about ended his career and life. It was during a minor-league game in Guelph, Ontario. A spectator carelessly threw an ice-cream lid on the ice, where it froze fast. Rod, encouraged by yells of "Jeel-bare," was speeding down the ice for a short-on-goal, when his skates hit the embedded lid at twenty mph. The collision had about the same impact as running into a moving train. He tried to get up, but his feet weren't receiving the message. His brain had lost contact.

The New York Rangers sent him to the Mayo Clinic, so they could rebuild his back with bone from his left leg. Months later Rod returned to the ice, but in a complicated neck and body brace. Even when he was benched, he couldn't sit down: the brace was so constricting he had a choice of standing up or not breathing. Still he skated. (I'd already learned that hockey players are insane from Jill Mikita.) One day Rod's spinal fusion gave way, and another operation had to be performed, and once again it took him months to recover. This time the injury healed, and Rod, as we all know, skated to superstardom with the New York Rangers. Today, at thirty-three, Rod Gilbert has become the all-time Ranger scorer, member of the All-Star team that beat Russia, owner of four race horses, a discotheque in Montreal, an apartment in New York City, wife, and a brand-new baby. Things happened fast after he met her that night in Duncan's.

Judy is a "now" girl—very much a product of her own generation. She has lived, by her own admission, a self-indulgent, pleasure-seeking life. Engaged five times, with one of the all-time great collections of frat pins, Judy has always seen fun as the aim of her action. A high flier, literally as well as figuratively, our swinger was pregnant and grounded when I met her. From the time I walked into her Manhattan apartment she tried to assure me she was really "into" marriage and motherhood. But she didn't sound very convincing, and I had a feeling she'd rather be passing out hot towels during the day on the DC-10 and spending her nights at Duncan's.

Their apartment is ultra-modern, decorated in red, white, and black, and overlooks the East River if you can get around one tall building obstructing the view. Judy answered the door munching on an apple. She didn't look five months pregnant. She didn't even look pregnant. "If it wasn't for that damn building, the view would be incredible!" she exclaimed as I looked out the window. "I sure do get mad at that building, now I have to stay home and look at it!" And then she went on to tell me how much she *loves* staying home, how she's *glad* to be out of her old life. "I've had the great freedom, great fun, the bars, clubs, dating. Now I want a home and baby. Of course, it's still fun to see the gang at Duncan's once or twice a week—Rod goes there a lot on his nights off. He has Monday night off from marriage. I have the same night off, but it's difficult to go out with the girls now I'm five months pregnant—it just isn't the same. . . ." Her voice trailed off, and she looked at her apple. There wasn't much left except the core. "I have to eat normally now because of the baby!"

Watching her gobble up the apple, core and all, I asked what she'd eaten before. "Junk!" She grinned. "I'm *crazy* about junk—hot dogs, hamburgers, and most of all Ring Dings!"

"Ring Dings?"

"Yeah, they're divine. Chocolate and marshmallow. Yum. My doctor told me to cut out the booze, crappy food, and *especially* Ring Dings. One thing about having this baby—it's forcing me to live a normal life. I'm not up half the night at Duncan's, that's where all the jocks hang out in New York. It's fun. I used to go there all the time," she said wistfully, "but my life is healthier now. Having a baby is good for me, but in some ways it's a pain in the ass."

Judy and Rod, it seems, have had an understanding from the beginning about their nights "off." Judy was supposed to go out with friends for dinner and to the theater, and Rod was free to play boccie (the Italian bowling game) at Il Vagabondo's or see his friends at Duncan's. The problem was they bumped into each other at Duncan's all the time, and that was *not* the idea. Everything was settled once Judy got pregnant. She stayed home, and Rod went to Duncan's. But there were more serious topics to discuss (I thought optimistically) than their Monday nights off, and one of them was the violence in professional hockey. Fresh from talking with Jill Mikita, who has always been repulsed by the brutality of the game, I asked Judy if it bothered her that the man she loved was participating in such a perilous sport. She looked at me with wide eyes that seemed to say, "He *is*?" Then she nibbled on her apple, thinking about it for a while. "Hmm," she said, clearing her throat, "well, you detach yourself. He's number seven—*not* my husband—when he skates. Just number seven. Of course, so far I haven't seen him *get* hurt, and I do go to almost all the home games. I really don't know if I'd go mental or just say, 'Oh, number seven's hurt.' It just hasn't happened, and I don't think about fear." It's probably healthier not to be plagued with Jill Mikita's fears, but somehow I could just hear Judy, as they carried Rod out on a stretcher, say, "Tsk, tsk . . . there goes old number seven."

She claims she doesn't think about jock lovers either and is annoyed with other superstars wives who do. "I wish they'd stop bitchin'! I'm *tired* of the subject!" I wanted to run across the room and kiss her because I was, too. "If a woman is married to a good-looking guy," she went on, "and he's success- ful in whatever field he's in, other women are going to be attracted. So what? I expect women will always find Rod attractive. So? I'm not concerned. . . . I haven't been given a reason."

But there's one thing about her husband's career that is much more upset- ting than either the injury factor or the "girls." The plain simple truth is, it interferes with their sex life. "It's a pain in the ass" to Judy, and this time I think she means it literally. The fellows, she complains, abstain from sex be- fore a game in order to conserve energy and are too beat up afterward even to *think* about it. Plus being away from home 60 percent of the time doesn't help matters. "It's an *exhausting* game. Hockey couples *can't* have normal sex!" She bit into her apple. "Of course, what's normal? Who knows? It's for sure I don't know anymore. Rod believes sex is enervating the night before a game—and after a game he's exhausted." It's either feast or famine, and dur- ing the hockey season it's famine. It's enough to drive a girl to Ring Dings. But off-season, according to Judy, their sex life perks up. "It's damn fortu- nate that when I met him it was off-season—or we never would have gotten anywhere. It wasn't until the play-offs that I got pregnant, for heaven's sake!" She leaned back and got a dreamy look on her face. "Summers are just great. Rod changes. I change. We play more. Life is fun! Once the season starts, though, he's another man. *Everything's* centered on hockey. But I was prepared for it. I don't cry and think I'm unattractive just because he leaves me alone. I know he thinks he needs all his strength for the game. Rod really protects his body, just like a surgeon would guard his hands. I mean, it's his business—his body. He doesn't ski, play tennis, or participate in any sport that would cause him to cross his muscles." Suddenly she put her apple down and giggled. "Whatever *that* means."

Judy served me coffee and cookies and commented how bad she thought coffee was for me. "I'm a naturalist." She beamed. "I don't like coffee or Coke or anything with drugs. I'm really into fresh fruits and vegetables. . . ."

"What about Ring Dings?"

"I'm off Ring Dings. . . . I told ya I'm giving up junk. Nothing but good food for me—and sunshine and water. My favorite thing is to camp out on a beach and sleep under the stars. I play tennis at the Fifty-ninth Street Tennis Club, golf at Fresh Meadows, and horseback riding in Central Park. In the winter I ski. I'm an outdoor girl—that is, when I'm not pregnant. 'Course, I do love to go to Duncan's and see everybody. That's where I met Rod. Most of our friends are jocks, and they hang out there, too. Would you believe a lot of the wives can't hack it? Not Duncan's, but the life, ya know? The guys are away a lot, and it's hard to be alone—hard as hell on your sex life. Phil Esposito's wife couldn't hack it; now he's going with a darling girl. We're all good friends. We pal around with Namath and Walt Frazier, too. It's fun! Now let's see, where were we? Oh, yes, I *love* people and parties and clothes. Halston is my favorite. He designs so young and sleeky. Everyone thinks it's strange that I buy my clothes in Montreal, but we go up there to see Rod's parents, and—*God*, I'll be glad to get back into my nice clothes after the baby arrives! Speaking of the baby, I gave Rod a baby book, and he reads it out loud at the dinner table and when we're in bed. 'Have you eaten properly?' " she mimicked her husband. "He's getting interested in the coming event. [Somehow it was difficult to envision one of the fastest, toughest hockey players in the world reading a baby book out loud in bed.] Everything is *super* with me. I love New York except for that damn building that gets in the way of our view. . . . But I've said that. That's the trouble when you ad-lib, you get into trouble and repeat yourself."

I found Judy's ad-libbing charming, but it does get her in trouble or to be more specific, it got Rod in trouble. Lots of trouble. After thirteen years with the New York Rangers, Rod Gilbert played out his option year and became a free agent on June 1, 1975. He was looking for a bigger salary, a no-trade clause, and a better deal all the way around. The New England Whalers were negotiating with him, and this made the Rangers even more interested. He was, in short, in a beautiful bargaining position. Suddenly Judy popped up and publicly announced that she "refused to leave New York." All negotiations collapsed around Rod like a balloon punctured by a pin. The Whalers, believing he'd never leave New York, withdrew their offer, and the Rangers, who were thinking of matching the Whalers' bid, immediately lost all interest. The night he announced the imbroglio on CBS, Jim Bouton signed off his sportscast with: "Gee, she sure knows how to hurt a guy's bargaining power."

Last I heard, Rod was back with the Rangers at his old salary—thanks to Judy's ad-lib.

So? So Judy loves New York! If more people felt that way, Abe Beame wouldn't have so many problems. And don't think for a moment that just because she's had a baby—Chantal Gabrielle (Daddy's middle name) Gilbert—and isn't on the scene these days and has bought a five-story town house in the Eighties that she's become domestic. Keep the faith at Duncan's. I have a feeling it won't be long before Judy returns to her Halstons, Monday nights out (she's hired a Haitian maid to make it possible), and Ring Dings. The hell with the New England Whalers!

The Cheerleader

Who wouldn't envy my life? If I were married to an accountant, this wouldn't happen—the excitement, the traveling, the fun—not even other basketball players have it so good!

Beth Havlicek* is the kind of girl who, if John were in the middle of negotiations, would be the quintessence of diplomacy. Unlike Judy Gilbert, she would probably announce publicly that she would go *anywhere* John's career would take him, including Zanzibar, and the truth is she would. Where Judy is completely zany, honest, and spontaneous, Beth is circumspect, conditioned, and carefully programmed. Everything goes through her computer. Everything! Even her continual cheery presence.

If you had to cast the role of cheerleader for a movie and Beth auditioned along with 500 other girls, you'd pick Beth Havlicek. She's bouncy and cute with long corn-silk blond hair and Paul Newman bright-blue eyes. She speaks in a rippling, bubbling way with a slight Ohio State twang—and always rapturously about John and basketball. In fact, sometimes it's hard to discern whether she's real or an annex to the public relations department of the NBA. Anyway, Beth is probably the perfect wife in the perfect life of John Havlicek.

Bill Russell, coach of the Seattle SuperSonics and one of the all-time great basketball players, gave John the ultimate compliment, after extolling his basketball talents and spectacular career with the Celtics, when he said, "John is a better person than he is a player!"

Strange as it seems, John Havlicek has had a difficult time living down his reputation for being a gentleman on and off the court, which includes no smoking, no drinking, no swearing, no chasing, no bad manners, ever—not even to the press. All this has earned him the title of Mr. Clean in some circles. Beth is the kind of girl Mr. Clean would marry. One woman, whose husband is a lesser star with the Celtics, pointed out that Beth was popular with the entire team. "*Everyone* likes her! The coach, the guys, even the wives. But why not?" the woman went on. "She's Miss Pollyanna!" Her meritori-

---

*John Havlicek, a forward with the Boston Celtics of the NBA. In his twelve-year career with the Boston Celtics, Havlicek has established himself as the most consistent star in basketball. He has helped the Celtics win seven world championships and was named the Most Valuable Player of the 1974 championship series between Boston and Milwaukee. He is in twelfth place on the list of all-time scoring averages and has been named to the All-NBA team five times.

ous assessment came off with a slightly astringent bite. "Beth doesn't *mind* that management frowns on wives traveling with the team; she doesn't *mind* that John's away more than he's home, and when he's home, he's pooped from running around that damn court; she doesn't *mind* that he misses birthdays, holidays—even Christmas! Those guys are often playing on Christmas. I complain like hell, and so do the other wives, but Beth never even grumbles to the girls, much less John. Now that simply isn't normal. How can a woman love basketball *that* much? Tennis, golf, skiing, swimming . . . maybe. But basketball?"

Beth loves basketball. She never misses a home game, sitting quietly most of the time and only demonstrating her cheerleader personality when John makes a spectacular play—but always keeping her eyes on him. Most people in the public eye have to take criticism once in a while, but it's their reaction to that criticism that is always interesting. The essence of Beth's personality comes to surface when asked if she minds bad press—that is, reading or hearing critical remarks about her husband. "Who'd want to criticize *John*?" she asked with real pain in her eyes. "If there has been any, I wouldn't read it anyhow, but I don't think there ever has been. John never, never plays badly. The team may lose, but John always plays a good floor game—even if he may not be making every basket." Her clear blue eyes had an "I hope you understand" look: "You see, John is the *best*. He truly is a superstar!"

It's all too perfect, but it didn't begin that way. They'd met and dated at Ohio State, but the real beginning was the summer of 1967. It was a balmy June night in Beth's hometown of Painesville, Ohio. Lights flickered everywhere, and in a town that pretty much goes to bed at 9 P.M. you just knew something unusual was going on. Painesville had been invaded by basketball players from all over the country. They'd come to see their pal, "Gentleman John," get married. At the rehearsal dinner the night before the wedding all the Ohio State players, whom John had played with in his college days, rose to toast John and Beth. Bobby Knight, now a coach in Indiana, gave an amusing speech, and more toasts were launched. John Havlicek, who didn't drink, was drinking. Friends kept filling his glass. Soon a worried Beth whispered some words of advice in his ear, "Take it easy . . . you're not *used* to that stuff!"

Beth finally wore out, but before she went home, she assigned Jerry Lucas (now with the Knicks) to watch over John. Jerry took care of him all right. At 4 A.M. a deathly ill John Havlicek was carted out of the country club and taken to a lakeside cabin where a group of his friends were staying for the wedding. He was unceremoniously dumped on a cot while the stag party raged on for another few hours of what might have been the biggest bender in basketball history.

The next morning in church, walking down the aisle on her father's arm, Beth looked up and saw John. "I couldn't believe it. There he was standing up by sheer willpower. He had *completely* lost his color. He looked bloodless except for his red, pained eyes. As we approached the altar, I could see he was trembling badly." They faced the minister, who immediately became aware of John's appearance. "Do you think," he whispered, "that you can make it through the singing of the Lord's Prayer?"

"No," John said.

The lovely soloist, a girlfriend of Beth's, was signaled to sit down, and the service was abbreviated. Cut, in fact, down to the "Do you take this woman to be your lawful wife . . .?" John was able to get out one more word, "Yes," and then Beth supported him down the aisle.

The reception wasn't exactly run of the mill either. Beth stood alone in the receiving line while John lay prone on a bed upstairs with the basketball emergency squad trying to revive him with oxygen. That was their beginning. Beth got John. John got his first and last hangover—and Jerry Lucas got the blame.

Today the Havliceks, with their two children, five-year-old Chris and two-year-old Jill, spend their time between a contemporary in Weston, a suburb of Boston, and a lovely old ranch house they purchased in Columbus, Ohio, where John is vice-president of a housewares business and where they hope ultimately to retire.

The first time I saw Beth was at lunch at the Ritz Hotel in Boston. In between mouthfuls of chicken salad she gushed about John—what a humble person he is (his friends say he is); how he idolizes Bill Russell; what a spectacular career he's having; what a great businessman he is, and how carefully he has planned for their future. "But what thrills me most about this life with John," she said in a tingly voice, "is the *traveling!* We've been all over the world promoting basketball." John, it seems, is very active in the Basketball Players Association and promotes basketball for this organization, as well as for the State Department, all over the world.

Beth informed me that in a few months she and John would be going on a State Department tour of the Far East, bringing John's basketball clinic to Korea, Thailand, Burma, Malaysia, Taiwan, and perhaps even Red China. "Who wouldn't envy my life? If I were married to an accountant, this wouldn't happen!"

It didn't even happen to John Havlicek. He got word from the State Department that a basketball clinic for that part of the world was last on the list. And the trip was canceled.

Several months after our first meeting I dropped by Beth's small house in Melrose where they were living before moving to Weston. It was a rainy afternoon, and I felt just like the weather, damp and limp. By contrast, Beth looked positively perky when she opened the door. Bright-eyed, her long straw-blond hair cut shorter than when I last saw her, she was wearing her usual happy smile.

She led me through the small ultra-modern, ultra-unusually decorated living room and into the kitchen, where we sat, drank tea, and gossiped a bit—if you can call it that with Beth. Everyone she speaks of is "a wonderful person." She's a living example of "I'm OK—you're OK," the ultimate goal for all the disciples of Burns and Harris. I took a good look at her over my teacup. She's every Wasp mother's dream, the ideal "nice girl" for someone's "good boy," pretty and prim with that quality of circumspect enthusiasm which automatically deletes four-letter words. Her conversation is sprinkled with "golly" and "gee whiz." And I knew when I asked her certain questions, she wanted to say, "Go to hell!" or "It's none of your damn business!" but she's much too politely programmed for that. Her eyes would send a message—*Watch out! You're invading!*—but she was quickly in control again, diplomatically circling the question or simply politely ignoring it and going on to something else. The main thing for Beth is to come off looking sweet, polite, and optimistic. She succeeds at all times. Well, *almost* all the time. When I asked her if she was bothered by jock lovers hanging around her husband, her cornflower-blue eyes widened, astonished, as if her innocent world were being besieged. "I give them no part of my thoughts." She sniffed primly, then went on to show she had given them a great *deal* of her thoughts.

"There are two kind of jock lovers. The first is the real sports lover, gals who just love the sport—so they go to all the games and hang around the superstars. Sure, they love John Havlicek, but gosh, it's hero worship—an innocent kind of love. [I can just hear the other wives saying, "Oh, yeah?"] Maybe it should be called adoration. Adoration, that's it! Then there's the other kind. . . ." Beth looked as if she'd bitten into a lemon. "They're just blatantly out after the guys. They're not very nice women"—she pursed her lips—"but I'm not concerned about them. You see, I don't worry about John. . . . He's, uh, he's a family man. A real family man! And of course, he wouldn't. . . ." She never finished. Saved by the telephone.

While she was on the phone, I decided to brave one question that I just had to have an answer to about basketball players, since theirs is one of the most enervating of all sports. It took some courage, but when she hung up, I just blurted it out, expecting a no-comment answer. "Does all that running around on a basketball court interfere with a normal sex life?"

"Yes," she said decisively.

I was so startled I almost dropped my teacup.

"Yes," she repeated, nodding her head vigorously, "to the extent that you don't have sex before or after a game. When you're a basketball player's wife, you start from that premise at the very beginning of the marriage. These guys need *all* their strength!'' Her voice had dropped noticeably lower and assumed a this-is-confidential tone. ''You see,'' she went on, ''before the game is out because of emotional fatigue, and after a game is out because of physical fatigue. There are some wives, well, I know two former Celtic wives, who simply couldn't cope with this—and the fact that they weren't allowed to go to out-of-town games. They felt sexually frustrated and solved their problem by getting divorced. One of the gals is happily married to someone else now and, evidently, very relieved to be living what she calls a normal life. Frankly, I believe this complaint is an excuse or cover-up for other problems. After all, there are many other days and nights in the year, and the basketball season doesn't last forever.''

I couldn't believe it. Beth Havlicek talking unguardedly about sex and thoroughly enjoying it. Her eyes brightened as she leaned forward and said, ''It'll be fun to read what the other wives say about their sex lives. I can't wait to read your book. . . . I've often wondered about football players.''

I pressed on, taking advantage of her interest in the subject. ''There's a general conception or misconception that when it comes to sexual performance, uh, athletes are better than other men because they're in top physical condition.'' I took a deep breath. ''Do *you* think they're better?'' I'd gone too far.

''Better than what? Better than other men? I haven't tried other men,'' she snapped.

I smiled weakly, and somehow I knew she hadn't.

''But let me tell you, John is in top physical condition. He really takes good care of himself. He's not overly neurotic or anything, but he wouldn't think of skiing or playing touch football with the guys in the neighborhood or anything that could possibly hamper his basketball career. . . .'' As one Celtic fan put it, ''Nothing has hampered John Havlicek's career. At thirty-six he's still running around the basketball court while the rest of us are lining up for Medicare.''

One thing you can count on when you're with Beth—every thought always comes back to John. John's needs, John's ability, John's plans for the future. ''John has brains and a business back in Ohio! Our future is secure!'' She not only loves, relies on, and worships her man, but is fascinated by other people who do, especially other people who are ''somebody.'' Once at a party Dustin Hoffman was so thrilled to see the basketball star he practically climbed over people to shake his hand. Beth just ate it up. Dustin Hoffman—Mrs. Robinson's lover—making all that fuss over her John.

In August, 1974, Robert and Lola Redford invited the Havliceks to their home in Sundance, Utah, for two weeks. They spent long, lazy days riding, hiking, swimming, and playing tennis. (Much to John's surprise and Beth's shock, Redford beat John at tennis.) Halfway through the first week the two Washington *Post* correspondents Carl Bernstein and Bob Woodward arrived to discuss Redford's movie of their book *All the President's Men*. Beth found herself sitting in on many of their discussions as they tossed ideas for the movie around. One can't help thinking how incongruous this group was. Two housewives, a basketball player, a movie star, and two brilliant, aggressive journalists, all sitting around the rustic living room overlooking the mountains of Utah. I wondered about the conversation. Was it about Watergate? The movie? Did they kick around suggestions for casting Nixon? I asked Beth.

"Oh, golly, it's a relief to be asked that. Nobody *ever* asks me what we talked about."

"What do they ask you, for heaven's sake?"

"Well, almost everyone wants to know if Robert Redford is really as short as they've heard—and he's not tall, but gorgeous! And they want to know if he seems to be in love with his wife, and he does, and they want to know what she's like, and she's just lovely—really lovely. But most of all, they want to know—" She started to giggle at the thought.

"Yes?"

"They want to know what we ate while we stayed there."

"Who'd want to know a dumb thing like that?"

"Oh, my friends . . . people who are interested in food. Well, let me tell you," she went on as if I couldn't wait to hear, "they eat the same thing as everybody else—lots of hamburgers."

Beth loves celebrities, but most of all, she loves celebrities who love John. She informed me that most of them do. Movie stars and political gods have to have someone to worship, so why not "Gentleman John," whose incorruptible image lies somewhere between the basketball court and Mount Olympus.

"Wherever we go, John just knocks them out!" Beth trilled excitedly. "A perfect example of how all the biggies think John is a celebrity was when we stopped off in Las Vegas shortly after our stay with the Redfords. We caught Liza Minnelli's act at one of the big nightclubs. We were sitting back kinda far—John doesn't like any special treatment—and it was a good thing too, because I just let go and cried like a baby when Liza sang one of her mother's songs. Suddenly, she stopped singing and breathlessly announced that John was in the audience. The next thing I knew, the spotlight was on us! Me with my red, teary eyes and mascara rolling down my cheeks, and John with his mouth open in astonishment.

" 'Ladies and gentlemen,' Liza cried out, 'I've just found out that John Havlicek is here in this very room tonight! Can you imagine? The world's

greatest basketball star coming here to see *me!*' I just couldn't believe it,''
Beth said wonderingly, "Liza Minnelli saying that about my John." She
looked at me over her teacup, her bright-blue eyes sparkling. "That's how
celebrities feel about John. To them *he's* the superstar, and he *is* the best basketball player in the world. Of course, all this makes my life dreamy, and as I
told you before, this wouldn't happen if I were married to an . . . an accountant. Not even other basketball players have it so good. Our life is really
terrific."

I wondered. Wasn't there *anything* wrong? Not even one little problem or
dark cloud in their life. All the other wives had problems. Had I at last found
one with a perfect life? Didn't John have a slight flaw?

"Well, yes, there is one thing wrong," Beth conceded. She put her teacup
down, folded her napkin neatly, and thought about it for a few seconds as if
trying to determine whether she should make this highly confidential information public.

"What is it?" I asked, somehow relieved they were human after all.

"You see, John," she said, fidgeting with her wedding band, "is . . .
well, he's . . . when it comes to helping around the house . . . picking up
toys . . . straightening things up if guests are coming . . . well, John is
slow."

"Slow?" I said unbelievingly.

"Slow," she said firmly. "He may be Mr. Quick on the basketball court,
but at home he's the slowest man in the world!''

Just like the coach, the guys, and even the other Celtic wives, I liked Beth
Havlicek. Everybody likes Beth Havlicek. She's a "right nice girl," as Mrs.
Catfish would say. But nice girls don't make good copy, and that's why she's
the only basketball star's wife in the book. After spending six hours with Jane
West (former Laker star Jerry West's wife), I decided not to use the interview.
She was a carbon copy of Beth.

I explained my decision to my agent over the phone and told him that since
I was in California, I might as well see some wives of track stars.

"But you've only got one basketball player's wife," he complained.

"That's enough. All the wives are square, and the ones who aren't won't
talk. Besides, I'm not interested in basketball, and this is *my* book."

"All right," Jacques said crossly. "Go see Kam Seagren. They tell me
she's got the kookiest house in Hollywood, and it's become a boardinghouse
for all the track stars."

Kookie Kam

Jock lovers? They flatter me. They're saying, "Boy, what great taste you have!"

We're known as the battling Seagrens . . . we fight a lot!

The first thing you've got to say about Kameron K. Nelson Seagren* is that not only her name is unusual. The middle initial could stand for Kook, and no one who knows the lady would demur. But it stands for nothing—her mom and dad left it open. She can pick any name she likes whenever she gets ready. She can't make up her mind. There's a special fascination for names beginning with *K* in the Nelson family. Kam's father is Karl, her sister is Karla, and her daughter is Kirsten.

"I've come close to filling in the *K*, but I always change my mind at the last minute. Besides, it would spoil all the fun if I decided once and for all," she said.

Compared to Kam's house, the name business pales. It's in the middle of crowded, conservative Westwood, California. From the outside it's conventional enough, a two-story Spanish stucco with the usual neatly manicured lawn. But the inside! I still haven't decided whether or not I liked it, but after my tour I felt the pressing need for a Valium.

If houses reflect their occupants, the Seagrens are classic schizophrenics. When I was ushered into the sunken living room, I thought I was on the set of *Gunsmoke* and that, any minute, Matt, Kitty, and Doc would barge in. There were three ornate red velvet Victorian love seats, matching heavy red velvet curtains with prominent gold tassel tiebacks, Tiffany lamps, and numerous brass spittoons strategically stationed on the polished floor.

"Isn't it wonderful? It's just like a whorehouse," said Kam, who has probably never seen one.

It might have been like one for all I know, except for three medals on the wall: the 1973 Gold SuperStar medal, a silver medal from the fateful 1972 Munich Olympics, and a gold medal from the 1968 Olympics in Mexico. They were inconsistent with the Belle Watling motif.

---

*Bob Seagren, professional pole vaulter. Bob Seagren is the former world record holder in the pole vault at 18 feet 5¾ inches. Seagren won the gold medal in the vault in the 1968 Olympics and the silver medal in the 1972 Olympics. The former collegiate vault champion from Southern Cal (USC), he dominated this event in the late 1960s. A superb athlete, Seagren won the 1973 SuperStar Competition. Since joining the professional track tour, he has vaulted over 18 feet several times.

So was the enormous obstruction in the hallway, identified for me as a bird-cage. The top of this black wrought-iron contraption reached the ceiling of the second floor. It was big enough to hold all the whooping cranes still in existence, with enough space left over for fifty eagles in flight and thirty-five peacocks. It was vacant.

"I don't know what I'm going to *do* with that thing," Kam said airily, throwing a limp-wrist gesture in its direction, "but it might make a good playpen for the baby."

The dining room might have been the wine cellar at Windsor Castle. Wine racks camouflaged three walls, imprisoning some fifty cases of exotic wines. Two huge barrel drums, marked Dom Perignon, served as the buffet, and the dining table was right out of Tudor England, long and massive with high-backed carved chairs and set with pewter goblets and plates. King Henry VIII would have been perfect at its head, flinging turkey bones over his shoulders. Old Henry was there actually, surveying the room with jaundiced eye from a vantage point on the wall where he glared disapprovingly out of an enormous oil painting (copy).

"I'm just *crazy* about Henry," bubbled Kam as we strolled out of the dining room and up the winding stairs for the rest of the tour, "because he didn't lead a dull life."

She forgot to mention that he dispatched unwanted wives to their eternal rest rather more readily than most. He would have liked Kam, too, for a while.

When we got to the master bedroom, we were out of Tudor territory and into the French Normandy country scene. A tiny pink-flowered print engulfed the walls, draperies, bedspread, chaise longue, and big, puffy pillows, edged in black lace, on the bed.

"Black lace makes it sexy, don't you think? *Wait* until you see the bathroom. We've had all the modern tubs removed and replaced with those darling old-fashioned kind with brass legs." She stood in the middle of the master bathroom with her arms outstretched. "Isn't it positively *sexy?*"

It looked quite functional to me until I noticed the mirrored ceiling. "Sexy," I concurred, wondering exactly how the Seagrens spent their bathroom time.

The nursery, where one-year-old Kirsten was sleeping, was Bavarian Bambi-land. The crib was brass, shaded by a white, ruffled organdy canopy. It stood regally in the very center of the room and was surrounded by elves and oversized stuffed animals. Edelweiss were painted on the woodwork, and Bambi was leaping all over the murals. I tiptoed to the edge of the crib, looked down on the peaceful face, and wondered whether she ever woke up yodeling.

The rest of the tour turned up a guest room done in the Dark Ages, a bedroom that was American Depression (the best kind), a Victorian hallway, and a jet-age den. It was a house in search of a theme.

Another thing you've got to say about Kam Seagren is that she's an absolute knockout—a flawless beauty. Her reed-thin figure is curvy, her eyes green, and her hair long and flaxen. When we went to the Farmer's Market to shop for the ingredients to make a health salad for lunch, I noticed that every head turned as she walked by the crowded stands. She walked along briskly, pretending not to notice the attention she was getting, but I could see she was secretly pleased that I noticed it.

We poked around the vegetables, pinching avocados, and Kam noted that they were expensive, which reminded her it was a bore not to be rich.

"We're just barely making it. Not exactly deprived, but I want to be obnoxiously rich," she said.

Just then she leaned over to me and whispered that Clint Eastwood was standing near the lettuce, and we joined a few others who stood transfixed, watching him trying to choose between romaine and iceberg.

"I'd *love* a movie career like his," she said with an admiring glance. "I've already been in one movie with Joe Namath, but I want to make it really big."

She knows that if she's ever to become obnoxiously rich, *she'll* have to make it really big because the economics of track won't do it for her husband.

"Nobody's rich in the track world," she said. "No matter how hard they run or how high they jump, they can't make any money. It's not like other sports. You don't sign a big contract with a pole vaulting team. In track there are no Catfish Hunters or Peles. Of course, Pele's the exception when it comes to soccer players. They and track people are at the bottom when it comes to money."

Kam also realizes that Bob is running out of medals and age is slowing him down. She's never been one to rest on his laurels, and now she's showing an itch to move out and eclipse her husband's star.

"Our parents worry because we don't have a set income and because we spend what we earn. They warn us the beautiful pink bubble will burst." Kam clearly isn't worried. They make TV commercials, endorse products, and do promotions. There are bit parts in films—and the hope of eventual stardom. "The pins are rolling our way, and we live like it will last forever. It won't, I know that, but I'm not going to worry about it. I'm lucky."

Others who make their living from track and have no moonlighting to turn to are not so lucky. They go to the lucky ones for help.

"I don't know how it happened," Kam said, shrugging her lovely shoulders, "but I woke up one morning and realized I was running a boardinghouse filled with nonpaying guests. It wasn't only friends, but people we hardly knew. They just seemed to drift in. One time last year there was a pole vaulter from Maryland who was down on his luck and had no place to stay, so I gave him the Great American Depression room. The next day a couple from Australia, whom we knew briefly when we were down there for a meet, dropped in to live with us until they found a place of their own. They stayed nine weeks. At the same time a girlfriend of mine, who was a model, out of work and broke, moved in. There was no room, so she had to sleep with the pole vaulter, which would have been OK except they didn't dig each other sexually, so they were forced to sleep on opposite ends of a king-sized bed. Weird, huh? Wait a minute. Listen to this. The Australian guy, he never knocked on doors. I mean he would barge into rooms, his eyes popping and never say a word. I personally think he was out prowling around one night, looking for his wife. She had moved to another room because my sister and her husband had come for a visit and I gave them the Australians' room. Oh, dear, it's so confusing. Anyway, this Australian guy opened the door to Great American Depression and found the model in bed with the pole vaulter, and she looked at him and patted the empty space in the middle and said something like, 'You might as well get in here, too.' She thought he was looking for a place to sleep. He thought. . . . Oh, well, it doesn't matter *what* he thought.''

Feeding this bunch, said Kam, threw the kitchen into disarray, with as many as five eating shifts organized at dinner time. She said it was customary for guests to panic because they were afraid the food would run out before they were filled up. She said they practically stomped each other to get to the buffet line first; then they piled their plates rather than risk losing out on seconds.

"One track friend of Bob's used to pile up two plates and hardly leave a crumb for anyone else.''

I had seen no boarders during the house tour and suggested that she'd either gone out of business or this was the slow season. She said she'd boarded up the boardinghouse when Kirsten was born.

"I didn't want her to grow up in a wild atmosphere,'' she said. "The model, my girlfriend, took to going around the house in a bikini. I saw her working on my husband and decided that was carrying the share-the-wealth plan too far. I threw them all out.''

Kam served the vegetable salad out by the pool and gave me a quick summary of her life. She was born twenty-five years ago on tiny Balboa Island and lived most of her life in California. She didn't like school very much and was only a fair student. "After a while everything was a repeat of the eighth grade.''

But she was an accomplished equestrian and track star because of her father's influence. He bought her a quarter horse when she was small, and her love of horses and riding led to three national championships and more than 300 trophies in the thirteen to seventeen age group. When she wasn't riding, her father coached her in track. In the San Gabriel All Comers' meet she won the 100-yard dash, the long jump, the relay, and the 440. In 1965 she went to the Rose Bowl Track Meet, and when she finished her relay race, she wandered over to the pole vault pit to watch Bob Seagren, the man everyone in the track world was talking about. She joined a crowd of twittering women fans on the grass and riveted her attention on him, deciding he was for her, while he, oblivious to the fact that he'd become Kam's man, repeatedly tore down the runway and grunted himself over the bar, tending to business. Nothing substantial came of that first encounter because no one was there to introduce them, and Kam was called back to her own area. The official announcement had to be postponed.

Months later Kam watched Bob win the gold medal in the 1968 Olympics on television. She applauded his feat wildly in the living room of her home and in a frenzy of passion announced to her startled family that she was going to marry him one day.

It really wasn't much of a problem for her. When Bob came home from the Olympics, he noticed Kam's picture on the cover of *Teen Age* magazine. She was wearing a track uniform which, among other things, caught his eye. He was wondering how he could meet her. Needless to say, fate took a hand. It went like this:

The cover picture opened up interesting new possibilities for Kam. She was offered a job as hostess on her own half hour TV talk show called *Kam's Corner* (naturally). It was a hodgepodge of interviews, gossip, and advice to teenagers on Channel 9, a local Los Angeles station. She also received offers to model and do TV commercials, and it occurred to her that it mightn't be a bad idea to take some speech lessons and study drama.

Simultaneously, Bob Seagren's agent had lined the star up with several promotions and speaking engagements, and he recommended that Bob also take speech and acting to improve his presence.

Of course, Kam and Bob wound up in the same class playing opposite each other in a love scene from *Cactus Flower*. The wedding was a year later, and *that's* when the fight started—the fight that has ranged across thirty-eight countries, privately and publicly, ever since.

Everyone was at the church in Los Angeles at eight thirty that night except Kam. She had her television show to do, in addition to going through the elaborate, nerve-racking gussying up demanded of brides.

"I knew I was late, so I ran out into the street—I was in my wedding gown, remember—and tried to find a cab. Hah! Have you ever tried to find a cab in LA? I decided I could get there faster on foot—I wasn't a track star for nothing. I hiked up that gown in one hand, held the veil down with the other, and took off. I don't know what people thought when they saw me—either that I was late for my wedding or that I was trying to escape from it. It was embarrassing either way. By the time I dashed down the church aisle it was nine thirty, and I was huffing and puffing like I'd just finished the hundred yard dash in record time. I may have, for all I know. And let me tell you I hadn't wanted the *Lohengrin* wedding march, so I chose 'Good Morning, Starshine' instead because I like it better and it's not so gloomy. But while I was walking down the aisle, at nine thirty at night, gasping for breath and Bob absolutely livid, I realized that 'Good Morning, Starshine' was as out of place as a funeral march. Oh, well, we got through it.''

On their honeymoon flight to Australia they got into such a terrible brawl they almost got divorced in Hawaii. They patched it up, but when they reached Melbourne, they had another one—a street brawl this time. Kam was throwing packages, her umbrella, and a newspaper. She started to kick him in the shins and wound up taking off her shoes to throw at Bob in front of their hotel. A journalist came by a few hours later and wanted confirmation of the report he'd heard that they'd been fighting. Kam smiled sweetly at him, denied the story and, to convince him, invited him into the hotel room. In the middle of gushing about how wonderful it was to be married to the great champion pole vaulter, the phone rang. Her call to Mother back in the States had come through. Carefully, she took it in the other room, but her cries could be heard out in the hall, and the reporter got an earful. Between sobs Kam shouted to her mother over a bad connection, ''I'm coming home to get a divorce!''

Then in Spain, Bob asked Kam, who knows a little Spanish, to be his interpreter at a press conference. One reporter asked if he was looking forward to making a record jump the next day. Bob told Kam to tell the reporters he'd suffered an injury and didn't think he'd be competing. The next day Bob's agent called and asked him why he'd made such a dumb remark as the one that had appeared in all the papers.

''What dumb remark?'' asked Bob.

His agent read it to him: ''I'm not going to compete tomorrow because I've eaten too much paella.''

Bob hung up, yelling, ''Kaaaaaaaammmmmmmmm!'' and the battling Seagrens were at it again.

When friends say the Seagrens air their differences, it's frequently a literal truth. They have their best battles at 20,000 feet. Once, flying to San Francisco for a meet, Bob and Kam staged a yelling match that left both sets of parents and the other passengers slack-jawed, plugging up their ears and cringing in their seats in embarrassment. The stewardess kept asking them nervously to tone it down. She might have been asking an earthquake to pull itself together for all the response she got. It was Bob's old, deaf grandmother who eventually broke up the fight. She was taking her first plane ride to see her grandson pole vault. She leaned from her seat across the aisle, tapped Bob on the arm, and gave him and Kam a sweet smile and said, "Isn't flying fun? So smooth and quiet!"

They all cracked up.

Friends have warned that someday they'll go too far and there'll be no neutral ground to return to. One athlete's wife in Los Angeles, who knows the Seagrens well, believes that instead of building a good marriage, they're staging a contest to determine who will emerge the stronger.

At a party recently, the Seagrens were introduced to a couple who'd just moved in across the street.

"We don't *need* an introduction," the new neighbor's wife said acidly. "We feel as though we've known you a long time. We certainly know all your business. We hear your voices every night over the traffic."

When the Seagrens settled down to housekeeping after the stormy honeymoon, Bob had already set ten world records and had his gold medal. His beautiful model-track star-equestrian-television hostess-wife was also moving nicely. The year 1973 in their small apartment in Santa Monica was a very good year for both. Between television commercials, promotions, superstar money, speaking engagements, and movie parts, they made enough to buy their home in Westwood Village and start their boardinghouse operation.

Today the boarders are gone, but the house is still full of friends and fun. The regulars are Rod and Mary Laver, Anne and Jim Ryun, Babbs and Willie Shoemaker, an ever-changing collection of movie starlets, doctors, lawyers, businessmen, and Gypsy Boots.

Boots is a sixty-seven-year-old health addict. He and his followers are frequent visitors at the Seagrens'. According to Kam, Gypsy is the original hippie and loves to come over to discuss diets with the track stars.

When I visited the Seagrens, I missed out on all the fun. No boarders, no brawls, screaming contests, or even dirty looks. They seemed to be loving. Bob strolled in and spoke of his hopes for winning the SuperStar competition in Florida (he didn't). Kam offered him a backhanded compliment when she commented, in his presence, "Groupies are around Bob all the time, but they flatter me because what they're saying is 'Boy, what great taste *you* have!' "

They smiled at each other a lot and brought the baby downstairs and played with her. They looked like such a beautiful family. You wanted them to stay together always because they look so perfect together, if for no other reason. But you can't help wondering when you leave that sweet domestic scene if it's just another commercial and if, once the door closes behind you, the Seagrens will be at it again.

Laughing Anne

*I had a dream the night before the race, and in my dream, Jim fell
down. I didn't warn him . . . I've often wondered if I should have
. . . if it would have made a difference.*

When various sports personalities in Los Angeles knew I was going up to
Santa Barbara to see Anne Ryun* they all asked me to be sure and mention
their name to the Ryuns. "Say hello—give them our best!" Ask them when
they're coming down off the mountain." It struck me as peculiar, as if the
Ryuns were living on a different planet, instead of two hours away. "Find
out," one sportscaster suggested, "if the Ryuns are beginning to feel
spooked. . . ."

And so I knew before I headed up that way, that Jim and Anne were living
outside the heady world of superstardom—in some kind of self-imposed exile
in Santa Barbara. There was talk of Jim's hard luck and the big question.: Did
he believe it?

Jim Ryun, up to May, 1975, held the world record for the mile which he
ran in 3:51.1 at Bakersfield, California, in 1967. But misfortune has followed
him everywhere since that time, and it's a wonder he doesn't feel spooked.

The first time he tried for the Olympics in '64 he was a junior in high school
in Wichita, Kansas. In spite of the fact that he could run as "fast as lightning," he didn't make the semifinals because he got the flu. The second time
he tried for the Olympics it wasn't the flu but Mexico's thin air. In the 1968
Olympics at Mexico City, Rod Clark, of Australia, collapsed at the end of the
1,500 meter race. The altitude got to Jim, too, who knew, with his shortness
of breath, that he'd have to push it to win and decided the race wasn't worth
killing himself for. Kip Choge Keino, from Kenya, who was used to high alti-
tudes, won the gold medal, and Ryun came in second. His disappointment
was monumental.

In 1972 he tried again. This time Anne and his parents went along as a
cheering section. In Munich they watched him in a race that should have qual-
ified him for the finals. He trailed behind the other runners, which was his

---

*Jim Ryun, professional track runner. Jim Ryun established a world record in the
mile run (3:51.1) that endured for eight years. One of the most famous track stars in
the world, Ryun dominated the middle-distance races in the 1960s. (He also set a
world record in the half mile run.) Ryun won a silver medal at the 1968 Olympics in
Mexico City but lost his chances for a gold medal at Munich in 1972, when he was accidentally tripped. Ryun joined the professional track tour (ITA) in 1973 and has established several professional records.

style, and about 500 yards before the finish line, he started running hard. As he moved out to run around the pack, a Pakistani runner threw an elbow into him. Jim wasn't prepared for it and fell. Another runner accidentally spiked him as he went down.

His heartbroken family stood up in the stands, yelling, "Get up! Get up!" He did—but it was too late. He finished last. The disillusioning thing for Jim and Anne, though, was the politics that followed. The officials claimed Ryun had fouled a man, but the film of the race indicates there were no officials around. Jim's petition for acceptance into the next day's race was turned down. The press did their usual "Thrill of Victory—Agony of Defeat" stories, and close friends of Jim's started whispering about his being "snakebit." The track world agreed he'd had entirely too much hard luck to make it a coincidence.

Publicly, Jim looks at the Munich Olympics as bad officiating and the Mexico City Olympics as the end result of a bad choice in location. He has said many times that it was politics, not luck, that was against him.

Today Jim Ryun is on the public relations staff of the International Track Association, is a national spokesman for Post Cereal, and works with numerous track clinics and boys' camps throughout the West. It all sounds good on his résumé, but the Los Angeles jocks who know him say his track career is pretty well shot. He has been severely hampered by hay fever and asthma, and lately his breathing problems have caused him not to be able to finish races he has started. Watching him on national television slow down and drop out of a race hasn't endeared him to his fans. His fame is fading, his world record was beaten by Filbert Bayi, of Tanzania (3:51.0), in May, 1975 (which in turn was surpassed on August, 12, 1975, by John Walker of New Zealand—3:49.4), his earnings are meager, and the glory, recognition, and invincibility that once surrounded his name have been replaced by a jinxlike aura.

"He was once a great athlete," the sports crowd in LA say about Ryun, "but SOL—short on luck."

With this information I headed to Santa Barbara.

The Ryuns live in a middle-income tract section—the kind advertised in the newspaper as "Get back to the basics and buy a commonsense home!" However, their one-level house is not like the others. The last one on the street and nestled up to the foothills of the Santa Barbara range, it allows them to look out their kitchen window and see cows grazing. Of course, on the other side of the house they look out on rows and rows of houses just like theirs. I like their furniture. It came from Sweden. They spotted it in a store window in Stockholm when they were there for a meet. Made out of blue pine, it's beautiful, sturdy, and natural-looking, just like the people who live there.

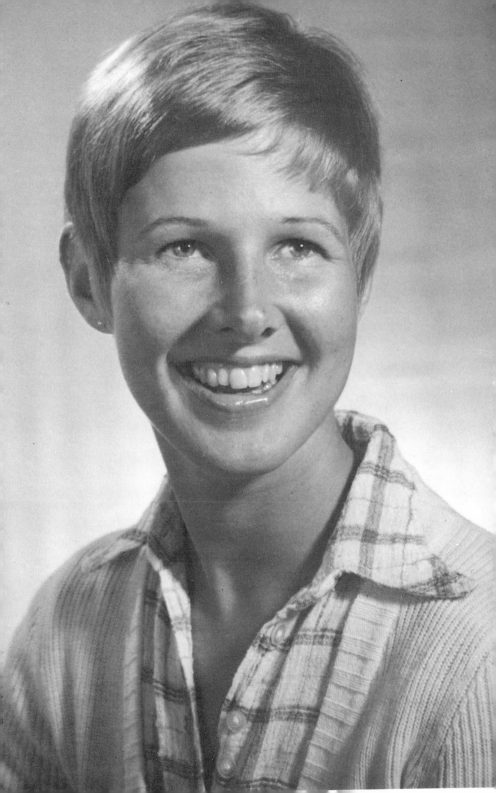

Anne and Jim greeted me at the door arm in arm. Jim looked as if he were holding a pocket-sized Kewpie doll next to his tall, lanky figure. This diminutive girl, with yellow-blond, closely cropped hair, looks like the little Dutch boy in the cleansing powder ads. She had no makeup on, and her skin was all pink and glowing. I made a mental note that like all the other wives I'd interviewed, Anne had a great figure—only to find out later that she was five months pregnant and still a size eight. Her blue eyes twinkled, and her face had that kind of upturn to it that looked as if she would probably smile in repose. I figured something pretty funny had been going on between them because Anne never stopped laughing from the time she opened the door.

By the end of the day I realized it's "jubilation time" *all* the time with Anne Ryun.

In terms of financial security, Anne is the poorest of all the wives (with the exception of Mary Lynn Rote), yet the happiest wife in the bunch. It's difficult to say whether her joy comes from her religion or her religion comes from her joy. She's a strange girl, not like any of the others. For one thing, she laughs all the time. I mean *all* the time. It's not phony, forced, sardonic, or even a nervous twitter; it's a genuine happy childlike laugh.

"Tell me about Kam Seagren, is she well? Isn't she beautiful? And that adorable baby—did you *see* Kirsten? They're such a handsome family. I wish we could see more of them." She laughed through every question, and when she ran out of questions, she laughed some more.

It was annoying. We aren't conditioned to hear someone laugh all the time over absolutely nothing. First I thought, *For God's sake, what is she laughing about? Is she psychotic or just plain balmy?* I decided to ask her. "Have you ever noticed . . . that—"

"I laugh all the time?" She laughed delightedly. "Yesssssss! But mostly I notice how glum other people are!" The thought made her laugh all the more.

I suddenly wondered if I looked glum and managed a positively sickly smile. "Do you laugh when you're pleased, when you like something, or does everything really seem funny to you?"

"I laugh all the time."

Jim came in the room and sat down, tall, boyishly handsome, and exceedingly serious. He smiles once in a while but *never* laughs. "Anne is a happy person, "he said quietly. "But sometimes I get the feeeling people could be offended because they think she's laughing at them. Of course she's not."

I mentioned that neither one of them appeared to be bitter over the bad luck that seemingly followed Jim around at the Olympics.

"I don't believe in luck!" Jim answered seriously while Anne laughed and shook her head. "God has his way. Sometimes it doesn't look like I've had good luck, but we know there is perfect timing in all things."

I gave him the messages I'd brought from Los Angeles, and he smiled and said, "We aren't bothered by being out of the swim—out of the mainstream. We're not publicity-seeking people. Besides, why should we go down there? We have our life here. Our friends aren't big, glamorous names, but they're all good, down-to-earth people. . . . "

"All of them are Christians," Anne said brightly.

"Yes." He nodded. "You can be sure of that!"

Religion is the most important factor in the Ryuns' lives. They live, breathe, feel, and radiate their religion.

"We're interested in a new spirit of Christianity. It's not so much a religion as a way of life. It's living a good Christian life!" While other wives talk to their plants or cats, Anne talks to God.

"I'm in communication with Christ all the time . . . and He talks back to me."

"How is this accomplished?" I asked, feeling slightly uncomfortable.

"By listening. Listening is important. God speaks to us through friends, the Bible, through prayer, through nature, but if you listen very quietly, He'll come right into your mind and tell you what to do—tell you how things will turn out."

"Why didn't God tell you Jim was going to be tripped in the Munich Olympics?" I asked unfairly.

"Oh, He did. I had a dream the night before the race, and in my dream, Jim fell down. I didn't warn him because I thought it would upset him. I've often wondered if I should have . . . if it would have made a difference. I don't think so. It was meant to be. What counts is how we handle it."

Anne laughed softly and played with the only piece of jewelry she ever wears—a silver and turquoise cross. "The German Olympics proved to us all, with the death of those Israelis, that there is something in life much more important than winning a race!"

"Winning isn't against your religion, is it?"

"No!" Anne's hyacinth-blue eyes went wide. "Jim did his best. His best to win." And then for the first and only time that day she stopped smiling and added, "Those were stupid rules!"

Anne Snider Ryun was born in Sandusky, Ohio, one of seven children in a happy, religious upper-middle-income family. Anne claims the only exciting thing about her entire childhood was when the family moved to Bay Village, a suburb of Cleveland, and they lived down the street from the notorious Dr. Sam Sheppard. Anne went to school with the doctor's niece and remembered them all as "very sweet people. Years later, when I read what happened, I couldn't believe it!"

After public school, Anne attended Kansas State University, where she got her degree in elementary education. While she was there, she met Jim Ryun, who'd just broken the world's record in the mile run while attending the University of Kansas.

"I went up and asked for his autograph. He had just broken the world's record that afternoon, and everyone was so excited! But I didn't get it." Anne laughed merrily. "He was sooo upset about his track shoes that he wouldn't sign any autographs!"

"What about his track shoes?"

"Well, someone had stolen them. I suppose the person thought they were special since Jim had run in them when he broke the record. Jim didn't seem to care about any of the back patting or compliments that were by now coming in from all over the country. He was so mad about those shoes he even turned me down when I said, "Please."

The disappearance of those track shoes symbolically triggered the hard-luck syndrome for Jim Ryun. From that moment on things went wrong in his track career. But things started to go right in his personal life. Anne and Jim were finally introduced by mutual friends and married a year later in 1968. They moved to Topeka, Kansas, where Jim became a professional photographer working for a Topeka newspaper. It didn't pay too well, and in January, 1971, they "U-hauled" it out to Eugene, Oregon, the track capital of the world. Jim got a job as a photographer for the Bohemia Lumber Company and, by working out every day, started to get back into the track world he knew and loved. He was running well when suddenly his breathing went bad. The pollen season knocked him flat, and he stopped training. The Ryuns packed up their worldly possesions once again and "U-hauled" it down to Santa Barbara, where the climate seemed to agree with him, but where the bad-luck syndrome certainly didn't end.

Today the Ryuns seem to be settled in their little house with the blue pine furniture and the cows grazing outside—a house they say was built for children. Their children are beautiful. Heather, their five-year-old, and the two-year-old twins, Ned and Drew, have to be the best-behaved children I've ever encountered, besides being absolutely angelic-looking. It all seems too "Goodie two-shoes" to be true. But it is! The Ryuns, who have the most to be bitter about seem the least bitter. If others think they're down on their luck, the Ryuns smile and say nothing. Being with them makes you wonder. What *is* luck?

And how can one describe Anne Ryun? That she's happy and laughs all the time? That she's religious and talks with God? What is there to say about someone after you say, "She talks with God"?

I suddenly remembered Jim's remark about their not being publicity seekers and wondered why she'd granted me this interview. "God told me to go ahead,'' Anne rhapsodized. "I asked Him if I should do it and He said yes. I knew it would be all right!''

It embarrassed me, and I searched for some logical explanation for the astonishing things she was saying. "Anne,'' I blurted out, "you certainly have a great imagination!''

"Oh, it's not my imagination. God always tells me what to do. Not long ago I had a friend dying of terminal cancer. Everyone said she was doomed. Jesus told me she would recover, and I went to the hospital and prayed with my friend. I told her Jesus had told me she would get better—and do you know, she got well!'' Anne laughed joyously while I sat looking at her in amazement. "She got well!'' Anne repeated ecstatically. Then she smiled softly and added, "When it gets the toughest and hurts the most, just say' Jesus,' and He'll be there!''

"What do you, uh, do all day,'' I asked, eager to change the subject, "besides—''

"Besides talk to God?'' She laughed easily. "Well, I tend to my garden. I grow flowers for the old and sick.'' The next moment Anne was bounding into the kitchen, then skipping back toward me with a vase of flowers in her hand. "It's a jelly jar,'' Anne explained, "and I tie a big ribbon around the jar and put daisies and sweetpeas in the little vase and take them around to the old people's homes, to the hospitals. It cheers up a lot of old people who don't have anybody to love them—the flowers make them smile. Heather helps me. We have a wonderful time making them up and taking them around.''

Suddenly I had a vision of laughing Anne and beautiful five-year-old Heather showing up at the foot of some ancient soul's bed with their fresh daisies in the ribboned jelly jar. *Regina angelorum*—Queen of the Angels. It was absolutely a celestial image, and I didn't have the heart to ask her about jock lovers, or the insolence to ask if sex life is normal with a long-distance runner (besides, he hardly ever races), or the audacity to ask if she might be worried about the future (would you ask that of someone who has a direct line to God?).

I picked up my notebook and turned to go.

"Don't forget, Jeanne''—Anne laughed—"when the going gets the toughest and it hurts the most, say, 'Jesus,' and He'll be there!''

I nodded and hurried out to my car. It was late, and I wanted to make Los Angeles before rush-hour traffic. As I headed out of Santa Barbara on Highway One, I heard a siren. Motioned over to the side of the road, I waited while the biggest, toughest, meanest-looking policeman I've ever encountered got out of his car and strode over to my window.

"What's the charge?'' I stammered weakly while he started writing out a ticket.

"Speeding. Ten miles over the limit. That's really movin', lady. Let's see your registration."

I opened the glove compartment and, methodically at first and then frantically, shuffled through a ton of papers, maps, bottle openers, a small flask (where did *that* come from?) and swore softly under my breath at my friend who'd let me borrow his car. Finally, I gave up.

"You'll have to come along with me to the station."

My heart froze. "Please. I've borrowed a friend's car. . . . I've come up here to do an interview with Jim Ryun's wife—you know, the track star? She'll tell you. I mean, I didn't steal this car," I pleaded, beads of perspiration trickling down my face. My hands were trembling on the steering wheel as I looked up into his cold eyes and stony face. I knew he was going to arrest me. "Jesus," I swore out loud, just thinking of what was ahead.

Suddenly his leathery face broke into a beaming smile.

"I see you *were* with little Annie Ryun!" He nodded toward the back seat. "She brings the same thing to my mother out in the rest home. Hurry along or the daisies will wilt!" He was gone.

I sat there a while until the trembling stopped, and then I turned around and looked in the back seat. There were sweetpeas and daisies stuck into a jelly jar and tied with a big green ribbon. A note on the seat simply said "Anne."

Mrs. Junior

I love Kyle, but I hardly ever see him. . . . He's out drumming up money.

What I really mind is being called Mrs. Junior.

Mary Lynn Rote* picked me up at the airport, and before I closed the car door, she was right into what was bugging her. "If the New York Cosmos can sign Pele to a seven-million-dollar contract that will pay him about two million dollars a year to play soccer, *why* does my husband have to play for seven thousand dollars?"

It sure makes her angry. Kyle Rote, Jr., is a top scorer for the Dallas Tornados and was a member of the U.S. National Team which defeated Poland and Bermuda, and in 1974 he won the nationally televised SuperStar Competition over such athletes as Bob Seagren and O. J. Simpson.

All that, and he was worth just $7,000!

"I'll never forget when Kyle signed his new contract, after reading about some of the superstars' contracts like Catfish and Csonka. It seemed absolutely ludicrous," said Mary Lynn as she drove through Dallas traffic. "We went to Lamar Hunt's office—he's one of the richest men in Texas . . . in the world. The Hunts are oil people and he owns World Champion Tennis, the Kansas City Chiefs, part of a hockey team, and the Dallas Tornados. We sat around his plush office with Lamar in his custom-made suit and the two of us in our seedy cottons, negotiating. Lamar was trying to squeeze Lyle down a few hundred dollars, and all I could think of was how little those dollars meant to him—and how *much* they meant to us.

"Lamar put his feet up on the table, and I noticed he had a hole in his shoe. I started laughing, and I couldn't stop. Mr. Hunt thought I was off my rocker, but I never said anything."

Mary Lynn told me without bitterness that when Kyle was drafted by the Tornados in May, 1973, he received $50 a month and $40 a game. "We lived on tuna fish. I created two hundred things to do with tuna. Today Kyle won't touch it. I don't blame him."

*Kyle Rote, Jr., professional soccer player. The son of a former all-American and New York football Giant star, Kyle Rote, Jr., has excelled in soccer since his days at the University of the South. In his first season with the Dallas Tornados Rote set a team record for assists, led the league in scoring, and was named the league's Rookie of the Year. He played on the U.S. National Team and won the nationally televised 1974 SuperStar Competition over such athletes as Bob Seagren and O. J. Simpson. Rote placed second in the 1975 SuperStar Competition.

It was only after being picked Rookie of the Year that he could command that $7,000 figure. Soccer is the lowest-paying sport in America. The average salary is $2,500 a year.

Mary Lynn is twenty-three, self-conscious and insecure. She thinks she's homely. She asked me if the other wives are pretty. Before I could answer, she blurted, "My nose is too big."

I assured her, truthfully, that her nose was fine. Indeed, her facial bone structure offers great beauty potential, which she squanders. She seems to take great pains to make herself look unattractive. Her wheat-blond hair is allowed to hang in limp, stringy strands. It looks as though she had cut it herself in the dark.

Part of the trouble is a deathly pallor she could disguise with makeup if she chose, which she doesn't. Her face is so chalky it borders on being albino. She is painfully thin. For good reason. She was born with kidney and bladder defects and spent the first nine years of her life bedridden. She recently had surgery to remove a bladder obstruction, and she hadn't fully recovered when I saw her. She sat in ill-fitting jeans and a cotton shirt in the living room of the little corner brick house in North Dallas, drinking tea and talking. Two cats spread themselves out near us in total disinterest. Mary Lynn turned to one of them.

"Are you hungry? Well, I've been neglecting you. Come on, Ten Pin, here, Alley, let's go get some dinner."

She disappeared for several minutes and returned, collapsing on the couch, exhausted. The exertion had tired her. She thought a moment, as though trying to pick up the thread of her narrative.

"The Hunts. They're really very nice in every way, except when it comes to paying for contracts. We see them socially once in a while, invited to their house for parties. But I don't like to go. Everyone's older, you see? I'm always wrong or I should say I'm never right. Norma Hunt and all her friends are so . . . so chic. They always seem to know the right thing to wear. If I wear a simple dress, they're done up like they're goin' to the opening of the opera. Once I wore a gorgeous dress from Neiman-Marcus' boutique, and everyone else was in a halter top and pants. We were invited to a picnic over at their estate, and I wore blue jeans. Everyone else was in a long flowered-print dress. I'm just . . . wrong."

Mary Lynn picked up a kitten that had wandered into the room and cuddled it.

"Another thing. I can't keep my mouth shut. I have a terrible temptation to tell both owners, Lamar and Bill McNutt, 'Why don't you pay my husband enough to live on?' So you see it's better that I stay home. It upsets me to see

the way they live, knowing we can't save a dollar and that Kyle has no pension plan or hospitalization or life insurance or benefits like other athletes have.''

Most Americans don't know it, but soccer, the most popular sport in the world, has had a hard row to hoe in the United States. Americans, who spend more on sports than anyone else in the world, won't get it up for soccer. Even Pele couldn't draw flies in his first American season.

In the spring of 1967 an effort was made to introduce soccer on a large scale to New Yorkers. The New York Generals were playing the Los Angeles Toros at Yankee Stadium. Fewer than 5,000 people came, and the price of admission was only $2 per family. Somebody spent a quarter of an hour on the loudspeaker explaining how the game is played. Then ushers handed out leaflets called *This Is Soccer.*

Soccer bombed in New York then, and only in 1975 did it show signs of maybe making it someday. Until the stands are jammed with paying guests, as they are for other sports, soccer players will remain the po' boys of the sports world. So what is Mary Lynn supposed to do in the meantime?

''Kyle loves the game. He's good at it, and he wants to play.''

When she speaks of the future, she hugs her cats tightly.

''We're frustrated. Kyle doesn't know what he wants to do. We can't make a living at soccer. He's studying theology at SMU now. He studied law for one year but decided that's not for him. I'll bet the wives of those rich football players don't have problems. Maybe we'll move away from Dallas. Kyle has talked about going to the Pacific Northwest, but he knows he can't make a living there either. It's a vicious cycle.''

To make ends meet, Kyle supplements his income with speaking engagements, promotes soccer balls and shoes and automotive supplies and, with Mary Lynn's help, runs a summer camp for retarded children for two weeks each summer. They work with 150 boys and receive $500 for it.

Most of the time the Rotes are separated, especially because Mary Lynn cannot travel.

''I love him, but I hardly ever see him. So last year I went back to school to study speech pathology because we're both into helping retarded kids. But I worked so hard on my courses that Kyle and I didn't see each other at all. I had only one semester to go, but Kyle said he wanted me home so he could see me more often, so I quit. Well, let me tell you that even though I'm no longer at school and stay home all the time, I *still* don't see him—so I think I'd better give up trying and go back to school, get my degree, and do something with my life.''

She tossed a cat into the air the way one would play with an infant.

"I'm a women's libber!" she declared proudly. "Kyle is a male chauvinist pig. He thinks women should be barefoot, pregnant, and in the kitchen. He'd like me to sit here and wait for him to come in the door and shower him with affection."

I assumed, out loud, that since she is a women's libber she wouldn't do that.

"Oh, but I do. I sit here and wait for him to come home and shower him with affection."

She kissed one of her cats to emphasize her feeling.

"I love him. A women's libber and a male chauvinist pig *can* live happily together. It's bad enough when they call me Mrs. Kyle Rote, but when they call me Mrs. Junior, that's too much. I'm Mary Lynn Rote. I want to be independent—within the limits of our marriage, of course."

She admitted it would be difficult because they had become public property.

"Sports does strange things to people. Look at Kyle's father. He's in the airfreight business now, and he's so sad. Fame and money never solved his problems. He's been divorced twice, and now his career is over, and he's alone and unhappy. He made big money for many years, but now most of it's gone. We don't want to end up that way."

She said she'd like to have children someday but didn't think she could have any of her own, but Dallas County Welfare was looking for emergency foster parents and she'd like to adopt a baby.

"Having children isn't the answer, but taking care of the ones who are already here might be. But gee, it's hard to think about it when there is no financial security."

I asked her why she doesn't go out more often and, since she doesn't, what she does with herself all day.

"I'm grossly uncoordinated, awkward, blundering, clumsy, and all thumbs," she said. "I bombed in tennis and golf, swimming bores me, the sun bothers my skin, so I do everything inside. I play the piano and flute, do needlepoint, water my plants, and talk to my cats."

As if on cue, one of the cats jumped up on my chair and curled its tail around my neck. I knew it was an expression of affection, but I wasn't accustomed to it, and I froze. Mary Lynn noticed my discomfort and took the animal, cradling it in her arms and cooing into its ear.

"This is Bowling Ball," she said at length, holding the huge, fat, furry, whiskered tom up in the air. "Ten Pin is the one on the mantel, and Alley is over on the window ledge."

I nodded to each. I had noticed that they had made coleslaw of the upholstery, which wasn't much to begin with. She called them her permanent cats, pointing out that in addition, she houses six rotating cats and four rotating dogs.

"They're good company for me. Last week, I was in the hospital, and Kyle didn't even know it. He was on some kind of promotion trip, and no one knew where to find him. I talk more to my cats than I do to him. My friends call and invite me to dinner and even offer to provide an escort, but I say no, I'd rather stay here with my cats. I talk to them, and sometimes I forget they can't talk back to me."

This pale blue-eyed girl, who seems undernourished, is an unusual mixture of an introverted woman with certain spinsterlike qualities and the charming naïveté of an innocent who has yet to venture out into the world.

Mary Lynn Lykins was born in Chattanooga, Tennessee. Her father restored furniture.

"He was a craftsman," she said, "and we were poor, proud and happy."

She entered the University of the South, an old Episcopalian school (she and Kyle take religion seriously) in Sewanee, Tennessee, in 1970, the year the school went coed for the first time, and "Did the guys ever resent us!"

Not all of them. She met Kyle there. She was dating one of his fraternity brothers at the time (familiar story).

"Kyle was a big shot, president of the student body, on the newspaper staff and on the track and soccer teams. He was following in his father's footsteps [Kyle Rote, Sr., was an all-American football star with SMU and was later All-Pro with the New York Giants]." Kyle was a student lab instructor in beginning psychology, and Mary Lynn took the course. They never had a formal date. She had gone to a basketball game alone one night, and he saw her and sat next to her long enough to ask idly if she were going to a picnic given by mutual friends the next day and, if so, he would see her there. She hadn't thought about it one way or the other, but now she was sure. The next day was windy, and she found Kyle flying a kite at the picnic. He seemed deeply engrossed in the bobbing, swooping dot in the sky. She watched for a time, neither of them speaking. Then suddenly he said, "I've been drafted by the Dallas Tornado soccer team. If you wanted to, you could come to Dallas with me as my wife." A line straight out of an old Hollywood Western.

"He looked at me with wide serious eyes, and I knew he wasn't just fooling. I had never, ever gone out with the man, never! Come to think of it, I haven't gone out with him much since we've been married either."

They were married on campus the day after Kyle graduated. He was twenty-one, and she was nineteen and had completed only two years at the university.

In the very beginning, Kyle's contract arrangement, $50 per month and $40 per game, gave them $400 a month to live. That was the tuna fish era. But they decided to go to the Virgin Islands on their honeymoon. They rented a cheap hotel room with a kitchenette in St. Thomas. For their very first married dinner, they invited a soccer couple over for spaghetti, the newlyweds' "old reliable." Mary Lynn was anxious to show she could handle herself in the kitchen and was determined to make the event a success. Kyle went out and bought some wine. Everything was going swimmingly. The sauce was ready and bubbling on the stove, she hadn't forgotten to get the grated cheese and Italian bread, the table was set with candlelight and wine, the spaghetti was done to a precise al dente, and she announced she was ready for everyone to take a place. The main course was coming in. She lifted the boiling pan to the sink to drain off the water and the noodles went down the drain. Kyle took everyone out to dinner.

Ten days after they were married, Kyle gave Mary Lynn a ticket to one of his games in Dallas and told her to stay in her seat when the game was over and not to stir until he came to get her. Otherwise they'd miss each other in the crowds. When the game ended, Mary Lynn did as she was told. One hour later she was still sitting there keeping company with 65,000 empty seats and a sympathetic cop, who finally had to tell her she had to move along.

"He was always forgetting me," she said. "After we married, I worked for an insurance company and Kyle was studying law at SMU. We had an arrangement. Whoever took the car each day was supposed to pick up the other person. Whenever I had the car, everything was fine, but when he took it, I never knew. Once he had the car and I was waiting for him. He didn't show. I called all over town—nothing. Then, on a hunch, I called his office, and there he was. He wanted to know what was keeping me."

After one year Kyle decided law wasn't for him, and he turned to theology. Mary Lynn had quit her job to study speech pathology in pursuit of her interest in brain-damaged children. And that was the year they had a lucky break. Kyle was invited to play with the U.S. national team in world competition.

"I'm sure they wanted to see what Kyle Rote's kid could do," said Mary Lynn. "That's the part he doesn't like, being somebody's kid. During the finals I was sitting next to an eighty-year-old man, you know the kind, he knew everything and everybody in sports, and he was going to give me the benefit of his knowledge—all of it. He never stopped identifying people for me. He pointed to Paul Warfield and called him O. J. Simpson, he got Stan Smith mixed up with Dick Anderson, Ernie Green became Reggie Jackson, and Pete Maravich was John Havlicek. I let him ramble on, and Kyle came up to speak to me. When he left, the old man said, 'Now that's one I don't know.' I told him it was Kyle Rote, and he said, 'He certainly has kept his age well.' Later when Kyle was accepting the trophy and check, the old man shook my arm and said, 'Amazing his winning against all those young fellas. Doesn't he look good for his years!' "

That check Kyle received was for $50,000 and it bought them their little one-story house in Dallas, but not much more.

"I love music," said Mary Lynn into Ten Pin's furry softness. "Shall I tell you what I would really like to be, in my wildest dreams? I'd like to be Beverly Sills, the opera star."

Mary Lynn certainly doesn't have the best life-style of all the wives, nor has she found solutions to all her problems, but chances are things will get better. Besides, there are great possibilities such as: The public will begin to appreciate soccer; management will then pay American players more money; Kyle will sign a fantastic contract; Mr. Hunt will repair the "hole in his sole"; Mary Lynn will be called by her own name instead of Mrs. Junior; she will have real children instead of cats; and one day she will venture outside and find the sunshine, and loneliness, like tuna fish, will be a thing of the past.

I called Jacques from my hotel room in Dallas to tell him I was on my way home with a trunkful of tapes to write the book. "Listen," he said in a tone I knew only too well to mean he had more work for me, "come back to New York by way of Cincinnati. I'd like you to talk to Vickie Chesser, the little model who's going to marry Johnny Bench."

"Aw, I've got enough baseball players to fill two books. I wanna come home."

"My God, you knew he was a baseball player! You're improving! Go to the Netherland Hilton in Cincinnati. I tell you this is a hot couple. Bench just met her, and they're getting married in two weeks. The story of how they met is supposed to be wild . . . there are all kinds of rumors . . . smoke her out, OK?"

Little did I know that I would be the one to be smoked out.

The Hotdog

Johnny is such a doll! I love him! He knows I'm a hotdog!

We have something special.

Vickie Chesser, a gorgeous twenty-five-year-old honey blonde from South Carolina, whose background of Swedish, Irish, and Cherokee Indian has produced a face of flawless beauty, will have entered the ranks of superwives by the time you read this. When I met her, she was three weeks away from becoming Mrs. Johnny Bench.* Rumor had it that Johnny Bench, the Cincinnati Red superstar, saw her on an Ultra Brite commercial while watching television one night, picked up the phone, and asked her to marry him. It isn't quite true. Vickie did the toothpaste commercial, but Johnny never saw it. In fact, up to their wedding, in February, 1975, he still hadn't seen it. Their meeting, however, and his subsequent proposal two weeks later are almost as bizarre as the rumor.

Johnny Bench, the handsome twenty-seven-year-old prize bachelor of baseball, had left a trail of broken hearts ever since he became an All-Star catcher in '65. While he was collecting baseball awards and looking for the right girl to fit the glass slipper, Vickie Chesser, the daughter of a retired Navy chief, was trying to figure a way to get out of South Carolina.

She realized that peering into a microscope at the University of South Carolina was no passport, so she changed her major from biology to broadcasting and started looking into a mirror instead. The mirror told her she was "the fairest of them all"—and the judges in the various beauty contests she entered confirmed it.

In 1970 she won the title of Miss South Carolina and came in second in the Miss U.S.A. Pageant. That same year South Carolina celebrated its three hundredth birthday, and Vickie became queen of the tricentennial celebration. She accomplished what she'd set out to do since the day she dropped biology,

---

*Johnny Bench, catcher for the Cincinnati Reds. Johnny Bench has established himself as one of the most sensational players in baseball today. He broke into the major leagues in 1968 and was voted the Rookie of the Year. Since then he has played in eight All-Star games in a row. In 1970 he led all of baseball in home runs (45) and runs batted in (148). In 1972 he again led the sport in home runs (40) and RBIs (125). He was voted the Most Valuable Player in the National League in '70 and '72. In 1975 he hit 28 home runs and knocked in more than 100 runs for the fifth time in his career. He was also one of the stars of the 1975 World Series, which Cincinnati won.

but what is a beauty queen going to do in South Carolina after she's won all the contests?

Leave.

She arrived in New York with $400, a degree in TV broadcasting and, like thousands of other girls who come to the Big Apple to seek fame and fortune, a burning ambition to make it. She found a $40-a-week walk-up and started making the rounds of the model agencies. But unlike thousands of other girls, Vickie wasn't destined to walk up four flights for long. She signed with Wilhelmina, one of the top model agencies, and soon was appearing in magazines and television. The mirror wasn't wrong. One year from the day she arrived in New York City she'd found her way into one of the toughest businesses in America and was earning in the neighborhood of $100,000.

And she found her way to Duncan's one day, too, without the help of Judy Gilbert, and it changed the course of her young life. Vickie had just finished doing that Ultra Brite commercial when she sauntered into the popular East Side Manhattan pub, and owner Frederick Tuckerman recognized the smile. One night at dinner. he introduced her to a bachelor friend, George Barley, who started taking her out. George made the mistake of telling her that he was one of the country's two greatest bachelors.

"Who's the other one?" Vickie asked sweetly.

"My best friend, Johnny Bench!" He grinned at her. "It's a toss-up as to which of us is the best catch around. Of course, Johnny's more famous—but *I'm* more lovable."

The word "famous" attracted Vickie's interest like a magnet. When her father called from South Carolina, Vickie asked him if he'd ever heard of Johnny Bench?

"Why, he's just about the best baseball player around," he answered. "Why? Do you know him?"

"Not yet!" She smiled and hung up.

George, who mentioned Johnny Bench's name to Vickie, made a second mistake. He mentioned Vickie's name to Johnny. "I'm dating the most gorgeous doll!" he told his friend proudly, displaying a picture of the beautiful Vickie. "She's the most sensational-looking model in New York!"

Three minutes later Johnny was screening people at Duncan's who might have her phone number. One hour later he rang her up and introduced himself. "I'm calling to ask you to come to Las Vegas and spend New Year's Eve with me," Johnny said boldly after *very* few preliminaries.

"Are you crazy? I don't even know what you *look* like!" But she knew who he was and kept the conversation going.

"Look, what have you got to lose?" Johnny teased. "If you don't like me, you can always leave."

Vickie is simply not the kind of a girl to let opportunity slip away. After all, he was rich, famous, and single, and those kind of men don't come around the bend very often. She must have smiled to herself over how easily he had fallen into her hands.

She agreed to meet him but insisted that she see him first in his hometown of Cincinnati, where she also had friends. If they liked each other, she'd go on to Vegas with him.

Johnny must have smiled at how easily she had fallen into his hands.

"See you at the airport, honey."

"But how will I know you?" Vickie giggled. "You'd better wear a name tag."

"Don't worry," said the confident Johnny. "I know what *you* look like. I'll find you."

She arrived at the Cincinnati airport three days after Christmas. Johnny was waiting. He stood well in the background and watched blond and adorable Vickie helplessly searching the crowd. He didn't make a move, just stood there taking her all in.

Vickie remembers looking around the vast room and becoming suddenly uneasy. "Everyone seemed to be greeting someone else. I expected someone to come up and take my hand, say, 'Hello,' or 'Are you the one?'—but nothing. Suddenly I saw this dark-haired fellow leaning up against the wall, sort of smiling at me. Everyone else was eighty years old, so I knew it had to be Johnny. As I approached him, he just leaned there, grinning at me, the rascal. It was very sexy. At that precise moment I knew something wonderful— something—uh, very different was about to happen."

Something happened all right, behind George Barley's back. His best girl and his best friend met, looked each other over, liked what they saw, and set out for Las Vegas to ring in the New Year.

In Vegas, they played a lot of Twenty-one, went to all the shows, and held hands at dinner—but the nights weren't quite what Johnny had in mind. The beauty queen from South Carolina kissed him a demure good-night, fled to her own room, and bolted the door. She was worried that Johnny might think she was one of those girls, jock lovers, who run after the superstars. Of course, this just fanned the fire, and to put it mildly, the celibacy act in Vegas was a pain.

"Johnny couldn't understand it, and frankly, I cried a lot. But you see, I was worried about what he might think if I slept with him right off the bat—so I slept alone, and quite honestly, it wasn't much fun."

Aw, but they were destined to satisfy those urges. First, however, they had to go through another ordeal. Parting. "When we said good-bye at the airport, I almost died! But two weeks later he called me in New York and proposed!" A look of ecstasy came over her face, and she told me, "I shouted, 'Yes, yes, yes,' into the phone."

Maybe she was the first girl who'd bolted the door.

Relief was just a few days away as they got together for the second time in their lives and planned their wedding. In baseball circles the word went out. Johnny Bench had been caught and was marrying the Ultra Brite Girl. The announcement came three weeks and three days after his first phone call.

Lunching with Vickie Chesser two weeks before her wedding in the Palm Court Room of the old Netherland Hotel in Cincinnati was an experience I'll never forget. For one thing she talked right through a fire.

After listening to her story of how she met and fell in love with Johnny, I wondered why they'd picked February 21 to get married.

"We played blackjack a lot in Vegas on our first weekend there together and thought it would be a cute idea."

"Cute?" I said, looking at her to see if she was serious. She was. "I mean, you just met in January. Hasn't someone suggested you wait a few months until you get to know each other?" It was none of my damn business, and I knew it when I said it.

Vickie picked at her salad and admitted that many of their friends and members of their respective families thought they should wait a few months until they knew each other better, but she wasn't listening to any advice. What did those people know about her feelings? "Why should we wait?" Her green eyes went wide. "We've both been around . . . really around . . . and we know what we want. A month is enough. . . . We already know each other. I feel I've known Johnny all my life!"

How many trillions of times have those exact words been spoken? (I remember saying them myself. Twice.) We discussed some of the problems other wives married to sports stars have suffered, and Vickie tossed off their problem of loneliness as "their own fault" and reckoned *she'd* never be lonely because she wasn't going to leave Johnny "for one minute."

"I love him, and we're going to do *everything* together. Oh, I know about those out-of-town games. I'll handle that. [She didn't say how.] I know what I'm getting into—I mean, regarding Johnny's baseball career."

The acrid smell of smoke drifted by our table. I sniffed the air. Someone had burned something. Maybe a piece of toast. I took another sniff. Maybe a whole loaf. It was coming from the hotel kitchen—I could see it drifting under the double doors. Vickie kept on talking. She was convincing herself that life with Johnny would be free of all the pitfalls other athletes' wives had discovered over the years. The words were rushing out, in between sighs of "I love him soooo." Then her eyes would go green and serious. "We are just *not* going to get in those ruts. We're aware of the problems, but we'll avoid them." The smoke was now pouring out of the kitchen into the dining room.

"There have been girls in his past," she noted with a slight pout, "but those days are over. We're going to be *one* couple who'll remain loyal—and constant to each other!"

The smoke started to make me cough, and I fanned the air with my menu as she went on. "I know all about those awful women—the groupies. Those pesty women are always around, but once we're married I *know* Johnny will be strong enough when he's out of town playing ball to, uh, to . . . wait. Yes, strong enough to wait."

"Wait?" I coughed through the smoke.

"Wait to come home to me!" she said, beaming at the thought.

Suddenly the Cincinnati Fire Department rushed past our table, yellow slickers flying, dragging a big hose. I looked around the room. There was a sense of absurdity to the scene—people looking up from their meals in astonishment, then grinning in amusement as the firemen ran through the sedate old dining room. Smoke was now belching out of the kitchen in thick yellow clouds. The cook was running around in circles. The manager was fanning the air with his handkerchief, trying to tell his customers that it was nothing. Vickie hadn't noticed any of it.

"Johnny," she said, brushing back her silky blond hair, "is deeply in love, and when you're deeply in love, you are *loyal.* I know I won't have to put up with other women or worry about him at out-of-town games, and he won't have to worry about me getting in, uh, trouble. We're both grown up. And besides, we have something very special."

There was a lot of noise from the kitchen. I wondered what everyone was waiting for. Were we all expecting an order to evacuate? Why weren't we running outside?

"Johnny knows baseball is Greek to me," Vickie bubbled, "so he uses a little game at the ball park to keep me interested. If he beats on his chest and lets out an Indian war whoop, he's referring to Geronimo. You know Cesar Geronimo, the Reds' outfielder! When they play "The Star-Spangled Banner," Johnny looks up at me, and I throw him a little kiss. It's cute the way he turns his cap around. . . . He's such a doll! I love him! He knows I'm a hotdog!"

I could feel a fireman's slicker rub against my arm as he rushed past with another heavy hose. I wondered if the fire was under control. Vickie still hadn't noticed and was chattering merrily away about her wedding dress.

"Halston designed it, and it's fab, just fab! I was worried about having a proper write-up in the Cincinnati papers. . . . I mean, I wanted a good, really *super* description of my wedding dress on the society page, but Johnny told me to quite worrying. 'Honey,' he said to me, 'never mind about the society page. You're going to be on the *front* page!' "

By now the smoke was giving me a headache, and I suggested we leave.

Vickie looked lovingly in a mirror and sighed as if the effect weren't quite up to what she'd expected. "The rain coming over here has ruined my hair," she said, patting her hair, which didn't look at all ruined. She added a touch of lip gloss to her pink smooth lips with her finger, concentrating very hard on the operation. Suddenly she wrinkled her nose like a rabbit and sniffed the air.

"What's going on in here?"

"Just a little kitchen fire," I said as we walked through the chaos and out into the lobby.

"Come upstairs and see the Hall of Mirrors!" she said gaily. "That's where we're going to hold our reception. It's such a beautiful room!" She skipped up the wide red-carpeted staircase. "It's going to be fab! Wait until you see all the mirrors. We're having nine hundred people at our reception!"

I had an immediate vision of 900 baseball players lifting 900 glasses in a toast to the bride in a Halston wedding dress with letters spelling "Hotdog" across the bodice.

My thoughts were interrupted as Vickie danced into the Hall of Mirrors and stopped and smiled at her reflection, little knowing that one year and twenty days later her super marriage would end in divorce. Suddenly there were thousands of her stretching back into infinity in the long mirrored baroque room. Thousands of Vickies with their superfaces, superfigures, and superplans, all shimmering in hope and expectation. Supergirls marrying superstars—and a whole new crop of superwives are born.

Afterword

I suppose there are always those conclusions. What can we say about the group as a whole? What have we come up with after $9,000 worth of airplane tickets, hotel bills, rent-a-cars, long-distance phone calls, 180 one-hour tapes, 90 yellow legal pads, 15 boxes of typing paper, three erasers (?), 24½ peanut butter sandwiches, washed down with at least 300 cups of coffee and tea?

Well, we have a few facts: The majority, twenty-five out of thirty, of the wives resent jock lovers, worry about their husbands' fidelity, and admit to jealousy, although most of the women say their husbands "would never!" Twenty of the wives confessed to chronic loneliness, ten found it extremely difficult to deal with fame, nine had severe identity problems, six lived in fear of the threat of injury or death to their husbands, six had fears for the future, three worried about kidnapping, and—one finding I certainly didn't suspect at the onset of my journey—most of these women, eighteen out of thirty, are deeply religious. The two that seemed to have the happiest lives were the most religious.

There were some other common threads. All the wives told me they loved and admired their husbands (I believed all but one); all said their family came first (I believed all but two); every wife said she was happy with her life in spite of her problems (I'm convinced that only two were).

All the athletes' wives are physically fit, with nothing short of sensational figures (when not pregnant). Most of them met their husbands in high school or college, more than half these women were cheerleaders, and fewer than half have a college degree. I found three wives interested in intellectual and cultural pursuits and all the rest solidly entrenched in the physical world. After examining my notes, I came up with twenty-two tennis players and fifteen golfers, three were taking flying lessons, and—another unexpected finding—twenty-four wives do needlepoint! What's this thing with needlepoint? A mutual liking which almost won, in terms of numbers, over their mutual hatred of jock lovers. Come to think of it, hasn't it ever been so? She who sits and waits. Didn't Penelope weave a shroud for twenty years while she waited for Odysseus to come home from Troy?

If nothing else, I came away from this odyssey with the definite feeling that for the superstar husband, the sport is first. Therefore, the dominant force in the lives of these couples is the sport. The sport calls the shots. When it dictates "Thou shalt not sleep together before a game," the husband sleeps at a motel. When it dictates "Thou shalt be away all but 60 of the 365 days of the year," the couple learns to adjust to separation. When it dictates "Thou shalt concentrate first, last, and always on thy sport," everything else comes second. That's exactly where the wife comes, second.

Does this ring a familiar bell with wives of successful doctors, lawyers, politicians, or businessmen? Of course it does. It's the same. The career calls the shots, the "star" follows the call, and the wife follows the husband. Emmy Cosell was right, but what I didn't know, nor perhaps did she, was that basically there's no difference between these wives and the wives of successful, dynamic men in any field.

If the marriage succeeds with superstars in the sports world, it's probably because of the wife. She is the one who has to do all the accommodating. Karolyn Rose seems to be the exception, but isn't it convenient that she happens to be crazy about baseball? Winnie Palmer is a good example of a wife who has made her marriage work because of "accommodating" all these years. Mary Laver swallows her loneliness and gets on with Rod's business, Barbara Nicklaus stands by for a phone call that may mean forty for dinner. This book has no comment to make about the rights or wrongs of accommodating, nor will it go into a philosophical discourse on what *should* be. The facts are: Out of the thirty women I interviewed, all are accommodating but one. (In that case he accommodates her, so it works out the same.)

One thing they are unanimous on: They are all curious about each other. I'm sure of selling thirty books. Winnie Palmer wonders about Linda Miller, Pam Csonka wonders about Marguerite Simpson, Linda Petty wonders about Judith Allison, Nancy Seaver wonders about Karolyn Rose, Daniele Killy wonders about all the American wives, and all the American wives think football wives have it the worst, including football wives, and can't wait to find out if it's really so.

We posed some questions at the beginning of this quest. Are their lives super? I would say, generally no. No more or less than yours or mine. There's an occasional smashing life-style, but even Helen Stewart, I have a feeling, looks out of her villa over the mountains toward Monaco and envies the life-style of the princess in the palace.

Are these wives married to supermen? No. Superathletes, but difficult men. Are they superwomen? No. As a group I'd say once again they were average, with class A, B, C, and a few Ds sprinkled in, but no failures.

And the big question: Are they superwives?

You'll have to make up your own mind about that question, but while you're thinking about it, name another group of wives who have to put up with things like forced separation; the Tuesday Rule; a $2500 fine for sleeping with their own husband; loss of privacy; going to the hospital alone in a cab while hubby's playing in a game, holding off labor while the tennis match is going to the third set; fighting off jealousy while jock lovers track down, swarm all over, and attack your man; praying that he won't be killed in a race or his ear mistaken for a puck and hoping his knees will support him after retirement; learning how to cope with the threat of permanent injury, forced retirement, being traded; handling the emotional, physical, and educational problems of child rearing by yourself; sitting in the stands while an entire stadium boos or throws garbage at your mate; listening to gossip about his behavior away from home; reading cutting criticism in the newspapers about his performance; trying to figure out a way to save money when the big income lasts for only a few years and you're taxed to death; coping with the feeling of being small next to greatness; trying not to be swamped by the very anathema fame brings to your family life; putting up with being stared at, whispered about, shoved out of the way, and ignored; straining to get love from a man whose very way of life brings on an intense form of self-concentration; worrying about what you'll do when he's "over the hill" at thirty-seven and knowing that he's scared shitless when the whole world is convinced he's a hero.

My answer is yes. Who else could live with these jocks but SUPER-WIVES?